CLIMATE-PROOF
your
PERSONAL
FINANCES

HOW (AND WHERE) TO SAFEGUARD
YOUR FAMILY'S BUDGET AND LIFESTYLE

PRAISE FOR THIS BOOK

"David Stookey's primary argument, that climate change is coming out of the political realm and into our daily lives, is one of which we would all do well to be better aware."
— **U.S. Senator SHELDON WHITEHOUSE**

"Using a "no-regrets" approach, Stookey provides page after page of easily overlooked, practical guidance so that you, your family and friends will be more financially secure in an insecure world. Includes lots of references and links for more information as things change in the coming years."
— **JOHN ENGLANDER**, oceanographer and author of *High Tide on Main Street*

"This book is full of thoughtful advice and practical tips for weathering the ecological and economic storms on the horizon. Stookey writes with a humane sensibility and grounded realism that invites us to act not from fear, but from pragmatism and possibility."
— **CHUCK COLLINS**, senior scholar, Institute for Policy Studies, cofounder of the Resilience Circle network, and author of *Born on Third Base*.

"This important book brings into sharp focus the dramatic and direct impact climate change will have on our local communities and their residents. It is an invaluable and unique resource for community leaders and citizens in planning for the shortages of food, water, energy and increased costs and health risks that will arise. It presents a compelling case and an excellent blueprint for civic leaders and individuals to take strong measures now to get ahead of the curve."
— **EARL M. LEIKEN**, Mayor of Shaker Heights, Ohio

"A very good book. Uncommonly well-researched with solid advice on how you can protect not just your finances, but also your most valuable assets—your home and family. An invaluable roadmap, which includes up-to-date links to many resources so you can drill deeper into individual topics. I'm very impressed with this book and I'm looking forward to using it as a reference for my own work regarding quality of life in different U.S. cities."

> — BERT SPERLING, author of *Cities Ranked and Rated*, creator of *BestPlaces.net*

"When I opened *Climate-Proof*, I was instantly reminded how we need to think about the economic impact that climate changes will impose on the private sector, our governments—and especially the finances and comfort of our families. I encourage readers to consider their own security, in particular if they live in a sensitive coastal zone. The rising waters will bring rising costs—so thinking and planning now will protect you and your family long-term."

> — LAUREN H. CARSON, RI State Representative. Chair, Special House Commission On Economic Risk Due to Flooding and Sea Level Rise.

"Think there's nothing you can do to protect yourself from climate change? Nonsense. David Stookey lays out in simple, accessible language dozens of easy steps you can take that boost your personal bottom line and the planet's. This should be required reading for financial advisers coast to coast."

> — MICHAEL H. SHUMAN, author of *Local Dollars, Local Sense: How to Shift Your Money from Wall Street to Main Street and Achieve Real Prosperity*

Read *Climate-proof* if you want to . . .

Visualize the financial impacts of global warming.
Warming is only beginning to affect your wallet. If you can see the bigger costs coming soon, you have a better chance of dodging many of them and protecting your way of life.

Gauge the consequences for your family.
A look at your own family's budget under warming conditions lets you see where you are vulnerable financially and how you might prepare to make changes that reduce your risk.

Understand that place matters.
Some hometowns will feel painful effects from warming; others are naturally immune. A few are preparing to protect their residents; most are not. You can predict where you're more likely to thrive or suffer.

See why we can't prevent warming, so we must adjust.
Yes, we must all try to limit the change in global weather patterns. But it's too late to prevent big costs over the next decade or two; they're already baked in. This book is about how to cope with what's on the way.

Adopt a no-regrets response to climate disruption.
Even if you aren't sure whether nature is really huffing and puffing, building with bricks, not straw, means fewer regrets for your family.

See which actions and attitudes won't help your family.
Over the next decade, you can boost or trash your family's finances and wellbeing depending on which actions you take. By avoiding certain actions and hopes, you can position yourself defensively.

Find ways to actually prosper from climate change.
Climate change will create new jobs and investment opportunities. Seeing these coming and getting in on them can be critical to your future.

Get the timing right. Act ahead of the crowd.
Americans are going to wake up to the dangers and opportunities in front of us, perhaps with a rush. It will pay to be the first to take certain actions.

Adopt attitudes that put you ahead.
Beyond improving your physical and financial circumstances, certain attitude changes will help your future happiness.

Don't bother reading if you want to . . .

Be persuaded climate change is real.
If you are a climate skeptic, this book doesn't argue with you. But it will suggest why you should be taking some just-in-case actions anyway.

Save the planet.
We should all be trying to save the world from warming. There are lots of good books about how we can do that. This book instead concentrates on reducing the impact of warming on your finances and wellbeing, including dangers that may not be obvious today.

Examine national political solutions.
There seems little hope today that Washington will protect us from the effects of warming. State and local initiatives are more promising.

Learn survivalist skills.
Homesteading, storing a year's food, stocking your gun safe—all these may seem like sensible protections to some. They don't to me, and this book does not explore such survivalist actions.

Consider other threats.
Climate change is only one threat in the coming decades. This book does not cover additional dangers, such as declining education, resource scarcities, ineffective antibiotics, vulnerable data, growing income disparity, and the paralysis of American democratic processes, to name a few.

CLIMATE-PROOF *your* PERSONAL FINANCES

HOW (AND WHERE) TO SAFEGUARD
YOUR FAMILY'S BUDGET AND LIFESTYLE

David W. Stookey

Savvy Families Institute
Newport, RI

Published with *Where-To-Live Indicators* covering
every U.S. hometown, free online at SavvyFamilies.org

Library of Congress Control Number: 2016904254

ISBN-13 978-0-9973958-0-8

ISBN-13 978-0-9973958-1-5 Kindle version

ISBN-13 978-0-9973958 Ebook version (EPUB)

Edited by Chris Murray

Cover and interior designed by Joanna Detz

Printed in the United States of America

BISAC Subject Codes:
- Business & Money / Personal Finance / Budgeting & Money Management
- Business & Money / Economics / Environmental Economics

DEDICATION

To our sons. Ben has lived off the grid, runs his car on waste vegetable oil, and works for an organization promoting sustainability. Alex is a professional at growing green things. And Pavel's Navy unit is the one most likely to help in natural disaster areas around the world.

And to their generation of Americans who, over the coming decades, will deal with far bigger threats and tougher decisions than their parents face today.

TABLE OF CONTENTS

PREFACE..i

P A R T   I   DEFEND AGAINST GROWING EXPENSES 1

1 Gauge your financial vulnerability.................................. 2
    Small margins of safety 2
    Family spending at risk..3
    Family income at risk..4
    Family assets at risk 5
    Sneak attacks on your finances.....................................5
    Your first defense: a family budget. Ugh! 7
    Your geographic vulnerability 10

2 Retain secure access to food.......................................12
    How our food costs will increase................................ 13
    Holding your food costs down 20
    Where to live for better food security......................... 30

3 Hold down your energy costs 33
    How our energy costs could change............................. 34
        What could keep energy prices down........................ 34
        What could keep energy prices up............................ 36
    Keeping your energy costs low 42
    Where to live for low energy costs 48

4 Avert health costs 53
    How our health costs will increase.............................53

Holding your health costs down 58

Where to live for lower health costs 60

5 Secure low-cost transportation options 63

How transportation costs will increase 63

Costs we will pay through fees and taxes 63

Costs we will pay directly, on and off the road.........................66

Keeping your transportation costs down....................................69

Where to live to get around cheaply..74

6 Avoid rising state and local taxes 78

How our state and local taxes will grow 78

Potential cost #1: Taxes..85

Potential cost #2: Fees in lieu of taxes 85

Potential cost #3: Send the bill to our children 86

Potential cost #4: Cuts in services 87

Warming costs come on top of other urgencies.......................88

Holding your state and local taxes down....................................89

Where to find lower state & local taxes 99

7 Protect against rising federal taxes 104

How our federal taxes will increase 105

Getting the most from your federal taxes..................................112

Where to live for low federal income tax 114

PART II   PROSPER AS YOUR SURROUNDINGS WARM...........117

8 Keep home costs down, your home's value up..................118

How housing costs will rise and home values will fall.................118

Rising domestic water costs 120

Safeguarding your home and its value......................................123

Destruction of value caused by warming.................................. 128

Understanding your home's investment value 131

Where to live to protect your property value 133

9 Choose financial investments prudently **139**

How warming will affect assets 140

Investments with recognized upsides 140

Other investments with long-term downsides 150

Information as key to investing well 153

Defensive investing 155

Where to live for better investments 156

10 Work in a good job market **158**

Choosing careers in the face of warming 158

Industries likely to wither 160

Industries predicted to hire 161

Developing the right skills 168

Helping to create local jobs 170

Where to live for better job options 172

11 Understand how much place matters **175**

The risks in your hometown, and others 177

A good place to live: one last indicator 182

PART III   **DEVELOP A CLIMATE-PROOF MINDSET** **190**

12 Adopt attitudes that protect you **191**

Think mobile. 191

Think simple. 195

Think provident. 199

Think multi-generational. 200

Think sharing. 202

Think self-reliant. 206

Think compassionate. 207

Think vigilant. 211

13 Get started now! **212**

Think no-regrets. 212

Getting ahead of the crowd 217

Your own tipping points 221

Is this your family? 225

Acknowledgments **228**

The Author **230**

INDEX **231**

PREFACE

The effects of warming have started a slow-motion train wreck of financial costs and lifestyle disruptions for many of us. This book proposes ways we can protect ourselves.

We will examine how a shifting climate is threatening not just the natural environment around us but our personal finances. We'll talk less about sea-level rise and more about its impact on our taxes and home value, less about drought's impact on the soil and more about its effects on our grocery and water bills.

Certain hometowns will help climate-proof their residents; others will expose everyone living there to financial pain. We'll examine how much location matters, and explain how to evaluate your town for its ability to protect you from the effects of warming.

Of course it's critical that we try to stop warming or, to be realistic, slow it down, and there are plenty of good books about how we can do this. We should all be joining in this effort. But to slow warming is different from protecting ourselves against its effects. In this book we'll focus on protection.

This is not a calamity book. Yes, we need to see the wide variety of negative impacts that American families will feel as our country warms up, but it's more important to learn what we can do about them by examining a wide assortment of examples. Above all, we should appreciate the initiative, ingenuity, and cooperation American families can draw on to fend off these growing pressures.

In the face of warming, each family member can take initiatives to preserve healthy, vibrant lives. Young or old, we should all be thinking about the impact of warming on our financial future, our career and lifestyles, and even our choices about where to live. After all, Generations X and Y, far more than their parents, face tough questions about how to earn, save, and thrive over the coming decades.

In this book we will address questions such as:

- How will my life be affected, compared to that of my cousin five states away?

- Do I need to protect my earnings somehow?

- Is the health of my kids threatened?

- Do I need to change my spending patterns, and how?

- Can I find a place to live where local and state governments have enough revenue and foresight to protect me?

There are dozens more questions, but "Is America warming?" isn't one of them. Warming was, until recently, doubted by a majority of Americans. Today, however, 75 percent of us,[1] and 98 percent of our U.S. Senators[2] have acknowledged the *Inconvenient Truth* to which Al Gore introduced us so presciently back in 2006.[3] They now agree that "climate change is real and is not a hoax."

Americans do not yet, however, agree about what causes warming or what we should do to slow it down. Whatever your beliefs on these issues may be, you can hold onto them and still benefit fully from this book. We are not discussing how you should prevent future warming, but rather how your family can dodge its financial effects. And it will be the majority's beliefs, right or wrong, and not yours that control many of your future costs—particularly the taxes, regulations and other government efforts to climate-proof your community.

To emphasize this distinction—that we are talking about actions to save your wallet, not actions to save the planet—I will seldom use the phrases *climate change* or *global warming*. These phrases have become politicized. I prefer to call what we face simply *warming*. I hope you will forget politics and semantics as you read and focus on what is about to happen to your family's bank account and your way of living.

How bad could it be? We will scan a wide range of financial pressures that are building now and the options that may be available for dealing with them. But to get an idea of the impacts of warming on American families, let's take a quick look at a single American city facing a single effect of warming.

Santa Cruz, California, a city of waving palms and pine trees, in a seaside county with its own mountain range and twenty creeks and rivers, is rated at "Extreme" risk for drought. As early as 2003 the city surveyed its residents and local businesses about how various levels of water rationing would affect them. These assessments come from the city's residents themselves, not from some environmental think tank or consultant.

At a 10-20 percent reduction, residents characterized the changes needed (reduced outdoor watering, shorter showers) as "inconvenient."

At a 20-30 percent reduction, they called the changes they envisioned "hardship." Drip irrigation will be required for landscaping. Some turf, shrubs and trees will be lost anyway. They will flush toilets by the rule "If it's yellow, let it mellow; if it's brown, flush it down." New domestic habits will become "disagreeable preoccupations." Fines will begin; multi-family dwellings will need rules and enforcers. Several employers in town will be "significantly affected . . . suffering large losses even during relatively moderate water shortages." Looking ahead, residents would bear "the economic and environmental cost of providing increased water capacity," perhaps with desalinization.

30-50 percent cutbacks would require rationing, perhaps with flow restrictors. Landscaping would be sacrificed, pools and common laundry facilities closed, and money spent to find and fix leaks. Lifestyles would be "significantly affected." Economic, health and safety impacts will be ubiquitous.

50-60 percent reductions will be "catastrophic" to residents' lifestyles and wallets.[4]

How unique are the problems that Santa Cruz residents face? Theirs is one of 29 counties across the country rated at *Extreme* risk from drought; 271 other counties are rated *High* risk, with many more at *Moderate* risk on the Water Supply Sustainability Index developed for the Natural Resources Defense Council.[5]

But wait—that's if there's *no* global warming. The ratings take into account only population growth, current water sources and demand. They don't consider changes in temperature, humidity and precipitation from climate change. When climate predictions are factored in, it's a different picture. The 29 U.S. counties at *Extreme* risk jump to 400. The 271 counties at *High* risk rise to 600. Under warming conditions, by 2050 one in every three counties in the lower 48 states is projected to have *Extreme* or *High* risk of drought. Santa Cruz' problem is not in some distant place: the problem is developing in a thousand counties across the country. And not in some distant time: water restrictions in Santa Cruz reached 25 percent in 2013.[6]

And thanks to the changing weather patterns across the country, drought is only one of the many risks that lie ahead for American communities.

Americans facing warming-driven uncertainties seem to be finding three ways to cope:

1. "Wait-and-see" is certainly the most popular. Even if we know it's warming, the great majority of us are doing absolutely nothing to protect our finances and lives from the threats we hear of. In fact, surveys indicate that, among all the developed nations, Americans are most likely to view climate change as "not a problem."[7]

2. Another group of us cope with uncertainty by manufacturing certainty. Extreme environmentalists, climate change deniers, survivalists and others have become inflexible about what lies ahead or how best to react.

3. A third path is what business calls risk management, what my mother called "a stitch in time," and what I am calling the no-regrets approach—taking actions early before the damage accelerates. This book is about that approach.

Despite the risks our families face, the financial costs from warming seem to be taboo topics. As of September 2016, if you search the web for *"climate change"* or *"global warming"* together with terms like *"personal financial planning," "Realtor," "family finances"* or *"personal budget,"* you get virtually no results. It's understandable that real estate agents are slow to admit that sea-level rise, flooding, and drought threaten many of their listings. Yet it's harder to understand why financial advisers are mum about the coming threats to family budgets. You would think that high-powered financial and property companies would be climbing all over each other to protect us:

"Rely on our firm for climate-savvy advice and management."

"Our extensive listings of certified *climate-safe* properties."

"Seaview Estates, elevation 70', model unit open."

But it's not happening yet.

This is both bad and good. Delay means the forces we need to protect ourselves, including public pressure, government action, and community effort, are slow to develop. But delay also means you can get a head start in making changes in your spending habits, your assets, and where you live before the rest of America wakes up and starts to compete with you for these opportunities. This book is meant to give you that head start.

In Part I of this book will examine major family costs: food, energy, transportation, healthcare, taxes. For each, we will identify the threats to your personal finances and the tactics you might use to protect yourself.

Part II covers your assets and income, particularly your home and investments, as well as your career, again looking for tactics you can use to skirt the financial pitfalls ahead. In particular, we will examine how much place matters to these elements in your life.

Part III will look more inwardly at our own attitudes: those that could endanger us and those that will help us deal successfully with the effects of warming. Then we'll look at questions of timing and initiative that can make our decisions and actions succeed or fail.

Beyond the book itself are several related tools designed to help you gauge the various threats and opportunities that have financial impacts specific to you. First, I have created a budget sheet for you to customize and annotate as you evaluate the threats and opportunities discussed. You will find it on the last page of the book. I invite you to cut it out and use it as a bookmark. (Alternatively, you can print a version from savvyfamilies.org/climateproof-budget-bookmark.)

The second tool to help you evaluate your personal situation and prospects is a set of thousands of local scorecards containing *Where-To-Live Indicators*. Communities vary widely in their vulnerability to the effects of warming, and you have free access to these scorecards for every Zip Code in America, showing data that measure the threats and opportunities peculiar to each location. You will find them at ClimateProof.org/where-to-live-indicators. Here is a sample scorecard.

kalamazoo MICHIGAN

DOWNLOAD   PRINT-FRIENDLY   COMPARE REPORTS   REQUEST ANOTHER REPORT   NOTES & SOURCES

WHERE-TO-LIVE INDICATORS

KALAMAZOO is in KALAMAZOO County, Michigan.

We have compared KALAMAZOO with other localities in the US, looking at measures of how well its residents are likely to fare facing the chief hazards predicted for American families over the coming decade.

Our accompanying **Notes & Sources** page tells how the ratings are developed and where to get more detailed information. We are always looking for relevant and accurate measures. Please suggest one we should begin using or comment on those we are using.

Kalamazoo, MI 49048
View larger map

View Larger Map

☥ Energy   [-]   C-

NEED FOR HEATING/COOLING Some localities require a lot more energy for home heating and cooling than others. With energy costs predicted to rise, we've looked at the need for heat and air conditioning in the KALAMAZOO area. The nearest weather station, 4 miles away, averages 6414 heating degree days and 174 cooling degree days each year. This result for this location: **D**.

SUNLIGHT Solar power installations pay off better in places with more usable sunlight. The closest measuring station is 4 miles from KALAMAZOO. This result for this location is **C-** for available solar energy.

WIND POWER Some places have higher average winds, making wind power more productive. The closest measuring station, 57 miles from KALAMAZOO, suggests the area has an average annual windspeed of 10.5 mph, giving it a **B+** for available wind energy.

NET METERING Solar and wind resources are more useful if the state has a good net-metering policy, allowing homeowners to sell excess electricity back to the local utility. Michigan has a statewide net-metering policy rated **A**.

My Reports

- **KALAMAZOO, Michigan**

♉ Health	expand [+]		B
⚘ Food	expand [+]		C+
● Water	expand [+]		B-
⬛ Housing	expand [+]		B+
☕ Transportation	expand [+]		C+
🖥 Education	expand [+]		C
♈ Security	expand [+]		A-
▤ Taxes	expand [+]		B-
$ Consumption	expand [+]		A+
☱ Jobs	expand [+]		A-
● Other	expand [+]		

Finally, here are a few questions you may have as you read . . .

Where do I find the footnotes? There are almost 500 of them and you'll find them online at savvyfamilies.org / climateproof-footnotes, not in the back of the book. Here's why. Most of my sources are online, and these days it's a lot easier for readers to click on a link than to type in a long URL found in tiny print at the back of the book. In fact, many of my sources can be found fastest just by typing keywords from my text into your search engine.

Some of the predicted expense increases don't seem very big. Why is that? It's because they are stated in terms of what economists call *real* growth— growth above general inflation. If average U.S. inflation is, say, 2% a year and both your income and your costs are growing at that rate, you don't really notice a change. If *real* growth in, say, your food costs is 2%, that may not sound like much, but after five years it's a ten percent increase *above* general price and wage inflation. Food would begin to crowd out other expenses in your budget.

Seems like things are moving fast. Where can I find updates to what I read here? You can follow—and contribute to—the news and comments pages at savvyfamilies.org / thelatest. We will post factual updates, plus new ideas for protecting ourselves, and stories about what others are doing. Posts and comments are categorized by the same topics as the chapters of this book.

PART I

DEFEND AGAINST GROWING EXPENSES

1 GAUGE YOUR FINANCIAL VULNERABILITY

Despite all of our wealth, prosperity and technologies, Americans have more to lose from the impacts of warming than most others around the world. True, we are not likely to look into the eyes of our starving children, watch disease spread among our friends, or be permanently confined to a disaster area. Nevertheless, compared to other countries, we have designed our lives around high levels of income, consumption, public services and financial assets. All are vulnerable to the many effects of warming.

Small margins of safety

And we face a further risk in the condition of the American family pocketbook. Many of us have virtually no financial resilience. A study published in 2011 by the National Bureau of Economic Research and the Brookings Institution found that about a quarter of Americans say they certainly could not raise $2,000 within 30 days, from all available resources, including family and friends. Another 19 percent could do so only with the help of a pawn shop or payday loan store. Amazingly, almost a quarter of households making between $100,000 and $150,000 a year said the same thing! This finding has been confirmed in many surveys through 2015.[1]

Recovery from the Great Recession has apparently not helped this huge number of financially fragile Americans. At the mercy of even small expense surprises or income disappointments, our household budgets cannot bend without breaking. Consider:

- The economy has improved since 2011, but we still put almost nothing in the bank. The savings rate of the average American family in 2016 was just over 5 percent, among the lowest in the developed world and down from around 10 percent in the 1970s and '80s.[2]

- Of those aged 50 to 64, about a quarter haven't even started saving for retirement.[3] Four in ten say they will need to begin taking Social

Security benefits before full retirement age, even though it will cost them a reduction in lifetime benefits of up to 30%.[4]

- Almost one in three Americans has some personal debt in the hands of a collection agency.[5] Most is mortgage debt, the rest credit card or auto-loan debt. This figure does not include payday loans which would add millions more Americans to the list of those unable to pay their bills on time.[6]

- An estimated two million Americans age 60 and older still have unpaid student loans, and more than 10 percent of that is over 90 days delinquent or in default. Unlike other debts, these loans will be collected, even if they have to be deducted from Social Security payments.[7]

- Early 2016 saw almost 900,000 properties in the U.S. in some stage of foreclosure.[8]

- Homeless populations now include capable, healthy, skilled middle-class Americans. A sudden job loss or family split leads to foreclosure or eviction, and these people have no savings cushion to fall back on. They find themselves in free fall, winding up in the street. Many of us can look at these people and admit to ourselves, "There but for the grace of God go I."[9]

It is so easy to ignore the tightrope so many of us are walking. As writers Paul Kingsnorth and Dougald Hine see it: "The pattern of ordinary life, in which so much stays the same from one day to the next, disguises the fragility of its fabric. . . not only the fragility of the fabric, but the speed with which it can unravel."[10]

With the understanding that many of us have little or no financial shock absorber, let's look at what the shocks from warming could be.

Family spending at risk

What are the chances your property will be damaged by increasingly frequent storms, that you'll lose electricity for weeks because your local generating station has no cooling water, or that someone in your family will catch dengue fever from a northward-migrating mosquito? Those physical risks are low.

But what about the financial risks? What are the chances you'll be paying higher taxes for disaster relief, storm drainage, seawalls, and health services in your area? Will your checkbook reflect outlays for higher-priced food and energy, home insurance, and auto maintenance? What will it cost to upgrade your insulation and air-conditioning, buy allergy medication, or join a community team when your kids' high school cuts after-school sports? Unlike your physical dangers, your financial risks are high.

Family income at risk

Needless to say, job loss can be a calamity. But the more insidious threat may be flat or declining incomes. For the many families who are only a few paychecks away from going broke, rising incomes would help them put away some savings. But experience over the last decade and predictions for the next are not encouraging. To begin with, the income of the median American household, adjusted for inflation, is today no higher than it was for the equivalent household in the late 1980s, despite more jobs, a doubling of the stock market, and overall economic growth.[11]

Many economic studies see average personal incomes still suppressed by factors related to warming. Jobs in agriculture, forestry, tourism and leisure, fisheries, and other industries may decline. Oil lubricates today's economy, so if we eventually cut back on fossil fuel use, that industry will contract and productivity in other sectors could go down, hurting wages.[12] And heat alone is an enemy of higher wages because it reduces our productivity. A 2012 study at General Motors concluded that, during periods in which temperatures exceeded 90°F for six days, assembly line output dropped by 8 percent. Other studies show that productivity—even indoors—is hurt by heat.[13]

Another uncertainty about jobs will be their location. It seems likely that, as the effects of new weather patterns hit some places a lot harder than others, your family's income could be protected or vulnerable depending on where you choose to live. We will talk about how you might take advantage of this disparity in Chapter 10 on jobs and Chapter 11 on the importance of place.

Family assets at risk

We have mentioned expenses and income, but these entries in your checkbook do not tell the whole financial story, as well as consider what you own—your savings, property, retirement accounts—and what you owe— the mortgage, car loan, and credit-card debt. For some, other assets not yet part of your wealth may arrive someday through inheritance. All these assets could get re-priced fast by warming.

We have seen it happen. The median U.S. household lost nearly 39 percent of its wealth from 2007 to 2010, largely through drops in house prices.[14] Much of this happened in just a few months as perceptions changed much more suddenly and dramatically than the underlying economics or our day-to-day expenses. We'll discuss these dangers and the opportunities to profit from them on your home in Chapter 8 and on your investments in Chapter 9.

Sneak attacks on your finances

There are additional costs from warming that won't go directly through your bank accounts. Even with an eagle eye on your checkbook, you may not notice them as they mount up.

Costs of neglect

What if our leaders can't raise the capital needed to prevent pollution from rainwater overflows? Or fix the tens of thousands of bridges, already "structurally deficient," which are threatened by warming?[15] Or repair the one in three of our nation's major roads already rated in "poor or mediocre" condition?[16] And what if raising the money to fight the physical effects of warming draws funds away from your schools or police departments?

Ducking costs may look like savings: "Hooray, we voted down that expensive project!" But the costs are going to hit you eventually, as damage to your health, your kids' qualifications for college, higher crime, the competitiveness of your town, the prospects for a good job, your car's lifespan, and more.

Beyond the declining quality of life you experience, it could be years before you begin to notice that your home is less valuable because your town has slowly become less attractive.

Costs via your neighbors

Even if your family maneuvers itself into the "just-fine-thank-you" category—an income that can be maintained, costs that won't jump much, and adequate savings—you will have friends, family, and neighbors who will be hurting.

Financial suffering elsewhere in our community has real costs to the rest of us. There is pain when people we know suffer. There are costs when we try to help our family or close friends, or support neighborhood charities and other helping-hand organizations. And malaise, stress and pessimism, not to mention crime and violence, have a way of suffusing throughout the community.

Costs to your children

Costs from warming will grow slowly, with higher impacts during our children's lives than our own. We claim we deplore this. Our politicians say, "Balance the federal budget so we don't leave our kids in debt." "Slow the growth of Medicare, or we're just taking money from our grandchildren."

Warming will cause other big costs that we will likely push onto our children. While this cost-transfer is sure to sweep the country, within our own family it can be different. It's possible to balance our children's needs with our current needs and for us to make adjustments—perhaps sacrifices—now for their future. We'll discuss this in Chapter 12 on useful attitudes.

Political strains cost everybody

In the many communities where climate-related costs will hit hard, social conflicts are predicted, with residents taking sides on questions of who pays. These tensions can paralyze local governments, as they have done to our federal government. In Chapter 11 on how much place matters, we will examine the real costs of squabbling over resources, inequality, and political polarization and what we could do locally to dampen the risks.

Costs of a nationwide slowdown

Millions of households are going to curtail their spending on some things in order to deal with the cost and income penalties from warming. Even if your family is not badly hit, the weakening of others can pull us all down. Consumer spending is, after all, more than two-thirds of the U.S. economy, and a recession hurts us all. As pressures from warming build, whether as a slow squeeze or a sudden crash, they could trigger a recession or worse. Our household budget, no matter how solid it may look today, may need further actions to shield it from a national slow-down.

Your first defense: a family budget. Ugh!

Chances are it won't be a sudden revelation, like the disappearance of your job, the destruction of your property, or a financial crisis in your community, that makes you realize what's happening to you. If you're like most, your finances will be in gradual, insidious decline—stagnant incomes, steadily rising costs, erosion of your assets—which you fail to notice or which you gradually accept as the "new normal."

To avoid death from a thousand cuts, you need to notice and monitor any degradations of your family's finances and lifestyle, and to make adjustments, big and little, to climate-proof your finances. There's one critical tool for that. Dave Ramsey says it best in his really practical *Total Money Makeover: A Proven Plan for Financial Fitness*: "The dreaded *B* Word enters the picture here. You must set up a budget, a written budget every month. . . I assure you that virtually none of the thousands of winners I have seen did so without a written budget."[17]

The business maxim, "If you don't measure it, you can't manage it," applies to personal finances too. I recommend that, before you read further, you make a list of what you're actually spending, earning and saving and refer to it while you read.

I know for many of us there's nothing more boring than a budget. It's just a list of numbers? It doesn't grab us like the TV specials and *National Geographic* articles on warming. But if you look closely at your budget, you may see the equivalent of suffering polar bears, shrinking coral reefs, and cracking farmland. It's an image of your family's financial life, and in that image you may, in fact, see future suffering, shrinking, even cracking.

The discussions throughout this book will mean more if you can see what's actually at stake for you in dollars and cents. Consider some what-ifs: your food bill goes up 25 percent over the next five years, your homeowner's insurance up 40 percent, your water bill 100 percent, and so on. A glance at your budget will tell you where you're going to find that extra money. Or not.

After you put this book down, there's the more usual reason to track a budget. Over time, it helps you see clearly when certain expenses are rising. Such increases are hard to notice day-to-day, and the total effect can become serious before you notice. Tracking your spending summaries each month can spotlight the insidious costs of warming. It can keep you from saying, "Don't worry so much, Honey. I can't really see what's changing."

Start with this budget bookmark. It's filled out for a notional family and shows only the items most vulnerable to the effects of warming. A blank version is on page 243, and you may want to take a pair of scissors and cut it out, fill it in, use it to mark your place in this book, and refer to it as you read. Prefer to print a copy or download an Excel spreadsheet? Do so from www.savvyfamilies.org/climateproof-budget-bookmark.

The following is just an illustration—a fictitious family, today earning around $70,000 (65% of American families earn less).[18] They have chosen to look ahead to 2022 and have chosen some what-if change numbers.

Using change percentages that are "above inflation" lets you compare the future in today's dollars. Throughout this book, the forecasts and projections are all *inflation-adjusted*, i.e. above inflation.

Notice what happened to this family's *Other* and *Saving* amounts, caused by some reasonable what-if changes to other budget items over seven years!

As you read below about the pressures from warming on various expense and income items, jot down change estimates for the effects on your family's spending. Supplement the predictions in this book with the *Where-To-Live Indicators*, plus other up-to-date information sources for which you should be on the lookout.

	2015	Change	2022
Earned income before taxes	70,000	1%	70,700
Other income before taxes	1,350	2%	1,377
Federal income taxes	4,800	5%	5,040
State/local income/sales taxes and fees	2,300	30%	2,990
Social Security and pensions	5,790	0%	5,790
Income after taxes	58,460		58,257
Expenditures			
Food, at home and out, incl. alcohol	7,800	10%	8,580
Housing (owned)			
Mortgage interest and charges	3,130	0%	3,130
Property taxes	2,000	15%	2,300
Insurance, maintenance, repairs	1,330	5%	1,397
Rent			
Utilities, fuels, and public services			
Natural gas	450	50%	675
Electricity	1,570	20%	1,884
Heating, cooling, cooking fuels	140	50%	210
Telephone	1,550	-20%	1,240
Water and other public services	600	50%	900
Transportation			
Vehicle purchase incl. interest	2,400	0%	2,400
Gasoline and motor oil	1,700	50%	2,550
Maintenance and repairs	960	0%	960
Vehicle insurance	1,200	10%	1,320
Public and other transportation	600	0%	600
Health care, including insurance	4,950	40%	6,930
Charity	1,810	0%	1,810
Education & reading	1,000	0%	1,000
Other	23,270		20,372
Total Expenditures	56,460		58,257
Saving, incl life insurance	2,000		0
Market value of owned home	166,000	0%	166,000

True, even the most accurate budget will not highlight hidden costs like those mentioned earlier. But few of us are aware of how even our in-your-face costs are trending, or sit down regularly to consider managing those costs. When we start to do this, the hidden costs may begin to creep into our consciousness.

There are plenty of budgeting aids.

You may find one of the online calculators easier to use than a hand-written table. The Expense Tracker, with its "Get Honest" button provided by Suze Orman, author of *The 9 Steps to Financial Freedom*, may be particularly helpful if budgeting is unfamiliar to you.[19] And if it seems too much trouble to write down your daily cash flows, you may want to use one of the online services that automatically gather transactions from your bank, credit card, and other accounts. The services, including Mint and Yodlee, will categorize most of the items for you, but each month you will need to look through and maybe correct a few of the computer's assumptions. It's a good chance to re-experience your month's outlays and receipts and maybe think about changing some of the patterns.

If you prefer to track your finances on a spreadsheet, you can type *"household financial budget template"* into your search engine to find a selection of downloadable templates for Excel, Google Docs or other applications.[20]

Want to compare your spending patterns against those of other households? Check the Bureau of Labor Statistics for household expenditures across the country by income level, age, education, etc. at 1.usa.gov/28Jx6Qa. Online calculators at bit.ly/28JKnZO will give you a rough idea of what average families are spending, based on income levels.

A habit of monitoring a household budget can make sure you see financial trouble spots as they develop and take steps early to climate-proof your lives—unlike many of your neighbors who may wait until their options become more limited.

Your geographic vulnerability

I'd love to be able to write something like "Over five years your water costs are predicted to go up 80-100 percent, your municipal taxes up 15-16 percent, electricity in your area up 20-30 percent," and so on. But with warming, such changes will vary all over the map—literally.

Geography may be the dominant factor in how well your income, your job security, and the value of your home are shielded. Does your part of the country have natural defenses against flooding and drought, or energy and transportation costs? Is your hometown prepared to pay for new infrastructure or to attract new businesses? We'll explore these questions throughout the book, especially in Chapter 11 on how place matters.

With the help of the *Where-To-Live Indicators* mentioned throughout and available to readers on the SavvyFamilies.org website, you should be able to answer these questions. The data let you gauge how your expenses, income, and assets will likely be affected by warming compared to families in other towns across America.

Beyond where you live, how you think will influence the likelihood that your family savings, your skills, and your spending patterns will defend you from the effects of warming. A no-regrets attitude will likely insulate you from serious decline. And the mentality to survive a big downturn and recover, to retreat with a minimum of pain, and to redesign your life to be more climate-proof can be as important as just moving to a safer hometown. These attitudes will be discussed throughout the book, especially in Chapter 12 on useful modes of thought.

Footnotes for this chapter, Where-To-Live Indicators for all American towns, and other tools and resources are available at savvyfamilies.org/climateproof, as well as the author's updates, your comments, and other useful information.

2 RETAIN SECURE ACCESS TO FOOD

Most of us in America are oblivious to the price and availability of food. We hear about the costs of healthcare and energy. And taxes are a perennial American bugaboo. But food? Not so much. Just look at the buy-one-get-one-free items on supermarket shelves, the one-dollar short stack, the three-dollar Happy Meal. Of all the family costs discussed in this book, Americans may believe food is the least threatened. Hey, even the big drought in California didn't seem to change anything on our grocer's shelves!

Wrong. We may not notice it, but what we pay to feed ourselves is rising significantly—and it's not just avocados and pumpkins. Although 2015 was a relatively favorable year, in just the past decade food costs for an average family around the world rose 50 percent.[1] America has been more fortunate, but U.S. food costs have been rising faster than our general inflation since 2006.[2] That may not sound like much until we realize that general inflation has climbed 14 percent while median household income has grown way less than that.

Food costs take about 10-15 percent of total spending for the median American household.[3] When they grow faster than other costs, they crowd out those other purchases. It's happening, and there's no sign it will stop soon. What will your family budget look like if food rises another 20% or more in the decade ahead?

Many families are at real risk.

For millions, the rising price of food is bad news. Incredibly in such a rich nation, one in seven American households already have trouble feeding their families. More than a third of those are undernourished because they can't pay for food. Others are taking money that should go for heat or medicine to put food on the table.[4]

The two biggest factors boosting prices in the U.S. are climate-related. Bad weather has reduced harvest and storage, and the same conditions abroad have doubled export demand for American wheat, rice, soybeans, and other agricultural products.[5] World prices for these commodities influence what we pay at home.

HOW OUR FOOD COSTS WILL INCREASE

Our world is drying. Rain and meltwater from snow are the most obvious sources of water on our farms. That water flows into our streams and rivers and fills our reservoirs. But precipitation is changing across America, and for the most part that will make our food increasingly expensive.

The Colorado River is showing the biggest impact. In early 2015 Lake Mead, the largest of the river's reservoirs, was about 37 percent full—the lowest level since its creation in the 1930's.[6] The Colorado basin is the primary water supply for more than 30 million Americans. If we don't happen to be among them, we're still dependent on the watershed; it irrigates 15 percent of America's food.

A watershed can store water in multiple ways. When we can see the local reservoir half-empty, we understand we won't be able to water the lawn next summer. But when we ski the Back Bowl at Vail we're less likely to notice it is storing only half its normal snow.

Roughly 90 percent of the Colorado River's flow comes from winter snow falling in the Rockies to form a frozen reservoir. This snowpack melts slowly in the spring, feeding the river more or less evenly into the early summer. Less snowpack in Colorado means less snowmelt in the spring and less fruit and vegetables in the summer. Snowpack water storage is now threatened in two ways:

1. Temperatures have been steadily warming in the mountains, producing more rain and less snow. In the autumn, snowfields start building later; in springtime they start melting earlier. Even if total precipitation in the mountains doesn't change, less of it will freeze to be used during the growing season.

2. There's another reason snow is melting earlier. As warming provides less water to desert areas west of the Rockies, the soil becomes very dry. The southwest wind can then lift large amounts of dust and blow

it east onto the Rockies. When the snowpack becomes darkened by dust particles, it absorbs more of the sun's rays, melting faster in the spring than clean snow. Thanks to these two factors accelerating snowmelt, scientists are predicting a drop in Colorado River flow from 6 to 45 percent by 2050.[7]

And it's not just the Rockies. The same problem faces the farm-filled Central Valley in California, which relies on meltwater from snowpack in the Sierra Nevada range.

Our groundwater is disappearing.

The other great source for irrigating our agriculture—and for more than half of our drinking water—is groundwater. By pumping it out for current use, we are fast using up that source. Well levels are going down. The underground lake called the Ogallala Aquifer is what keeps huge areas of eight High Plains states, from South Dakota to Texas, from being uninhabitable. It used to water over 25 percent of the nation's irrigated land, but its level has fallen by almost 10 percent since 1950, in some places by 160 feet. The drop is accelerating. (China is doing the same thing to its North China Plain aquifer, and Premier Wen Jiabao has said the depletion of well water "threatens the very survival of China.")

The aquifer will take thousands of years to replenish the way it was formed, through rainfall.[8] This is true beyond the Ogallala. Observers have focused attention on Lake Mead, but that surface lake has been hiding a bigger water loss. In the summer of 2014, NASA discovered that a groundwater lake under the Colorado River bed has also been emptying thanks to decades of pumping by towns and farms in the area. Enough underground water has been lost to fill Lake Mead twice over— enough to meet the home water use of the entire U.S. population for eight years.[9]

While the drop in aquifer levels is not directly caused by warming, there is a strong connection. The more surface water we lose due to warming, the faster we pump our aquifers dry.

We're losing our topsoil.

When Iowa land was first farmed, the settlers found 14 to 16 inches of topsoil. By 2000, that average was six to eight inches.[10]

We usually think of farmland erosion as caused by flooding—heavy rains running off badly sloped, un-contoured, over-tilled or over-grazed fields, filling creeks with soil runoff, pesticides and herbicides. With more intense downpours caused by climate shifts, this danger is expected to continue, but drought too poses a danger. During the 1930s Dust Bowl topsoil dried up and blew away by the billions of tons, and it is now happening again.[11] Iowa alone lost enough topsoil each year recently to potentially cut $1 billion in yield from the state's 88,000 farms.[12]

In 2013, Boise City, Oklahoma, it was drier than in the 1930s, prompting *National Geographic* to send a photographer and writer to compare the conditions with images and reporting from Dust Bowl days. Today's dust storms have thinned out livestock herds, and residents are again moving away from the corner of America where Colorado, Kansas, Oklahoma, and Texas meet.[13]

Other effects are costly.

Rising temperatures have several additional effects. The first is gradual. Plant Hardiness Zones, areas of similar growing conditions that stripe across a map of the U.S., are moving north 10 miles a year. This means that good weather conditions for a particular crop are vanishing at the southern edge of its range and extending into new counties at its northern edge.[14] American agriculture will encounter problems migrating crops and herds as the land shows the effects of warming and will face increased costs to also migrate skills, processing plants, transportation methods and other infrastructure.

Another effect of heat is sudden. Heat waves kill crops, sometimes very quickly. Heat can also hurt dairy farming. Cows are highly sensitive to temperature changes; above 77°F output starts dropping.[15] Another industry affected dramatically is maple sugar. A quintessentially American industry, sugaring can suffer drops of 15-40 percent in output, thanks to decreased sap flow from warm spells.[16]

In Texas, government economists say the 2011 drought was the most expensive in the state's history, with $5.2 billion in crop and livestock losses. That's equivalent to one-quarter of agricultural production in a typical Texas year, and its effects on agricultural output last well beyond the drought year.[17]

In the Midwest's Corn Belt, increasingly harsh drought conditions may take a serious toll over coming decades. Some scientists predict corn yields could drop as much as 15 to 30 percent; soybean yield losses would be less severe.[18] And, of course, it's not just the research groups that are documenting change. Corn farmers in Iowa, oyster growers in Washington State, and ranchers in Texas are all coping with negative climate-related changes that they haven't seen before.

Each day Chipotle uses, on average, 97,000 pounds of avocado. Recently the company announced it may have to remove guacamole from its menu if warming continues to push up prices.[19] Drier and hotter conditions are predicted to drop California's avocado production by 40 percent over the next 30 years.

America's breweries are concerned by rising temperatures and droughts. Heat has caused the harvests of hops to fail, and water has been in increasingly short supply in some places. If brewers' risks and costs grow, the price of beer will be moving up.

In 2015, Libby's, which supplies more than 85 percent of the world's canned pumpkin, found their annual pumpkin yields reduced by half due to unusually heavy rains in early summer. The price of pumpkin-based products soared.[20]

In addition to worrying about the effects of warming on our crops, we need to think about the effects on a few key animals. Honeybees pollinate 70 of the top 100 food crops, supplying about 90 percent of the world's nutrition. Other plants depend on migratory birds like hummingbirds for pollination. Thanks to warming, NASA and other researchers are finding that migratory patterns are changing and bee colonies are endangered.[21]

Agricultural acreage could be shrinking.

As heat, drought and flooding increase, and irrigation costs reduce arable land and kill crops, one remedy for farmers is to leave their land fallow rather than planting and watching the crops shrivel. This may protect farmers—but not consumers. Over half-a-million acres were predicted to be fallowed in 2015.[22] Farmers naturally cut back on low-profit crops like lentils and tomatoes in favor of almonds, grapes, avocados and other high-profit plants that grow on vines and trees. As farmers make this shift to keep their incomes steady, they are raising the average price of America's food.

In Buena Vista, California, it has become more profitable for farmers to sell their water than to grow stuff with it. In 2014, this town announced it would auction off water from its aquifer and use the proceeds to pay local farmers $400 an acre to leave their fields fallow for the season. Bid prices came in at 3 to 8 times the normal cost those farmers pay for water.[23]

Over five years, the price of bulk water has risen tenfold. Water auctions have grown in Colorado and Texas, as well as California. There are more private sales too. Whether water costs farmers more or pushes their land out of farming, the pressure on our food prices is steadily upwards.

Water is not just for growing stuff.
The groceries we bring into our homes have likely been irrigated, but they have also been cleaned, cooked, canned, cooled, packaged, and transported using fresh water. A gallon of milk requires 880 gallons of water, including cattle feed and drink, to reach our fridge. The average hamburger takes more than 600 gallons. As water becomes more scarce and expensive, processing costs go up.[24]

Rising temperatures can mean new blights.
In 2014 Starbucks raised its prices between 5 and 20 cents. A 20-ounce, Venti-sized cup of brewed coffee, for example, went up to $2.35. We paid a dollar more for a bag of Starbucks coffee sold in the grocery. Folgers and Dunkin' Donuts packaged coffee had already gone up 9 percent, Maxwell House and Yuban up 10 percent. In the first half of 2016, the wholesale price of coffee went up 12%[25] because overseas high temperatures combined with heavy rains and dry periods have given rise to the coffee rust plague, which now infects 70 percent of coffee plantations. An estimated 22 percent of the international coffee crop was lost during 2013–14.[26]

Warming has shrunk America's cattle supply.
Long-term drought on the Great Plains diminished America's cattle supply to its lowest in sixty years in 2014 and pushed up the cost of steak at supermarkets and restaurants. With the number of U.S. cattle at a 60-year low, wholesale prices of beef surged 11 percent over 12 months through May 2014. The U.S. Department. of Agriculture forecasted retail prices for beef and veal would increase 6 to 8 percent in 2015.[27] Since then, conditions have improved somewhat, but with increasing drought

predicted over the next decade, we should expect further contraction in beef production.

As we pay our taxes, we're paying more for food.

The largest single purchaser of food in the country is the federal government. As taxpayers, we pay for SNAP (Food Stamps), WIC (Food for Women, Infants, and Children), and the School Lunch Program to help deal with the hunger of millions of our fellow citizens. Thanks to rising food prices, federal taxpayers paid $2.3 billion more in 2013.[28] In addition, rising nutrition-related health costs across the nation are borne by Medicare and Medicaid.

Taxpayers also pay $20 billion or so each year to farmers in direct subsidies under various farm bills. On top of that, we fund the Federal Crop Insurance Corporation, which sells insurance policies to corn, cotton, soybean and wheat growers, protecting them against weather-related revenue losses. Because the program doesn't charge premiums high enough to cover the growing losses, taxpayers cover the shortfall making it essentially a price-support program for farmers at our expense. It seems perverse to many that we gave farmers, most of them large corporations, $16 billion in 2013 while giving the hungry $2.3 billion. But both groups will likely ask for more from taxpayers as the impacts of warming play out.

On top of taxes, many of us voluntarily contribute to the costs of local food banks and soup kitchens to help feed the poor. The need for these services rises as the price of food goes up. In addition, Americans have always made contributions to charities that operate private food aid programs abroad, a need that is expected to grow dramatically.

Let them eat hake.

For anyone thinking to compensate for declines in landfood by eating more seafood, the news is not good. Since 2006 more than half the ground fishing boats in New Bedford, Massachusetts, the largest fishing port in the country, have given up fishing.[29] Decades of overfishing on the northeast coast and George's Bank persuaded the government to progressively cut the cod, haddock and flounder limits. By the summer of 2014, the cod stock had dropped to 19 percent of what scientists said is needed for a healthy population.[30]

Warming compounds the problem. In water temperatures above 68°F lobsters have problems molting, are more susceptible to disease, and are more stressed trying to keep cool. Before 1998, Buzzards Bay averaged 30 to 40 days a year when water temperatures were above 68. In each of the years since, the number has soared to 90-100 days.[31]

The overall results: seafood prices in the U.S. rose 9 percent in 2014 alone.[32] Overfishing has been the cause of current low production but warmer seas, made more acidic by absorbing CO_2, are now making it difficult to recreate healthy fisheries. Shellfish are a particular long-term casualty.[33] The same is happening to America's freshwater fish. The temperature of the Lower Platt River near Lincoln, Nebraska reached 97°F in the summer of 2012. Coupled with low river flows during one of the warmest, driest summers in history, this killed off tens of thousands of sturgeon, as well as catfish, carp, and bass. Across the Midwest, other rivers and species met the same fate.[34]

Commodities speculation helps keep food prices up.

When harvests increase we would normally expect the law of supply and demand to push food prices down. But U.S. Department of Agriculture data show otherwise. In 2010 a record high in wheat production coincided with record highs in wheat prices. The International Monetary Fund demonstrated the same disconnect, examining the doubling of the price of maize in April 2011 when the crop was plentiful.

A major cause of these abnormal prices seems to be speculation in the commodities futures market.[35] What a buyer is willing to pay for a commodity many months from now can influence the expectations of buyers and sellers when they set prices in today's market.

As weather events become more frequent and severe, farmers are likely to invest more heavily in commodity futures contracts to protect themselves, while speculators will find there is even more money to be made as these events make markets increasingly volatile. With futures contracts becoming more speculative, Wall Street's influence on food prices is growing.

Food distribution costs could be hit by warming.

How our food reaches us may become increasingly costly, but not for the reason that many environmentalists preach, food miles. Their proposition goes like this: since the average item on a grocery shelf has traveled 1,500 miles, we can save the costs of all that diesel and jet fuel by eating local food.

This turns out to be at best an exaggeration. Transportation is only a tiny portion of the energy used to grow, process, package preserve and deliver food. Studies have shown that in some cases food flown from New Zealand has used less energy from seed to kitchen than food grown near us.[36] In his eye-opening book *The Conundrum: How Scientific Innovation, Increased Efficiency, and Good Intentions Can Make Our Energy and Climate Problems Worse*, David Owen tells us "How far you live from your grocery store is of far greater environmental significance than how far you live from the places where your food is grown."[37]

No, the real reasons for us to be concerned about food transport are the increasing risks and unreliability in our national transportation system, discussed in Chapter 5. If, as many predict, our road, rail, and barge systems continue to deteriorate and weather creates more interruptions, the supply chain for food will need to build in more redundancy and rely less on just-in-time delivery. We won't hear about these adjustments, but they will add to food distribution costs.

HOLDING YOUR FOOD COSTS DOWN

So with food costs taking a higher percentage of our family expenses, and supplies of some foods in danger, is there a no-regrets set of actions to protects us? First of all, America's food companies will try to help by adapting, migrating and inventing, trying to maintain the availability of their products. In particular, water will be used more efficiently, and we can expect to see new plant strains better suited to dry and warm weather. But beyond the big industrial farmers, another sector of American agriculture will likely increase in importance, one that can help dampen the effects of shifting weather patterns in America's farming centers, and one which we as individuals can influence and encourage. That's local agriculture.

Local farming provides some protection.

It is hard for many of us to imagine why we need local farmers. In normal times their produce is more expensive; we can't buy it on a normal grocery-shopping trip; sometimes it's not even packaged and labeled.

But local farms can give us many benefits Big Ag does not. Most are not vulnerable to snowmelt in the Rockies or the Sierra Nevada and are not sucking the last decades' worth of water from the Ogallala, so these local farms are more likely to avoid disruptions and price fluctuations from drought. Their crops are more diversified than the endless monocultures of corn, wheat, soybeans, and rice, hence less vulnerable to crop-specific pests and disease. They use fewer chemicals to prevent those problems. Small local farms are also less vulnerable to a terrorist attack, a growing concern at the FBI and other agencies.[38] And, as local distribution strengthens, local farmers will be more and more locked into putting food on your table instead of some distant family's, adding to your food security if national supplies are disrupted.

Beyond improved security, local farmers generally provide the healthy stuff (think fruits and vegetables, poultry and eggs, beans and milk that are right in the center of the USDA's Food Pyramid), not the oils and fats (corn and meat) sitting at the top, labeled "Use Sparingly." And local farmers supply foods you can actually recognize, not the heavily processed supermarket products made with high-fructose corn syrup, polysorbate, bromated flour and other chemical ingredients. You're likely to eat more healthily as you increase your purchases from local farmers.

And local produce is something you can influence. Here are a number of ways you can help these local farmers expand and thrive.

Encourage protective zoning and land trusts.

In many communities, builders and real estate agents still consider farmland simply as future housing developments. Many farmers think the same way: "I'll keep on farming until I get the right offer. Then I'll go off to Florida, and they can do what they want with my land."

Local citizens can help change these attitudes by pushing their states, towns and counties to encourage small agriculture. There are dozens of ideas: passing state laws and town ordinances that help preserve farmland, reducing property taxes and regulations on farm plots, making permitting easy, etc.. The easier it is for farmers to buy contiguous land parcels, the more likely they are to develop into efficient farms, so you should support favorable zoning for farmers. Supporting land trusts lets their purchasing power compete against developers and preserve farmland. The availability of money to buy development rights can be a big factor in keeping the Wilson Farm near you from becoming the Wilson Estates.

You can encourage your local government to favor local farmers in their food purchases, offer unused city land for farming or gardening, make urban farms eligible for non-profit grants, and provide low-cost loans for urban farmers.[39]

Cutting government red tape can help. In Hancock County, Maine four neighboring towns passed Local Food and Self-Governance Ordinances declaring a measure of independence from state and federal food labeling and license requirements, which they say stifle farmers' markets, roadside stands, farm-based sales and direct producer-to-patron sales. The towns argue they have faith in their citizens' ability to educate themselves and make informed decisions.[40] Similar ordinances have been enacted in towns in Massachusetts, Vermont, and California. Dropping regulations to boost the sale of local farm products may spread as these market outlets become more popular.

Even big cities can encourage urban farming. In San Francisco, if the owner of an empty lot turns it into a vegetable garden instead of building a home or apartment block (and donates some of the produce to a school food program or food bank), the city will lower property taxes to virtually nothing.[41]

Strengthen farmers' markets.

Local food requires more than just land. To really support area growers, farm-to-table distribution channels are critical. Today's farmer's markets are not always doing that job. Although in some towns where there's a push by citizens, local food sales have grown explosively, in many others neither farmers nor food buyers seem very interested.

There are natural barriers to local food. For consumers, markets are weekly, weather-dependent, seasonal, pricey, limited in supply and, for many of us, distant. And there's no information: Are there blueberries this week?

From the farmer's point of view, few people shop at their markets (especially in bad weather), the per-unit cost of transporting produce by pickup to the market (and maybe back again) is high, and the hours devoted to selling rather than cultivating can make it much easier to simply sell to a wholesaler.

You may live in a town that has tackled these problems successfully and now provides local food plentifully and conveniently. The 65 farmers who sell at the Green City Market at Lincoln Park in Chicago serve 10,000 shoppers a week. There's a waiting list for farmers. If this is not the case in your town, you can think of ways to help strengthen demand at your local market. Introduce new shoppers. Start a carpool to a market with your neighbors. Offer a teenager the job of shopping for multiple families each week.

Another factor that keeps local farmers selling locally is the chance to supply nearby restaurants and schools. Hidden from us as grocery shoppers, these channels nevertheless serve the same purpose as farmers' markets, developing local farms' capacity to sell more fruits and vegetables. Michelle Obama's Healthy Hunger-Free Kids Act should help increase local demand. You can ask your restaurant server for dishes that are made from local products and encourage your school system and its citizens' committee to buy local.

Get your own farmer.

Sign up with a CSA—the channel known as "community supported agriculture"—that brings farmers and their customers closest together.[42] The typical CSA is a small farm on the outskirts of town growing fruit and vegetables in season and putting them each week into boxes labeled for individual members. As a member, you show up and take your pre-paid box home to the fridge. The farmer enjoys a paid-in-advance market, low selling costs, and low wastage. Members have "my very own farm" and a reliable supply of really fresh produce, often at competitive prices. If national supplies do become less reliable, how nice to have a locked-in personal source of food.

The concept seems to be scalable. Full Circle, based in Seattle, has expanded from a single five-acre farm to a service that works with 15,000 members and 400 farms from Anchorage to San Francisco to Boise. Although the company will sometimes buy food from out of the area—

and therefore out of season—to put in members' boxes, it still serves the function of locking in demand for farmers and supply for members.[43]

Encourage food cooperatives.

Food coops vary widely in their scope and purpose but are all designed to strengthen local farms, remove middlemen, and serve local consumers. Two hundred producer members in the Oklahoma Food Cooperative sell more than 6,000 items—including meat, produce, milk, and value-added items—to its 3,800 consumer members. Customers place orders on the Internet and receive them via member-operated distribution routes that cover most of the state. All products sold through the cooperative must be made in Oklahoma, and members always know which farmer produced their food.[44]

Cooperatives are usually owned by their local employees, make many of their purchases locally, and won't move to another town if things get bad. You can research the many economic advantages that cooperatives and other locally-owned businesses bring to their communities in the example-filled book, *Local Dollars, Local Sense*, by Michael Shuman.[45]

Check an online directory to see if there's a producers' food coop or a food buying club in your area. If not, ask around; you may find someone who needs only a little help to start one.

Support development of food hubs.

Regional Access, in the Finger Lakes region of New York, is a good example of what is called a food hub.[46] The Ithaca company provides many traditional wholesaler services: transportation, warehousing, and marketing of a farm's output. The difference is that Regional Access sells to chefs and specialty retailers, coops, buying clubs, institutions and individual families, most of them local.

The process is characterized in its simplest form as "one truck that goes to the city, and one delivery route."[47] Food hubs help regional growers collaborate on local marketing and distribution, thereby expanding food sources and distribution channels beyond just farmers' markets and CSAs.

Encouraging local agriculture is a way to insulate your family and community from the growing risks of a distant food supply. But of course it only works only if you've chosen a hometown with farmland, where local farmers face a relatively low risk from warming-related threats, and where nearby communities provide an eager market. We'll discuss below how you can identify these communities.

Dependence on local farms has its limits.

While local sources of food will be an important cost and supply buffer in the face of warming, it's easy to exaggerate how much local farms can provide. We may have a pleasant hazy dream in which we and our neighbors rely on the farms just outside our town, maybe an urban hydroponics operator or two, some community gardens, and our own backyard plots for the bulk of our food. The bad news is that reliance by all of us on local food is impractical.

Even the most hopeful scenarios—for instance a 2011 plan calling for New England to dramatically increase its food production—only aspire to 50 percent of a region's consumption.[48] First of all, there's nowhere near enough acreage close to our cities and suburbs to grow what the country needs. Then the growing and distribution costs of small farms are much higher than corporate agriculture's. And our eating habits, our town's land-use laws, and our shopping methods may all present barriers.

But even against these headwinds, we still have plenty of scope for increasing local food supplies. Currently, farm-direct sales across the country account for well under one percent of total farm sales,[49] but, as with other things discussed throughout this book, you and your town don't have to be average. Communities with nearby farmland, devoted farmers, favorable taxes and regulations, strong local demand, and inventive distribution methods can efficiently put lots of local produce on our tables. You can create some of these factors over time by your own demand and by encouraging other local residents to care about local food sources. Or you can move to a town that is already way above average.

What about growing some of your own?

If American farmers increasingly struggle to provide cheap food, can your family or neighbors plant a garden, learn canning, and harvest significant amounts of your own food? During World War II, Victory Gardens were everywhere. The government nailed up posters saying "It's thrifty. It's patriotic. Dig for victory!" and an estimated 20 million home and community gardens were planted. For a short period, they produced 40-50 percent of all the country's fresh produce.[50]

The "Special Period" in Cuba is an extreme example of coping with agricultural stress. Imagine our country's farmers suddenly losing access to petroleum products. Diesel is no longer available to help plant, irrigate, spray and harvest their huge fields. Fertilizer production drops dramatically. Food becomes scarce, and the government imposes rationing. People begin to starve. That's what happened to Cuba when the Soviet Union, Cuba's source of oil, collapsed in 1989, the U.S. refused to lift our 40-year embargo, and Castro refused to accept private donations from Americans. The average Cuban lost about 20 pounds.

Cuban families and groups started to grow their own food on any open land they could find. Organic by necessity, these plots eventually fed the Cuban population at survival levels until 1998 when Venezuela began to replace the Soviet Union as Cuba's supplier of cheap petroleum.[51]

Closer to home, and far less existential, the New Economy Transition group in Jamaica Plain, an inner suburb of Boston, has done more than most communities to collect and analyze actual data about the 28 community gardens (not including private backyard gardens) in their town. Their conclusion: "Community Gardens will never be able to grow enough food to feed the whole neighborhood. Even if all the undeveloped land was put under cultivation it could not do that (the requirement for 1 person is 1.2 acres!). What it could do, however, is provide most of the fresh fruits and vegetables we need to keep us healthy, while traditional farms provide the carbohydrates and fats."[52]

Would a home garden save money?

Even if home gardens can't feed everyone, could yours feed your family? How practical and cheap is a home garden? Here's one answer.

Roger and Jacqueline Doiron cultivate potatoes, tomatoes, carrots, zucchini, cabbage and 30 other vegetables and herbs on a third of an acre behind their home in Scarborough, Maine. A few years back, they weighed their year's harvest—834 pounds in all—and tracked what it would have cost at the market:

> Grocery store: $2,196.50
> Farmers' market: $2,431.15
> Whole Foods: $2,548.93

The Doirons' cost for growing that produce was $130 for seeds and supplies, $12 for a soil test, $100 for compost, and $40 for water, a total of $282. That's a big saving!

But, of course the family's labor is not included. Even at day-laborer rates, those hours would make the family's bounty more expensive than the markets'. Doiron says they did not include labor costs in the comparison because "We enjoy gardening and the physical work involved. If I am to include my labor costs, I feel I should also include the gym membership fees, country club dues, or doctors' bills I didn't have." Doiron has since developed the nonprofit Kitchen Gardeners International—35,000 people growing some of their own food and helping others to do the same— where information and advice about home gardens are available.[53]

How many hours a week does it actually take to cultivate a garden? The answer, of course, depends on its size, what you plant, whether you're a newbie and other factors. But you may be surprised to read in home-garden books that tilling and planting at the beginning of the season is estimated in single-figure hours, and watering and weeding at ten or twenty of minutes a day. Many gardeners say something like, "Time? I don't track it. Those are among the best minutes of my day."

How can a family free up time to spend in their own garden or the community plot up the street? Roger Doiron's answer is a starting place: "The average American watches four hours of TV a day."

More and more towns allow you to keep chickens.
The evidence is anecdotal, but there is a movement toward allowing city residents to keep chickens for their own use. Flock size is limited, and noisy roosters are prohibited, but there's a chance that your City Hall allows—or can be persuaded to allow—you to enjoy your own fresh eggs every day. And if you don't start thinking of them as pets, you might bring yourself to enjoy a home-grown chicken dinner occasionally.[54]

Cheap technologies are evolving.
A well-designed low-tech rain collection system can make a huge difference where water restrictions will likely be instituted.[55] And more and more urban gardeners are incorporating some low-cost engineering and chemistry into their mini-farms. Whether it's hydroponics, grow lights, grow tents, artificial soils, CO_2 exhalers, organic nutrients, worm

castings, or just simple rain barrels, you can grow more stuff under greater control in less space.

Learn from mentors.

Starting a food garden can be daunting. It takes skills that were lost to most of us generations ago. We would have to start vegetable gardening with a trowel in one hand and a how-to book in the other. Mistakes won't show up for weeks or months.

It can be easier, faster and more fun to get your garden to flourish with help from one or more knowledgeable neighbors. Apprenticing in a neighbor's garden, joining a garden club that isn't just about ornamentals, even going to classes can help you avoid major mistakes and discouragement.

A group in Honesdale, Pennsylvania created a fenced community garden with 25 raised beds. The group offers these beds to those who don't have their own backyard for growing vegetables and to clients of such poverty programs as SNAP, WIC, and local food pantries. The fee depends on ability to pay, and gardeners donate 10 percent of their harvest to a nearby nursing home. For everyone in the community, the group offers gardening classes and DIY workshops. Topics include how to build a cold frame, make a worm bed, and construct a rain barrel.[56]

You can find instruction at agricultural supply stores, garden centers, Grange and 4H Clubs, Agricultural Extension Offices, and other organizations that emphasize skills and supplies for smallholdings.[57] The Cooperative Extension Service of the University of California operates a Horticulture Center in Fair Oaks that includes a water-efficient landscape, blueberries and cane berries, demonstration vegetable and herb gardens, and areas for compost and vermiculture. They help vegetable-growing residents via phone and office consultations, plant clinics, workshops, youth gardening programs, and a speaker's bureau.[58]

The Foodshed Alliance in Bucks County, Pennsylvania, in addition to sponsoring farmers' markets, organizes farm tours, lectures, and workshops for amateur growers, runs a food book club and sponsors a micro-lending program to support producer-to-consumer efforts. The Alliance works with the local university, food bank, food co-op, chamber of commerce, and other community organizations to "improve availability of local, healthy, sustainably grown food."[59]

Ask if the local garden club is into zucchini and potatoes, not just begonias and morning glories. The club in Summit County, Colorado organizes the usual garden tours, beautification projects, and speakers program on floral topics, but it also contributes to the development of a community vegetable garden, and its website and speakers now offer advice and resources for creating a kitchen garden.[60]

As mentors, newly arrived immigrants with agricultural skills and strong ties to the land, are a resource. Including them in a project benefits everyone.[61] The Dallas Area Community Gardening Program recruits recent immigrants, allowing them to produce traditional crops otherwise unavailable locally, taking advantage of their experience to produce a significant amount of food for the household, and offering both groups a cultural exchange with other gardeners.[62]

Another place to look for mentors and equipment, for indoor growing in particular, is your neighborhood pot farmer. In states that permit cannabis cultivation, look for a "garden center" that specializes in lighting and other indoor growing equipment. Its customers are sure to be way ahead of you on hydroponics and other small-plot growing techniques.

True, most Americans don't see a risk to their food supply and have no interest in weeding their own vegetable gardens. But if you're looking ahead, you will see that the pressures that could make U.S. food more expensive may take years to develop. If your children grow up today with a small backyard vegetable plot, the whole grow-your-own thing will seem comfortable for them if they encounter seriously rising costs or declining availability of food in the future. [63]

And how about eating differently?

Two other practices can offset any food cost increases you're likely to see from warming. First, there's the food you eat but don't need; second, the food you buy but don't use.

Our families could spend less on food if we stopped overeating. Consider fats we add to our diet, like those in salad and cooking oils. Back in the 1950s, each of us happily consumed 45 pounds of added fats each year. By 2000 it was 75 pounds. In that period sweetener use rose from 110 to 152 pounds per person, with high-fructose corn syrup rising from zero to 64 pounds. Not surprisingly, the percent of Americans classified as obese jumped from 13 percent to 31 percent. It's over 35 percent today.

Eating less can save hundreds of dollars on food costs, but that's dwarfed by the thousands you can save in healthcare costs in coming years.

The second potential source of food savings is waste at home. The average American consumes 2,700 calories a day, but our food system wastes another 1,100 calories or so per person. Much of that is in production and distribution, but the average consumer still throws away around 30 percent of the grain products, seafood, fruits and vegetables it buys, and around 15 percent of the meat and milk. While there may not be much we can personally do about losses on the farm, in transit or at the supermarket, we can save hundreds of dollars a year by becoming more conscious of food waste in our refrigerators and on our plates.[64]

What about actually cooking for a change?

The cost of a heat-and-eat meal is several times the cost of its ingredients bought separately, combined and cooked at home. This means many families have a huge potential to save on food costs. But it means they must spend extra time to plan meals, buy ingredients, work at the kitchen counter, and stand in front of the stove, right?

Not necessarily. Look at the "Food" shelves in your local bookstore. You'll see "Easy" and "Quick" and "Simple" in many titles. One or two of these will supply hundreds of dishes that require hardly any more work to prepare than ready-to-eat packaged food—at a fraction of the cost.

WHERE TO LIVE FOR BETTER FOOD SECURITY

Not all towns and cities are going to have robust local food sources. If your hometown has the right weather, land, infrastructure and enthusiasm for local food, great. But if the community continues to think of farm plots in residential areas as nuisances, or if it doesn't let farmer's markets operate in convenient central areas, you may want to be living somewhere with a better attitude a few years from now.

Moving is a tough decision and, once it's made, a tough process. But, as we'll see throughout this book, the likelihood that you can dodge the effects of warming will be much higher in some places than others, and your ability to relocate could be the most effective means of climate-proofing your family's finances and lifestyle.

Pick the right agricultural climate.

It's important to live where things will grow well—not just today but in the future. Increasingly, good growing conditions will be at higher elevations and farther north.

Yourtown, USA

Check the Plant Hardiness Zones from the U.S. Department of Agriculture at bit.ly/plant-hardiness, plus their Plant Finder at http://www.garden.org/plants, to see where vegetables grow best— remembering, of course, that these bands are moving slowly north.

Less-than-weather conditions need not deter you from your own garden, but you may need to cover your beds, or invest in a greenhouse.

Are water problems on the horizon?

If a town is destined to have water restrictions, you may wonder whether family or community vegetable gardens will work. It pays to look ahead. Even if there are no water restrictions today, many parts of the country will increasingly need to conserve in the coming years. We will discuss other costs and problems of water shortages in Chapter 8 on the home, along with what you can do to protect yourself from them.

Don't overlook soil quality.

You are viewing a house to buy. You take notes, you take photos, and you take soil samples from the back yard. Soil samples? Yes, if you might want to grow stuff on your own lot someday, it pays to make sure you won't be pushing your seeds into salty, acidic or lead-contaminated soil. It's cheap and easy to bag a few samples, send them off to a state or private lab, and gauge your prospects for a backyard vegetable garden.[65]

Pick the right consumer climate.

If you want to live where the local food industry is strongly supported, the number of farmer's markets is one indicator.

Yourtown, USA

For detailed maps and data about local farming and food distribution, check the U.S. Dept. of Agriculture's Know Your Farmer, Know Your Food website at bit.ly/know-your-farmer. Check for CSAs at localharvest.org/locations.

Farmers' markets are listed at localharvest.org/farmers-markets. Roadside farms are listed at bit.ly/farm-stands. The U.S. Dept. of Agriculture maintains a directory of several types of local food sources at bit.ly/local-food-directory.[66]

Think ahead.

When we push our overflowing carts down the supermarket aisle, flanked by full freezers and endless shelves, steering around clerks busily replenishing the morning's purchases, it's hard to imagine that we have anything to fear from food shortages or price jumps.

And even if we conclude that we need to adjust our lives to dodge these costs, a no-regrets approach may not seem attractive today. For many, it's hard to see ourselves in the backyard holding a hoe instead of a mower. Or standing up to speak at a Zoning Board meeting. And what about standing at the stove? That's just not our style.

But the California and Texas droughts' effect on beef and vegetable prices suggests that we will still need to adjust to grocery prices that are rising faster than inflation and, for many of us, a lot faster than our incomes. A few key decisions—and, yes, lifestyle adjustments begun today—can help savvy families to at least partially insulate themselves from tomorrow's rising food costs and shortages.

Footnotes for this chapter, Where-To-Live Indicators for all American towns, and other tools and resources are available at savvyfamilies.org/climateproof, as well as the author's updates, your comments, and other useful information.

3 HOLD DOWN YOUR ENERGY COSTS

Until the global oil glut began in 2014, energy was an expense we closely linked to warming and the one we thought most about curbing. It was the topic that showed up most frequently in the media and the bookstores: hybrid cars, triple-pane windows, Energy Star appliances, vacationing closer to home, solar panels—a swarm of tips on energy conservation were buzzing around us.

Lately, thanks to overproduction around the world plus the new technique of recovering oil and gas through hydraulic fracturing, or fracking, prices for gasoline, heating oil and natural gas have dropped. But the oil and gas glut has somehow left the cost of our electricity untouched.[1] And, despite the energy-saving actions many businesses and households have taken over the past decade, overall energy demand, and our costs, are likely headed up. Because of warming, America is predicted to require 95 gigawatts of additional capacity for electric power, mostly for cooling, at an increased cost of $12 billion a year.[2]

We can meet those needs by burning more fossil fuels in more generating plants. Or we can install new solar arrays and wind turbines to power our communities, homes, and companies. Either way, Americans will be spending more on electricity and on the equipment that supplies it.

Here's an indication of how threatening both the prices and the environmental costs of fossil fuels may be. In the early 1980s, Gwyneth Cravens was a leader of the activists who successfully protested the Shoreham Nuclear Power Plant on Long Island. Thanks to Cravens and others the plant, although completed, was never opened. Thirty-five years later, in 2007, Cravens wrote *Power to Save the World: The Truth About Nuclear Energy*, reversing herself and arguing that nuclear power has now become essential to avoid the much greater dangers from warming.

Warming has also changed the mind of arch-environmentalist Stewart Brand, founder and editor of the *Whole Earth Catalog*. In his book *Whole Earth Discipline*, Brand lays out the many arguments against nuclear power that most of us believed back then and which he considers today to be dangerous myths.[3] In the face of warming, other dyed-in-the-wool environmentalists and anti-nuclear activists have been doing an about-face on their long-time objections to nuclear power.

American families spend a lot on energy. Average costs were $3,052 per person in 2012 (over $5,500 in some states). That's $9,000 for a family of three.[4] Unless we can take steps to protect ourselves, even a modest fifteen to thirty percent increase in this expense will put a budget squeeze on many of us.

That means a plan to reduce the energy outlays by our family and our community will be important. But before we look at what tactics such a plan might include, let's examine the forces pushing on our energy costs.

HOW OUR ENERGY COSTS COULD CHANGE

What could keep energy prices down

Fossil fuel costs are down.

There are reasons to believe that oil and natural gas may stay cheap for a long time. First, many of the exporting nations, including Venezuela and Russia, have become dependent on high levels of oil revenues and cannot afford to cut back on production until prices rise again. The result is a growing surplus on the world market, holding prices down. New sources from Iran are only adding to the glut.

Demand has been down too. Americans are making more economical use of energy today. Gasoline use topped out back in 2007 as hybrid, electric, biofuel and other technologies became more widespread. Today U.S. drivers get an average of 26 miles per gallon, an improvement, but in less than ten years we'll be buying new cars that average 54.5 mpg.[5] Electricity use is down too. In the U.S. it has declined since 2007, partly because of the recession but also because of more efficient electrical devices.[6]

Then there's fracking.[7] Those pipelines and hundred-car trains heading for refineries have been carrying dramatically cheaper crude oil and natural gas. 'Peak Oil' seems to have been postponed. According to

Citigroup, by 2020 the U.S. will pass Russia as the world's largest supplier of petroleum products. With its huge success, fracking has reminded us not to underestimate human ingenuity.

Renewable energy costs are down

Solar and wind costs are falling as well. The cost of electricity from photovoltaic panels has been dropping dramatically[8] thanks to increasingly efficient solar cells,[9] rising production volume, and more efficient distribution channels.[10] In 1980 the cost of wind energy was about 30-45 cents per kilowatt-hour; today it's less than 3 cents. Solar, geothermal and biomass energy production have dropped in cost too, thanks to maturing technologies.[11]

It's conceivable that the U.S. will follow Denmark's example. Encouraged by the success of their big wind farms, Danes have committed to getting over half of the country's electricity from wind by 2020.[12] There are many studies that find no technical or cost impediment to stop Americans from powering the country purely on renewable energy sources. A group from Stanford University says this can be done with wind, solar and water power by 2030.[13]

New energy sources are showing up too. Many farmers are waking up to the fact that, along with beef and milk, their cows produce huge amounts of methane. With 1,500 cows each producing about 100 pounds of manure a day, Fiscalini Farms in Modesto, California has installed two anaerobic digester tanks to capture methane from the manure. Heated to around 100°F, the tanks help bacteria convert manure to methane gas. Piped out of the digesters, the methane fuels a generator that powers the farm, heats the digester, and sends electricity back to the grid.[14] This is also being done at landfills, where methane is a product of our garbage.[15]

Other new energy sources include algae, which can be grown anywhere, and biofuel made from switchgrass which, unlike biofuel from corn, would not raise prices in the world's food markets. Eleven European countries have several thousand offshore wind turbines operating; five are finally being installed in America, off Rhode Island.

Increasing energy efficiency can help a lot

We waste huge amounts of energy today. Amory Lovins, long-time advocate of energy efficiency, has been an inspiration to me ever since I read his *Soft Energy Paths* in 1977. In his latest book, *Reinventing Fire*, he argues that industry, business and consumers already have big opportunities to save money by cutting fuel use through higher energy efficiency. This is true even without new taxes or regulations. Lovins sees $5 trillion in potential savings on the table over the next 40 years.[16]

On the other hand, despite these potential cost-savings, energy could soon be taking a much bigger bite out of the family budget, largely due to warming.[17] Let's look at some of the reasons, most of which have little to do with the cost of fossil fuels.

What could keep energy prices up

Electric utilities are threatened by water problems.
As heat dries our waterways, some electric utilities may need to cut generation, shutting down plants when their water source drops below the intake pipe.[18] Even without drought, warming alone can hurt electricity generation, since water above a certain temperature doesn't cool a power plant.[19]

In the 2012 summer drought, the electric plant in Powerton, Illinois had to turn off one of its two generators because the lake providing its cooling water became so hot the bearings overheated.[20] And, of course, the timing is always wrong: when our utility needs more cooling water during a heat wave is also when customers demand more electricity for air conditioning.

Too much water is a much bigger threat. Because fossil-fueled or nuclear power plants need so much cooling water, they are naturally sited next to rivers, lakes or oceans.[21] Yet increasing climate disruptions are making those locations risky. The Oyster Creek Generating Station, north of Atlantic City, New Jersey is designed to remain safe if seawater rises by 8.5 feet. Above that, the cooling pumps will be flooded. During Hurricane Sandy, a combination of high tide, area-wide storm surge, and wind-driven water reached 7.4 feet. The growing need to rebuild generating and transmission stations away from coastal locations will call for huge construction costs, which will find their way into our electricity bills.

Oyster Creek is not alone. Power plants supplying 53 percent of New York City's electricity currently sit within the 100-year floodplain, and by the 2020s, 87 percent could be in that danger zone. In addition, about a third of the city's electrical load comes through substations also in the floodplain. It could be two-thirds by the 2020s.[22] Utilities—and we, their customers—are going to spend big to climate-proof those plants or abandon them and rebuild somewhere else.

Renewables are another threat.

Surprise! Even green energy could wind up raising, not lowering, our electricity costs. Putting solar panels on our roof reduces the electricity we buy when the sun is shining, reducing our electric company's revenues. At the same time, we expect our utility to maintain all its costly equipment so we get electricity when the sun isn't shining.

Nearly one-quarter of the electricity in Gainesville, Florida now comes from renewable energy, thanks to a policy of net metering—paying residents, businesses, and solar farms for the solar power they feed back into the city's electrical grid. But the project worked so well that it began to threaten the revenues of the city-owned utility. Today the city is no longer encouraging new solar panels among its residents—a change of heart that will keep electricity prices higher.[23]

Hawaiian Electric Industries Inc. went one step further. Without notice, in 2013 they simply placed a moratorium on new connections to household solar panel installations. They have since relented and are connecting new solar customers, but the incident highlights the growing backlash among utilities against letting their customers blend in cheaper sources of electricity.[24]

Most utilities operate under the supervision of a state or local commission, which must approve their rates to make sure the customers are protected from monopoly abuse. Today the emphasis is beginning to reverse. Commissions are also obligated to protect the utility's profits. This used to mean protection against fuel or construction cost rises. Now it also means protection against lost revenues from net-metering and renewable sources. The results: higher rates are being approved for many utilities, exactly because renewable power is becoming cheaper.

Wall Street investment analysts agree that American utilities are in trouble from solar energy competition. In mid-2014, Barclays investment bank downgraded the corporate bonds of the entire U.S. electric sector, saying, "We believe that a confluence of declining cost trends in distributed solar photovoltaic power generation and residential-scale power storage is likely to disrupt the status quo."[25] This problem has to be resolved. Until that happens, what homeowners gain from renewables we may lose in utility rate increases and fees.[26]

Warming brings risks to gasoline and natural gas too.

Petroleum refineries require cooling. They actually use far more gallons of water than the gallons of gasoline and diesel they produce.[27] If water shortages interfere with production, those products could go up in price.

Fracking for oil and natural gas is facing several problems related to warming. The process is dependent on good water supplies, forcing it underground to fracture shale rock and release trapped methane. Nationwide the amount of water used for fracking is not significant, but 75 percent of our fracking wells are located in areas where water is scarce.[28]

Barnhart, Texas, for instance, has run out of water. There's no more. Drought and over-usage of the aquifer contributed, but the killer was when local residents sold the output of their water wells to energy companies. Those firms trucked it to nearby fracking sites, added chemicals and grit, and pumped it deep underground, never to be used again. The Texas Commission on Environmental Quality predicts that many more West Texas towns will soon be without water for the same reason.[29]

A second problem comes from environmental dangers. The small percentage of fracking water recovered above ground is sometimes cheaply dumped instead of expensively treated.[30] Pennsylvania confirmed in late 2013 at least 106 water-well contaminations in the state since 2005, out of more than 5,000 new wells.

And many fracking wells and methane containers have leaks.[31] Yes, burning methane puts out less CO_2 than burning coal, but in the process of getting shale gas from the well to the consumer, an estimated 12% of that unburned methane leaks into the atmosphere.[32] Scientists tell us that methane is dozens of times more potent than CO_2 at warming the earth, and that now total greenhouse gas emissions from natural gas are actually greater than from coal. Thus authorities may soon require fracking and methane transport operations to install more safeguards to make the process leak-free. This extra equipment could raise the cost of natural gas considerably or shut down many fracking operations completely.

So could the cost of lawsuits. The Oklahoma Supreme Court ruled in 2015 that citizens may sue fracking companies for damage from earth tremors caused by high-pressure injection. Before 2009, the state averaged two earthquakes over 3.0 magnitude each year. In 2015 that number had jumped to 857.[33]

The ultimate impact on low-cost oil and gas could be shutting down hydraulic fracturing altogether. The states of New York and Maryland have banned all fracking apparently based on public opinion, which runs heavily against fracking because of fears of water contamination, earthquakes, methane emissions, and toxic wastewater pools. Many California towns have banned fracking, and there is a strong movement for a statewide ban.[34] Whether or not fracking can be made safe, there will likely be many jurisdictions where its costs rise dramatically.

Warming depresses other renewable energy sources.

For years hydroelectric has provided around 18 percent of California's electricity, but the winter of 2013-14 was so dry (snowpack in the southern Sierra Nevada was about one-fifth of normal) that output diminished by a third.[35] An improvement in 2015-16 has left the area still below historical averages.[36]

Utility-scale solar power can be surprisingly dependent on water as well.[37] Photovoltaic panels don't need any, except in their manufacture, but big solar power plants—the kind that cover acres of ground with parabolic solar troughs focusing sunlight on a tube of water—require a lot. Although some water can be cooled and condensed for reuse, hundreds of millions of gallons a year are lost to evaporation and must be replenished.[38]

Anyway, low-cost fuel doesn't mean low-cost electricity. One might think that because a lot of utilities burn natural gas, and natural gas has dropped dramatically in price, our electricity bills should be going down. But they aren't. Natural gas prices, which are the biggest input to the electric system, have declined by 39 percent since 2008, but electricity prices are up by 40 percent. Cheaper natural gas saved the industry around $30 billion a year, but consumer rates still rose faster than inflation.[39] The U.S. Energy Information Administration predicts a continuing rise, not a drop, in residential electricity prices.[40]

Why hasn't fracking lowered the country's electric bills? First of all, only 27 percent of America's electricity is produced from natural gas; far more is from coal whose price has not changed much.[41] Second, fuel is only one of a utility's many costs. They need enough income to pay the far larger non-fuel costs, including debt service, construction, and maintenance.

Pressure is rising for a carbon tax.

The most serious threat to cheap energy may be a growing conviction that it's bad for us. A big rise in our energy costs could be consciously self-imposed, by the spreading consensus that burning fossil fuels causes warming and that a self-imposed tax is the only effective way to slow future climate shifts.

The purpose of a carbon tax is not so much to raise money (see below for details) as to artificially raise our cost of fossil fuels. This makes us want to stop using the stuff and start using such untaxed (non-carbon) energy sources as wind and solar. The tax would be collected from fossil fuel companies, which would, in turn, pass its cost on to their customers—and ultimately to consumers—in the prices of coal oil and gas and products or services that use those fuels. Clean sources of energy would not be taxed.

Nine New England states and California already have carbon-tax lookalikes, called cap-and-trade systems, that add tax-like costs to energy. Washington residents will vote soon on a statewide carbon tax.[42]

A quick word about carbon emissions: we hear that emissions have plateaued for the moment, what with the Great Recession, China's cutbacks in coal use, and energy efficiency measures around the globe.[43] That's good news, but it's a little like saying hooray, your caloric intake has stopped rising at 4,500 a day, when you know you need to drop back to 2,700 a day to stop gaining weight. Regardless of what you read about decreasing emissions growth, expect increasing pressure from public and private groups for serious cuts.

The causes of warming, its dangers, and whether a carbon tax would make the world safer are highly divisive issues. But as a buyer of carbon fuels, what a person believes about the causes of warming doesn't matter. If enough Americans come to support a cap or tax on carbon, we'll all be paying extra, regardless of our beliefs. The point here is not whether a carbon tax would be a good idea. It's whether, if it comes, you'll have prepared to minimize its impact on your family's budget.

Here are four things you should understand about a carbon tax:

1. **We would notice it.** Very rough estimates from the Congressional Budget Office (CBO) say that low-income households (before-tax income averaging $24,600) buy stuff that would incur about $440 a year in carbon tax. For high-income households ($245,700), the average impact would be around $1,720 a year.[44] The carbon tax at the gas pump, for instance, would be around 20 cents a gallon. Business purchase of carbon would also be taxed, of course, although the CBO does not calculate averages per firm. Overall, your carbon tax would not be huge but, for many of us, it would certainly be noticeable.

2. **But we would likely be reimbursed for the carbon tax we pay.** Washington could spend the carbon tax in many ways, but the easiest to sell to voters is to return it to us immediately and in full. To the government, this is "revenue-neutral." There are several ways to get the money back into our hands, but the least controversial is probably to write a check to each household or company, based on a general estimate of how much carbon tax such a family or company might have paid. Because of these rebates you are not likely to be out-of-pocket for more than a fraction of the amounts mentioned above.

3. **We can cut our carbon tax but still keep the reimbursement.** So, if we come out even, what's the point of the tax? The point is to give us incentives to buy less of what's now expensive because it's taxed—electricity, gasoline, natural gas—and to change our buying and living habits so we don't use as much of that stuff. By switching to solar for electricity, buying high-mileage vehicles, and driving and flying less, for instance, a family or business can pay less for energy but still keep the reimbursement. We come out ahead.

4. **The carbon tax is meant to seriously cut future expenses.** If the carbon tax works as expected, by cutting our carbon emissions and slowing the warming process, it should also lower the upward trajectory of many future costs discussed in this book. This will play out slowly over time, and would help our children and grandchildren far more than the current generation. But that's the point! If

governments take our money but give it right back in a way that reduces the long-term costs from climate shifts, a carbon tax would be a win for consumers, most businesses, and governments at all levels. Of course, a few businesses would lose out, and oil companies, traditional utilities, and related businesses are fighting any attempt to suppress demand for their products.

Beyond the effects of a carbon tax or other warming-related drivers, we must acknowledge that as this book goes to press the prices of oil and natural gas are very low compared to the past. Adjusted for inflation, you can buy a gallon of gas cheaper than at any time since the 1960's. Perhaps these prices are the new long-term norm, but much of that drop occurred unexpectedly in the past few years, and a likely return toward the long-term trend would mean a big hit to our family's gasoline and heating oil budgets

KEEPING YOUR ENERGY COSTS LOW

It's not too early to take some smart actions to secure cheap power and to live lower-energy lives in the future. How should savvy families prepare themselves to dodge the costs discussed above? What would a no-regrets strategy look like?

Weatherize your home.
This is the low-hanging fruit for many households. Compared to investing in a renewable energy source, or relocating to a more climate-proof town, nothing costs less and keeps more money in your wallet long-term than insulation and weatherization. Few homeowners realize how much heat they lose from their home in the winter and how much unwanted heat enters in the summer. Even fewer know how easy and cheap it can be to find these energy leaks and do something about them.

Most electric and gas utilities will send an expert to your home to do a free Energy Audit, or you can pay an auditing firm for a more thorough inspection. The auditors will arrive with an infrared camera, draft gauge, blower door, smoke-maker, combustion analyzer, watt meter and other tools. In an hour or so, you will know how much heat gets in and out of your house under the doors, around leaky windows, and in other easily-plugged ways; how efficient your furnace is; where you do and don't need more insulation, which appliances are sucking energy, how much heat goes out your chimney, and more.[45]

Most of these energy losses are cheap to fix, and tax credits and subsidies are available for the more expensive changes. Government and non-profit energy organizations estimate annual energy savings up to $600 per average home, or 30 percent of its energy bill.[46]

Drive an energy-efficient car.

A few years back our family traded in our Suburban for a Honda Civic hybrid. We've saved over $1,000 a year in fuel since. If we need a bigger vehicle for a few days, we rent one. Can you see a similar change in your family life coming? For us, it was the day we stopped operating the neighborhood school bus.

Evaluate residential renewables.

Solar costs are dropping and the market is growing. There's no scarcity of solar vendors with increasingly cost-efficient products out there. Solar City's photovoltaic panel plant will push out 10,000 a day when it reaches capacity in 2016. Those and other company's panels are setting records for watts per square foot.[47]

Wind turbines are limited by prevailing wind speeds and by zoning and noise ordinances, but a turbine may be preferable to solar in some locations. There is also no scarcity of advice on whether and how to add solar or wind power to your home's energy sources. That's a good thing, because there are umpteen variables you'll want to consider, from panel or turbine location to your utility's net-metering policy.

Look for community power opportunities.

For many of us, of course, residential solar or wind simply won't work. We rent, we have a roof with an east-west slope, or we're shaded or sheltered by trees or buildings. In many towns, that needn't prevent us from saving money on electricity through a shared installation nearby.

In Rehoboth, Massachusetts a 'solar garden' with 4,400 photovoltaic panels sits in a former cornfield, producing one megawatt of electricity. It is owned by a private company, Clean Energy Collective, which constructs similar community solar arrays across the country. Panels are sold one-by-one to nearby residents for about $400 each. Owners receive a credit from the electric utility for energy produced, about $100 a year. This payback means free electricity from the fifth year on. The effect is the same as having a rooftop panel, but without needing to have a south-facing roof or to pay the installation costs, which can run over $10,000 for most home installations.[48]

We can take initiatives toward energy self-reliance by encouraging a group in our neighborhood to get into the distributed generation game. For instance, a condo association, business, or other organization with a parking lot could add canopies with solar panels on top, sharing the electricity produced or the net-metering credits.[49]

Power cooperatives are a bigger possibility. As of mid-2014, the residents of Burlington, Vermont get their electricity from 100 percent renewable sources: wind, hydro and biomass. Burlington, home of the University of Vermont, is an environmentally oriented city of 42,000. Their Washington Electric Co-operative's 11,000 customers are now protected against price rises in fossil fuels.[50]

Even if you want solar on your own property, many private vendors let homeowners join together for discounted group purchases of panels and installation.[51]

What about living off the grid?

As we saw above, the dark side of expanding solar power production is its effect on local utilities' revenue. In areas where a utility is successfully pushing back with fees, surcharged rates, or outright refusal to connect, homeowners may eventually consider disconnecting from the grid altogether, storing the electricity they generate, and becoming independent of the utility.

The costs of home energy storage are dropping fast.[52] But, tempting as energy independence may sound, going off the grid won't prove attractive in most cases: if we install a system large enough to actually make us independent, we will have excess power much of the time. Since we can make a significant amount of money selling that power back to the grid, it makes economic sense to stay connected.

Time your switch to renewable sources.
With lots of salespeople out there ready to tell you how much money you will save by installing solar panels, it makes sense to know when grid parity is actually expected in your area. That's when the cost of electricity from residential solar drops to equal the cost of electricity from your utility. It's a complex prediction. Future advantages for renewables depend on lots of variables: your utility's cost of operations, interest rates, the continuance of subsidies, etc. Some states and towns are at grid parity already; others will get there soon; in still others, you will be smart to wait a few more years until your own solar panels or wind turbine can actually save you money.[53]

Yourtown, USA

There are several sources of grid-parity predictions by state and city. Perhaps the most useful is produced by John Farrell at the Institute for Local Self-Reliance. You can see his interactive maps and discussion at https://ilsr.org/newsolarparitymap.

Even when domestic solar panels produce cheaper electricity than what your utility provides, consider other factors in timing a decision to add renewable sources. Costs of solar panels and home or neighborhood wind turbines are all up-front. You buy and install the equipment, including the wiring, inverter, and batteries or tie-ins to your utility feed. After that the sun and wind are free. You sit back for twenty years and enjoy the free energy. (Okay, that's a slight exaggeration, but only slight.) But with 99 percent of the costs of your next twenty years' energy paid in advance, you will be smart to get your equipment:

- When it's least expensive. Later may be better, since costs are still coming down.

- When you can get the best government subsidies, tax breaks, and the acquiescence of your power utility. That's a bit of a guessing game, but push-back from utilities suggests that sooner may be better.

These considerations vary widely from place to place across the country, so you need to check local sources, not the national media. And when these factors look favorable, you still have to come up with the money. Here are a few ideas.

Find cheap financing.

If you can save money with a major energy overhaul—solar panels, a wind turbine, new insulation, a more efficient furnace or air-conditioning system, window replacement, or other upgrades—you might be able to borrow the costs as part of your mortgage. These Energy Efficient Mortgages are available on new loans or refinancings.[54] Each month your monthly energy bill is a lot lower and your mortgage payment is a little higher.

Another way to finance energy and water conservation upgrades to your home is to arrange for Property Assessed Clean Energy (PACE) financing. Stamford, along with ten other cities in Connecticut and many across the country,[55] offers PACE financing for energy efficiency improvements as well as solar and other renewable energy installations. You buy the improvements, get financing through the state's Clean Energy Finance and Investment Authority, and pay back the loan over 15-20 years— through your property tax bill.

Nowadays financing for solar panel installations can commonly be arranged through an installation firm. Solar City, a nationwide contractor for residential solar, offers at least two ways for customers to handle the up-front cost. A 20-year loan lets you own the system and make monthly payments geared to how much electricity is produced. Alternatively, a long-term lease, where the company continues to own the equipment, calls for monthly lease payments, like a car.[56] Most other big solar installers offer similar financing.

In some places, local governments can help too. Pendleton, Oregon offers interest-free loans of up to $9,000 for photovoltaic systems. Residents are expected to pay them off quickly using money from federal and state tax credits. The program has been extended to businesses and to weatherization work. Many other towns and cities across America offer financial support to renewable energy and energy conservation efforts.[57] Not all programs are promoted strongly, so it pays to ask your town offices and solar contractor what is available.

Seriously consider supporting new nuclear sources.

Older nuclear power plants are closing across America, no longer cost-competitive with new fracked fuels or renewable sources. But there are new nuclear technologies too, and they may be critical to some regions' power supplies. We need to keep an open mind to make sure these innovations are considered.

As Will Rogers said, "It's not what we don't know that hurts, it's what we know that ain't so." Nuclear is nowhere as risky as we've been led to believe. If someone suggests building a new nuclear plant, most of us will roll our eyes, maybe clench our fists. After all, look at all the death and destruction at Chernobyl, Three Mile Island, and Fukushima. And the 10,000 years of danger from spent nuclear fuel.

These prejudices against nuclear power run deep in America, but they bear little relation to the facts. Several commentators have noted that, with climate change, those who know the most are the most frightened, but with nuclear power, those who know the most are the least frightened. Here are the facts:

- Radiation, illness and deaths from nuclear accidents have been hugely exaggerated, creating public fear out of all proportion to the actual risks.[58]

- New reactor designs lower these risks even further.[59]

- Dry-cask storage of nuclear waste has dramatically lowered radiation risks.[60]

- Nuclear plant fuel or waste is not weapons-grade. Converting it into a weapon is far beyond the capabilities of all but the most advanced scientific establishments.[61]

- Security at new nuclear facilities in the U.S. is likely to be much stronger than at storage sites elsewhere in the world, lowering the likelihood that theft would be attempted here.

Countries vary widely in their acceptance of nuclear power plants. While Americans quiver in fear, and Germany has announced the shutdown of all of its nuclear plants within a decade, France produces 75 percent of its electricity from 59 nuclear plants. The results include cleaner air across France, fewer pollution-related deaths, relatively cheap power, low national CO_2 emissions, and freedom from Russian threats to shut off natural gas supplies.[62]

Sure, nuclear power has its risks, but they pale next to the alternative. Bill McKibben, author of *Eaarth* and leader of 350.org, which mobilizes awareness of global warming, reminds us, "Nuclear power is a potential safety threat, if something goes wrong. [But] coal-fired power is guaranteed destruction, filling the atmosphere with planet-heating carbon when it operates the way it's supposed to."[63] In addition, the smoke from burning coal and natural gas sickens and kills people. Lots of people. NASA has reported that nuclear power actually prevented an average of 76,000 deaths per year between 2000 and 2009, thanks to lower air pollution-related mortality.[64]

If we are to stop burning coal and natural gas for electricity, nuclear is the only alternative that seems able to fill the gap. America is unlikely to replace fossil fuels with solar or wind alone.[65] A researcher at Rockefeller University estimates that powering New York City would require wind turbines covering the entire state of Connecticut. And, megawatt for megawatt, wind turbines require 5 to 10 times as much metal and concrete (not to mention energy) to build as a nuclear plant does.[66]

One way we can protect our families from the effects of global warming is to convince our fellow citizens that we need to seriously consider rehabilitating the nuclear power industry in the U.S.[67] While older nuclear plants are shutting down, new ones are being licensed in Tennessee and Georgia.[68] Given their safety improvements over the old technology, it will make sense to support these developments.

WHERE TO LIVE FOR LOW ENERGY COSTS

With energy, again place matters. You get a greater bang for the buck by choosing a low-energy hometown than a low-energy home. You may say, "Hey, I'm willing to drive around town looking for low-priced gas—but moving across the country? Come on!" True, moving is not attractive to most of us. But when you look at the disparities in energy needs from town to town, alongside similar differences in healthcare, transportation, tax and other warming-induced costs, you can see the importance of where you live growing significantly over time.

Even if you're going to stay put, you can do your children a big favor by guiding them toward settling in a more climate-proof town. We will talk about the benefits and the techniques of mobility, particularly for the next generation, in Chapter 12 on attitudes and Chapter 13 on timing.

Choose a hometown for low heating and cooling needs.

Some localities are really hot or cold, calling for heavy home cooling or heating. The measure your HVAC contractor uses to gauge how big a heating or cooling system your house needs is the degree-day. For heating, it quantifies by how many degrees for how many days per year the outside temperature in your location is below "normal" (usually considered 65°F). Likewise, this measure is used to size a cooling system based on how many degrees for how many days the temperatures are above normal (usually 72°F).

The National Climatic Data Center calculates 30-year averages for heating and cooling degree-days at almost 10,000 measuring stations around the U.S. If your home is in Colorado Springs, you register no cooling degree-days in the average year, sparing you the cost of air conditioning. On the other hand, the city registers 9,474 heating degree-days, costing you a lot to heat your home. At the other end of the spectrum, Miami records only 105 heating degree-days but 2,179 cooling degree days, so the average family spends nothing to heat their home but quite a bit to keep it cool.

If you live in San Diego (around 1,000 heating and 100 cooling degree-days) or Honolulu (as low as 4 heating and 606 cooling degree-days) you spend the least overall to heat and cool your home.

Yourtown, USA

You can look up the heating and cooling degree-days for most U.S. locations at weatherdatadepot.com and other similar services. These data are shown in, and also incorporated into, the energy rating in the *Where-To-Live Indicators* available at SavvyFamilies.org/Where-To-Live-

Indicators. These numbers indicate what you will likely pay for heating
and cooling.

When you use degree days as a proxy for energy costs, remember that, for
most homes, lowering the temperature by a degree with air-conditioning
uses more energy than raising it a degree with oil or gas heat. So unless
you plan to get a super efficient air-conditioning system, cooling degree
days should be multiplied by 1.5 or 2 when compared to heating degree
days.

Also remember that what's a comfortable temperature varies from family
to family. An elderly couple may want their home at 80° in winter and 65°
in summer, while a young active family may be okay with the reverse.

Above all, remember that these degree-day measures are averages for
recent years. The next decade or two will look very different, as most
locations in the U.S. will increase their cooling degree days and reduce
their heating degree days.

Choose your hometown for better energy sources.

If you're thinking of moving for any of the reasons discussed throughout
this book, check the conditions for wind or solar power in your would-be
hometown. The National Renewable Energy Laboratory collects data on
how much solar energy hits various locations around the country. Called
insolation, this measure tells us how much electricity our photovoltaic
panels might generate.

Needless to say, some locations get lots of sun, and others not enough, to
make it worth installing solar panels. A whole lot of solar energy hits the
area around El Paso, Texas while a lot less reaches Seattle, Washington.
(We won't mention Alaska.) Latitude matters, of course, but weather
patterns do too. Cedar City, Utah is about the same latitude as Lewisburg,
West Virginia, but receives much higher insolation.

Yourtown, USA

The U.S. Department of Energy's National Renewable Energy Laboratory publishes insolation maps of the U.S. The annual levels for photovoltaic use are at 1.usa.gov/1ei7zh5.

In addition, the Scorecards at SavvyFamilies.org/Where-To-Live-Indicators gives every community a grade for insolation based on the nearest NREL reporting station.

Wind power has even more variation. The National Water and Climate Center keeps data on average wind speeds for many locations across the country. Wind speeds average 12.9 mph at Corpus Christie, Texas. At Hondo Airport, outside of San Antonio—only a four-hour drive south—the average is 7.2 mph. Near the extremes we find Cross City airport, west of Gainesville, Florida averages 4.2 mph, while Livingston, Montana records 18.0 mph average.

Yourtown, USA

You can look up the average wind speed for any weather station (often an airport) in the U.S. using the data from the Natural Resources Conservation Service at 1.usa.gov/1lRdi8S.

It may be easier, to check the Indicator Scorecards at SavvyFamilies.org/Where-To-Live-Indicators. We've listed a wind speed rating for each town or Zip Code, based on its nearest weather station.

The ability to generate cheap electricity from the sun or wind may not be at the top of your list today when looking for a place to live, but it could become an important factor as energy costs rise and the profits of traditional utilities are protected.

Check other energy factors when choosing a home.

Even if your area is generally sunny and breezy, individual properties can vary widely. Few homebuyers inquire about the chance to use renewable energy, but that could change fast. Once you've chosen a home, you may have given up any chance to use solar panels or a wind turbine. Check to see if any home you're considering will have:

- a south-facing roof or yard for solar

- south-facing windows for some passive solar

- a few trees and buildings to the south and southwest that block sunlight or block the prevailing wind from turning a wind turbine or providing cooling breezes in summer

Don't rely on the wind speed recorded at your nearest airport. Borrow a wind meter and check on your property. A hilltop location can give stronger breezes, while some parts of town are naturally sheltered. A few extra miles-per-hour of wind could mean the difference between an effective wind turbine and a waste of money.

Footnotes for this chapter, Where-To-Live Indicators for all American towns, and other tools and resources are available at savvyfamilies.org/climateproof, as well as the author's updates, your comments, and other useful information.

4 AVERT HEALTH COSTS

Ticks, mosquitoes, and sandflies bearing tropical diseases are moving north in the United States. The range of the particular mosquito that carries Dengue fever, for example, will extend across most of America by 2050 as the country warms.[1] At the same time the habitat of the blacklegged ticks that cause Lyme disease is predicted to expand dramatically westward across the country.[2] Other warming-driven changes will increase allergies and contaminated water, adding to our healthcare costs, which are already around $25,000 per year for the typical family of four and rising at over 6 percent a year.[3]

The federal government is projecting per capita spending on healthcare to grow at 4.9 percent a year through 2024.[4] That's far faster than other items in your budget, and that growth rate doesn't yet include the growth of medical bills thanks to warming.

One in five American families struggles with medical bills, including many who have health insurance.[5] And, for many of us, protecting against unpaid medical bills means protecting ourselves from the number one cause of bankruptcies in this country.[6] Families and communities can take steps to climate-proof their health and healthcare costs, but we need to know what is coming and where.

HOW OUR HEALTH COSTS WILL INCREASE

Allergies and asthma are spreading.
The ragweed pollen season is now a month longer than in 1995, thanks to warming weather. A recent study shows the number of patients reporting a sensitivity to ragweed expanded by 15 percent in just 4 years while sensitivity to mold grew by 12 percent.[7] One of the causes: as America gets hotter, ragweed and mold are more virulent.

The chances that someone in your family has, or will develop, an allergy are high. Two in ten Americans, but more than five in ten children, already cope with allergies. Over half of American adults, even those without symptoms, test allergic to one or more pollens.[8]

A few sniffles—so what? Allergies seldom kill (yearly deaths in the U.S. are a few thousand), but fighting them is very expensive. Sufferers make 17 million doctor visits and 30,000 emergency room visits each year. Directly or through our insurance plans, Americans are paying $1.3 billion to doctors, plus $11 billion to pharmacies and drugmakers to treat allergies.[9] Add in the cost of sick days at work or school, lowered productivity, and misery when a person is sneezing and sniffling, and the personal costs are high.

And that's before we consider asthma. The number of Americans with wheezing, breathlessness, chest tightness and coughing has increased more than 60 percent since the 1980s. If anyone in your family is or becomes an asthmatic, their lifetime out-of-pocket costs from childhood through old age could be over $7,000.[10] On top of that, allergies are a major cause of absenteeism, which depresses incomes and promotion prospects.

Heat waves drain municipal and personal budgets.

One of the dangers from warming is simply warmth. Heat waves killed more people than hurricanes, lightning, tornadoes, floods and earthquakes combined between 1979 and 2003. That puts heat among the deadliest natural disasters in America.[11]

Extreme heat events are predicted to become more frequent across the U.S., and the costs will be significant. This is particularly true for cities. They've been warming about twice as fast as the rest of the country.[12]

Chicago is a memorable example. On the first day of the 1995 heat wave, the temperature hit 106°F, and the heat-and-humidity index rose above 120°F. During the following days, Chicagoans suffered under daytime temperatures in the 90s and low 100s. At night it was in the low-to-mid-80s. Patients were turned away at 23 hospitals, which were overwhelmed and closed their emergency rooms to new patients. Many lost electricity for a while. Heat danger depends on not just the temperature but also how long it stays hot—and by the time cooler air returned a week later 700 Chicagoans were dead.[13]

Researchers at the Union of Concerned Scientists predict heat waves like the deadly one in 1995 in Chicago will occur three times a year by the end of this century. Emergency healthcare costs will grow dramatically. Heat-related deaths will quadruple by 2050, among our children and grandchildren.[14]

The growing health and other costs of heat waves go beyond deaths. California's two weeks of extreme heat in 2006, which killed 655, created 16,000 additional emergency room visits and boosted hospitalizations by 1,620. The result: nearly $5.4 billion in extra healthcare costs, paid not just by those affected, but by all taxpayers.[15] And although temperatures are higher in the South and Southwest, serious heat waves can strike any part of the country.

Of course, medical treatment was not the only cost. Families spent extra money to crank up their air conditioners. Many stayed home, losing time at work and school. When the grid went down for up to two days, others had to leave home to find air conditioning.

Today, as Americans face higher use of air conditioning, the EPA is also phasing out production of Freon, a danger to the ozone layer but still the most common refrigerant. Freon prices tripled in 2011, and that means higher prices for cooling and refrigeration.[16]

Although cities are heating up twice as fast as rural areas, many authorities have been slow to prepare plans and take actions to meet this growing problem.[17]

Warming puts pathogens into our water.

Beach lovers know all about closures caused when storm water runoff from increasingly wet storms put bacteria into the water, but the dangers of warming to our health and our personal finances come in other, sometimes indirect, ways. In New York, a lawsuit was filed against the city by a group of fishermen who claimed their catch from shellfish beds was poisoning customers, thanks to massive releases by the city of raw sewage during superstorm Sandy. Authorities, in fact, closed the shellfish beds for about two months as a health hazard.[18]

It doesn't have to be a hurricane. New weather patterns mean rain is coming in increasingly big bursts. A new-normal rainstorm can easily overflow a town's sewer and waste treatment systems, dumping fecal matter and other raw sewage into the streets and nearby waterways. Sometimes the stuff can enter our drinking water sources. Waterborne diseases spread easily under these conditions.

Even without overflows, warmer water also breeds algae, which can produce toxins. Residents of Toledo, Ohio have been stocking up on bottled water every spring because the annual summer algae bloom on Lake Erie makes tap water dangerous to drink.[19]

Preventing these threats is increasingly costly to cities and their residents.[20] The EPA is requiring the Northern Kentucky Sanitation District to spend $1.2 billion to eliminate massive sewage contamination of the Ohio River by 2025. Sewer rates for residents have been rising 10-15% per year and will likely continue upwards at that rate.[21]

Another example: Plagued by raw sewage overflows during heavy rains or rapid snowmelt, Portland, Maine has introduced a "stormwater fee." To encourage residents to replace driveways with permeable pavers or lawn, the city charges any property with more than 400 square feet of impervious surface a fee, for instance $6 for 1,200 square feet of impervious surface. The fees will be used to fund the $170 million needed over the next 15 years to upgrade its sewage-stormwater systems.[22]

One might think that local taxpayers should be able to find the money to cope with sewage problems caused by the slowly warming atmosphere above us. But those costs will arrive on top of some big bills already overdue. Even before the effects of warming, many sewer systems across the country already need massive improvements. The American Society of Civil Engineers gives America a grade of D for its wastewater infrastructure and estimates that we will need $298 billion over the next twenty years to maintain the country's wastewater and stormwater systems, even before considering the effects of warming.[23] Three-quarters of that is for fixing and extending pipes. Since 2007, the EPA has required affected cities to invest more than $15 billion in new pipes, plants, and equipment to eliminate overflows.

How much more expensive could it get to deal with these health hazards? The National Association of Clean Water Agencies expects to see an average of 5 percent increases every year in sewer costs for many years.[24] At that rate, these costs would double on average across the country in 14 years. Depending on the condition of your wastewater infrastructure, your community could face higher increases.

In harder-hit areas, EPA affordability guidelines say that the town should be able to charge up to 2 percent of median household income for wastewater fees.[25] When you consider that the same family spends only 4 percent on clothing and 5 percent on entertainment and recreation, rising sewage costs seem likely to have a big impact on lots of families.

Mental health problems are predicted to grow.

Problems from warming may cause you persistent low-grade annoyance, and annoyance is stressful. Research on stress, summarized by the American Psychological Association, predicts that climate disruptions will cause a steady increase in depressive and anxiety disorders, post-traumatic stress disorder, substance abuse, and suicides.[26] Many will be the result of a specific event, such as a drought, flood, damaging storm, or heat wave. Others will build up over time from the many effects of warming.

Stresses include pressures on personal finances, strained relationships with family and neighbors, and the worry that the surroundings we love are deteriorating. Symptoms include a disrupted sense of continuity and belonging, decreased community cohesion, increased personal aggression, domestic abuse and intergenerational strife, more violence and crime, and heightened social instability.[27]

The likelihood of these problems goes up in neighborhoods where infrastructure cannot protect against storm damage, flooding, and drought, where racism and economic inequality are high, where education levels and an understanding of climate change are low, and where large numbers of young children or seniors live.[28]

Even if they do not make your own family depressed or anxious, new burdens from warming may be causing many less fortunate members of your community mental and emotional stress, in turn swelling the budgets of your town's health, community support, and police departments and increasing your local taxes and fees.

Health facilities may be damaged by warming.

In Santa Cruz, California, which we visited in the Preface, where drought has reduced domestic water consumption by 35 percent, there is concern that, if things get worse, hospitals and clinics will simply not have enough water to operate reliably, forcing them to cut services, handle emergencies only, and transport long-term patients out of town.[29] Do you live in one of the 400 counties in the U.S. with the same long-term water risk as Santa Cruz?

HOLDING YOUR HEALTH COSTS DOWN

With America's riches and resources, rising risks from asthma, allergies, and communicable disease are likely to spur new preventives and treatments. Sanitary engineering standards will rise. There may be new approaches to individual and community mental health.

But we shouldn't count on the medical cavalry to get to us in time. And, even if it does, the cost of new treatments will likely put further financial strains on government and health insurers, and inevitably on us. Here are some of the ways you can adopt a no-regrets attitude toward keeping your health costs down.

Take precautions in your home.

No matter where you choose to live, you can take steps to reduce your family's susceptibility to heat waves, allergies, asthma, and pollutants. The American Red Cross website contains lists of preparations and to-dos during a heat wave to keep your family and neighbors safe.[30] There are other good sources of advice for reducing allergens and asthma triggers in the home. Allergists and your family physician can give advice, often accompanied by fact sheets and instructions.

Make sure your town is taking precautions.

If you live where growing health dangers are predicted (see below how to check), you may be able to persuade officials to take steps to help climate-proof your family's and neighbors' health costs.

Many cities have drawn up defense measures against heat, allergies and asthma, and pollution.[31] Look at them online. Some include measures to reduce exposure to heat waves. For instance, unlike many municipalities that have only a cursory plan for helping residents get through a heat wave, Boston has mapped out and rehearsed extensive actions: educating the public in advance, warning residents early, directly contacting at-risk residents (the elderly, disabled, mentally ill, homeless), keeping air-conditioned libraries or community centers open longer, and others.[32]

Taking their cue from Atlanta (already know as "The City in a Forest"), Los Angeles and Denver have committed to planting a million trees. Although trees do remove some CO_2 and pollutants from the air, this greenery's main purpose is to keep the cities a little cooler during heat waves. The trees shade buildings, sidewalks, roads and parked cars during the summer, reducing their temperatures. If the trees are deciduous, they let the sunshine through in the winter. Many other cities and towns across the country are doing the same thing.[33]

New York, Seattle, Philadelphia and other cities have mandated white roofs to reduce heat absorption and curb the "heat island effect," the phenomenon that makes a city's average air temperature 2-5°F warmer than its surroundings and up to 22°F warmer in the evenings.[34]

Over 150 plant species, including shrubs, vines, and two trees, are growing on top of Chicago's City Hall. The garden is designed to improve air quality, save energy, soak up stormwater, and lessen the urban heat island effect. Chicago is second, after Washington, DC, in square footage of green roofs, and is aiming at one billion square feet by 2022.[35] Other metro areas are expanding their green roof programs, slowing runoff, reducing temperatures, and providing habitat for bees, birds, and butterflies.[36]

More ideas are being developed as the problems worsen, so an open mind toward new approaches along with the financial capacity to implement them will be important in your community.

If you believe that such citywide protections are beyond your influence, you could be surprised. Along with a few other articulate hard-pushing residents, you might discover it's easy to galvanize the press, civic organizations, and City Hall into widespread agreement on these changes.

WHERE TO LIVE FOR LOWER HEALTH COSTS

Your health will be better, and your medical budget lower, in certain locations than others. If, as America heats up, you can live away from allergens, summer heat, sewer overflows and other health threats, you'll avoid both high medical bills and high health insurance costs. If you can live outside jurisdictions with looming sewer problems, in particular, you'll save on local taxes and fees.

For many of us, this means we should at least learn our hometown's health advantages or disadvantages. There are two related tactics here: (1) Live where health problems such as heat, allergies, asthma, pollution, and emotional stress are low. (2) Live where the costs of treating those problems are low.

Live in a low-allergy area.

Given the discomfort and cost of lifelong allergies, it makes sense to choose a hometown where pollen and mold are scarce. Decades ago many allergy sufferers did just that by moving to Arizona and New Mexico where it was too dry for molds and too barren for pollen-producing trees.[37]

Asthma is particularly costly. In 2009 it averaged $3,259 per sufferer every year, with severe allergies far more expensive.[38] So if you or a family member has asthma, allergies, or any other expensive chronic condition, you can protect the family budget from high long-term medical costs by choosing a hometown whose hospitals and practitioners have proven to deliver above-average quality at below-average cost.

Today, Knoxville, Tennessee is ranked worst for allergies among 100 U.S. cities by the Asthma & Allergy Foundation of America. It has high pollen counts, high numbers of allergy medications prescribed, and lots of board-certified allergists practicing there.[39] Other cities' rankings are available at the AAFA's website, AllergyCapitals.com.

Yourtown, USA

Looking ahead, the National Wildlife Federation publishes a map of tree pollen potential under two levels of warming, plus a list of the

worst cities for asthma, spring allergies and fall allergies at
bit.ly/NWFallergies.

Unfortunately, this map covers only half of the U.S. In SavvyFamilies'
Indicator Scorecards at SavvyFamilies.org/Where-To-Live-Indicators,
these AAFA data are used in creating our Health grade.

An NWF study picks Arkansas, Iowa, Maine, Minnesota, New
Hampshire, New York, Pennsylvania, Vermont, and West Virginia to
have "large increases" in pollen. Other states will have moderate
increases; some states lower. The worst cities are apparently easier to
identify than the best. You can search for the latest articles with headlines
such as *"Ten Best Places for Asthma Sufferers."* But be careful—most of
those are looking back at the historical record, not ahead at a warmer
future.

Live where sewage pollution is likely to be low.
The EPA tells us that 40 million Americans in 772 communities—mostly
in the Northeast, Great Lakes, and Pacific Northwest—live with
combined sewer systems, the designs where sewage can mix with
stormwater runoff.[40] The rest of the country is free of this pollution risk,
which will likely grow as our weather patterns change.

Yourtown, USA

To find out if a particular town has the potential for sewage overflows,
check the list at bit.ly/CSO-list. Or just spend a few minutes on the
phone with someone in the public works department, asking about the
extent of past overflows and what is being done to prevent larger ones
in the future.

If your town has pollution problems and you are not leaving, you may be
able to reduce the costs you are going to bear by joining neighbors to
push for engineering solutions to threats earlier rather than later.

Live where medical costs are low.

As you may know, what you pay hospitals and doctors varies widely across the country—for the exact same health outcome. The average cost per patient day in 2013 in a Wyoming hospital was $1,170. In Texas, it was $2,242; in Washington State it was $3,154.[41] The variation within any state from one "hospital service area" to another can be great as well.

And quality of care does not correlate with cost. In many places, you can purchase less expensive medical care that is in fact well above average in quality.[42]

Yourtown, USA

Cost and quality ratings are compiled for every U.S. "hospital service area" by Dartmouth Medical School and published in the Dartmouth Health Care Atlas.[43] The latest figures are available online at www.dartmouthatlas.org and are remarkably easy to use. The data are available at SavvyFamilies.org/Where-To-Live-Indicators. The Footnotes for this chapter at savvyfamilies.org/climateproof-footnotes indicate where to find additional sources of cost and quality data for your locality.

If you stay where you are, damage to your family's health and the rise in your healthcare outlays may be slow, steady, hard to notice, but costly. However, if you move to a town with lower healthcare costs and good quality, you should see both immediate improvements in your symptoms and slower increases in your bills.

Footnotes for this chapter, Where-To-Live Indicators *for all American towns, and other tools and resources are available at savvyfamilies.org/climateproof, as well as the author's updates, your comments, and other useful information.*

5 SECURE LOW-COST TRANSPORTATION OPTIONS

When we think about how to control our family's transportation costs, we tend to look around for a cheap gas station, a reasonable mechanic, or a we-will-not-be-undersold car dealer. But those are just the surface costs. Beyond fuel, maintenance, car payments, and insurance, we should prepare to shelter ourselves from expanding taxes, tolls, service fees and other less visible costs, many of which are set to rise as a result of warming.

HOW TRANSPORTATION COSTS WILL INCREASE

Costs we will pay through fees and taxes

Warming is hammering infrastructure that is already crumbling. Hotter surface temperatures, greater erosion from runoff and wave action, and rising sea levels are driving maintenance and replacement costs up. Roads, bridges, airports and ports are all increasingly in danger.

Some of the new costs will make the headlines. If you were in New York after Hurricane Sandy died down, you saw the storm-surge debris in the streets—fourteen feet above the normal high tide line. You couldn't take the subway because stations and tunnels in the country's largest system were flooded and its electric controls corroded.[1] Taxpayers in New York had to come up with $5 billion to fix the storm's damage.

Tropical Storm Irene dropped up to 11 inches of rain across Vermont in 2011. Roads were washed out and some towns isolated for up to two weeks. Not in the headlines were the costs to Vermont's rail system. Eighty separate work projects were authorized by FEMA for the repairs to tracks and bridges.[2]

In the summer of 2011, a section of Interstate 69 in Marshall, Michigan buckled from the heat, pushing pavement slabs up several feet to form a barrier like a skateboard ramp. Officials say the surface temperature of 116°F was too hot for the concrete. Many U.S. roads will need to be rebuilt to withstand increasingly hot summer temperatures.

Rising water and storm waves will hurt roads too. Michigan has had to quickly move a stretch of highway US-41 back 100 feet from a shoreside cliff that was eroding out from under it. The cost was $3 million for a two-mile repair. About 60,000 miles of America's roads along the seacoasts and Great Lakes are already exposed to flooding from storms and high waves.[3]

But most of our transportation problems are not so dramatic—just costly. Many of these costs are compounded by the need to rebuild to new higher engineering standards to resist the effects of warming. We know how to do this. New asphalt mixtures and concrete materials, larger drainage culverts and, erosion-resistant footings and new ways to raise roads are all available to us. We just have to find the money for them.

Bridges are especially vulnerable.

Given the beating that warming will inflict on our roads, it is worrisome that the average age of a bridge in the U.S. is 42 years.[4]

When engineers detect a bridge in danger, they usually have no remedy except to close it. A bridge over the Delaware and Raritan Canal in Franklin Township, New Jersey was inspected in 2014 and received a structural and functional score of 7 out of 100. It was immediately closed. Ninety-three bridges in New Jersey got a rating of "serious," "critical" or "failed."[5] The Delaware River seems to have it in for bridges. In 2014 more than 75,000 vehicles per day were forced to detour through downtown Wilmington because a major bridge on I-495 had begun to tilt.[6]

Your state may face bigger repair costs than others. We will look below at how you can find out.

Airports and seaports are in trouble.

A preferred location for airports has always been next to the water so planes don't take off or land over buildings. The result: many airports are right on the shore.

Consider New York's La Guardia and Kennedy International airports: The levees that protect runways and buildings are only a few feet above the sea. With increasing storm surge and rising sea level, these levees are not expected to protect the facilities much longer. LaGuardia's runways were flooded during Hurricane Sandy. Had the storm arrived at high tide, the water could have entered the terminal buildings.[7]

After the storm, the New York airports were closed for three days, and thousands of passengers were inconvenienced. But the real impact on Americans is not the clean-up and inconvenience; it's the coming cost of protecting these and other airports across the country. Twelve of the nation's largest airports have at least one runway within 12 feet of current sea levels.[8] Authorities will need to spend large amounts on higher levees, raised runways and rebuilt terminals to protect property, traffic, and revenue.

Even more exposed to sea-level rise and stronger wave action are our 600 commercial seaports. More than 80 percent of America's offshore oil and gas from the Gulf of Mexico comes ashore at Port Fourchon, Louisiana. It's the only port in the U.S. capable of unloading the largest oil tankers, so it also handles about fifteen percent of America's imports of foreign crude.[9] A 90-day closure of the port would knock up to $7.8 billion off of America's GDP.[10]

This could happen. Louisiana Highway 1 is the main road leading in and out of town. It carries 600 eighteen-wheel truckloads of offshore drilling equipment each day. Studies predict that by 2030 the highway will be underwater at least half the time, effectively closing the port.[11] A new elevated highway must be built soon.

As warming begins to permit new sea routes through the Arctic and centuries-old trade routes and port volumes begin to change, we are building new facilities in one location and abandoning them elsewhere. But we cannot simply walk away from endangered port properties. Many include contaminated industrial land that must be protected from flooding.[12]

Costs we will pay directly, on and off the road

Fuel costs may go up—or not. As we discussed in Chapter 3 on energy, these days economists and energy pundits have become more tentative when forecasting the price of a gallon of gas. However, many non-fuel costs are reliably predicted to rise through the next decade and beyond.

Taxes on fuel are likely to escalate.

Even without considering warming, it seems inevitable that we will soon be spending more, one way or another, to maintain America's roads and bridges, our airports and seaports. Our Federal Highway Trust Fund, which provides the money to build and repair federal and some state roads and public transit across the country, as well as state transportation budgets, used to be fully supported by fuel taxes. In mid-2015, federal and state gasoline taxes averaged a little over 52 cents a gallon, depending on the state: in Alaska it's 26 cents, in Pennsylvania 70 cents.[13] That may sound like a lot, but today it's nowhere near enough even for normal maintenance, let alone building new transport infrastructure or dealing with the damages from warming.

Congress passed the FAST Act in late 2015 to provide multi-year funding for U.S. transportation, for the first time in years. But the funding levels are not enough to make a dent in the nation's deferred maintenance. And there is still uncertainty, since payment will come out of General Revenue, not from a dedicated, sustainable revenue stream.[14]

To find enough money for state and local roads, by early 2014 twelve states had passed or were seriously considering increasing their tax on fuel.[15] In addition to gas taxes, tolls, and fees, there's a strong possibility that our states and cities will need to turn to higher income or property taxes and to commit us and our kids to new debt. And, if governments have trouble finding the money to keep bridges open and potholes filled, they could always take money from some other programs, cutting services like education, police, fire, or public assistance. We will discuss this threat in Chapters 6 and 7 on taxes.

There is pressure for higher user fees.

If higher gas taxes are unpopular and there is resistance to raising general taxes, what about higher tolls, a weight-distance tax on truckers, increased registration and driver's license fees, and other charges? If you believe users should be the ones to pay, some of these seem like equitable ideas. But many roads need costly repairs or improvements that can't wait for those fees and tolls to accumulate.

There are hidden costs.

To the extent we don't fix our bad roads, whether caused by the ravages of changing weather or by neglect, money will leak out of our pockets in subtle ways. A transportation research group estimates that, in Michigan alone, the costs per motorist of driving on congested, deteriorated roads that lack some safety features add up to over $1,000 a year per motorist. This comes in the form of additional vehicle maintenance costs, tire wear, lost time, and wasted fuel as a result of slow traffic, plus the costs of traffic accidents.[16] Closure of a typical freeway section during peak traffic hours can cost commuters and commercial traffic up to $200,000 per hour in economic activity, while also placing stress on drivers.[17]

Lost passenger productivity is another cost. I can seldom read on my local transit bus because of the road bumps, and when I tried to hand-edit the manuscript of this book while a car passenger on Interstate 95, I gave up thanks to the road-surface cracks, ruts, holes, rhythmic bumps and irregular patches.

The current costs of mending America's roads and bridges—not to mention our airports, seaports, rail systems, and inland waterways—plus protecting them from the future degradations of warming, are already much larger than any imagined sources of funding for them. Whatever lawmakers decide, we will likely feel the tax and fee increases from multiple directions.

Transportation would feel the pinch from a carbon tax.

If enough Americans become convinced that we need to cut down on carbon emissions to limit the warming process and protect our grandchildren from even bigger financial pain, our politicians may give us a carbon tax. Ten states have small ones already.[18]

The Congressional Budget Office looked at the effects of a tax on climate-changing gas emissions. As we saw in Chapter 3 on energy, a household in the lowest 20 percent in terms of income would pay roughly 1.8 percent of their before-tax income. For households in the highest 20 percent, it would cost about 0.7 percent."[19] That's at a carbon tax level of $20 per metric ton, predicted to be a good start for incentivizing us to burn less carbon. To have full effect, the carbon tax would need to rise over time.

It's important to understand that a carbon tax, unlike a gas tax, is not a way to increase funding for road maintenance or other transportation needs. Rather, its purpose is simply to increase our transportation costs so we choose less energy-intensive ways of getting around. More details about how a carbon tax works follow in Chapter 7 on federal taxes.

Energy costs hit our wallets in many, many ways.

The price of fuels will be in the news every day, but you won't hear much about the larger but hidden transportation costs that find their way onto the price tags for our goods and services. Casey Dinges, a senior managing director of public affairs at the American Society of Civil Engineers, calls it "kind of a drip, drip, drip scenario. There's not a galvanizing thing there to get people's attention. The real impact of poor infrastructure is just this kind of grinding negative effect that it has on the economy."[20]

River freight is cheap. A barge carries a ton of grain 500 miles using one gallon of fuel. A semi-trailer can move that same ton only 60 miles per gallon.[21] But barge traffic is endangered by warming. The great flood of 1993 was a catastrophe along 500 miles of the Mississippi and Missouri Rivers, bringing rail, truck and marine traffic to a stop. Major east–west traffic was halted for roughly 6 weeks in an area stretching from St. Louis west to Kansas City and north to Chicago, affecting one-quarter of all U.S. freight that either originated or terminated in the flood-affected region.

In the future, the Mississippi, Missouri, and other major waterways are predicted to be shut, and the bridges that cross them temporarily closed, more often. These warming-driven incidents push up the cost of the commodities that are rerouted.

Drought can have the same effect as flooding. In 2000 and 2001, water levels on the Mississippi were at their lowest point in 35 years, reducing barge loadings by about 10 percent.[22] And, in January 2013, water levels on Lake Michigan and Lake Huron fell to their all-time lows since record keeping began in 1918.[23] When lake levels drop, cargo ships must run partly empty to avoid grounding.[24] Ships have lightened loads about 5 percent. For a ship charging $6 a cargo ton and making 40 trips a year, that would amount to about $1 million in lost revenue per ship.[25] This has to be made back by charging higher rates, which find their way into the prices of the stuff they carry and we buy.

Long-needed improvements to ships, channels, ports, locks, and breakwaters are planned that will help counter these problems, but the costs are in the billions.[26]

Of course, the news isn't all bad from a shipping standpoint. As warming lengthens summers in the Arctic, large ships will be steaming across the ice-free Arctic, saving 1,650 miles from Japan to New York, compared to the Suez or Panama Canals routes.[27] Likewise, warming will reduce the time the Great Lakes are covered by ice, allowing products to move by ship, cheaper than by truck, additional months of the year.

Another potential cost was mentioned in Chapter 2 on food. Most large U.S. manufacturing and retail businesses use just-in-time delivery. This cuts costs, but if a company keeps very low inventories, its operations can be brought to a standstill when delivery is delayed as little as a day or two. If climate disruptions are going to mess with our roads, bridges, and waterways, businesses will need to carry extra inventory to avoid scarcity and rerouting costs. Those carrying costs are passed on to customers.

When we consider that over two-thirds of freight in the U.S. travels by truck, it's easy to see that deteriorating transportation will impact the costs of things we buy.[28]

KEEPING YOUR TRANSPORTATION COSTS DOWN

As with many of the other effects from warming, you will no see rising transportation costs take a single big bite out of your bank account. They will nibble away until that big bite has been removed without your noticing. And, if you're a typical American, transportation is already the second-biggest item in your budget, at 17 percent; only housing takes more. There are actions you can take now to dodge future transportation costs from warming, plus the existing costs from neglect, which could save many percentage points on your budget year after year into the future.

Many of these climate-proofing tactics involve developing options for yourself—alternatives to the gasoline-powered, pothole-dodging, multi-vehicle travel on which so many of us have made ourselves dependent. Others call for new tactics for your hometown, which may be facing outlays on crumbling infrastructure.

First, let's look at your costs of getting where you need to go. If you can reduce your travel needs—getting to work, school, shopping, doctor's visits, the library, the pizza shop—you can reduce gas, maintenance, tolls, maybe even the cost of a second car.

Share car rides.
As an experiment, Josh Waldrum arranged his life in Austin, Texas around Uber and Lyft car-sharing and local home delivery services, so for a month he never sat in his own car or got a ride from a family member or friend. He found ridesharing to be "a lot cheaper" than owning a car and very convenient. His average wait time was around 4 minutes.[29]

The number and variety of on-demand services, particularly in transportation, are exploding. If warming is going to hurt the cost, comfort, and convenience of driving, it's easy to imagine on-demand services saving you a lot of money.

Of course, Waldrum encountered the most powerful impediment to car-sharing in America. Like most of us, he loves to drive. He reported that withdrawal symptoms when traveling without his hands on the wheel were painful.[30]

Rent a car or pickup when needed.
When you start seeing articles titled "The 10 Best Car Sharing Programs in the U.S.," you know there's something going on.[31] In 2014 over 1.3 million members used almost 20,000 car-sharing vehicles in the U.S.[32] ZipCar may be the best-known service, letting you jump into a car parked in your neighborhood and use it for a few hours or days, but there are others. The big car rental outfits have gotten into the game with Enterprise Car Share, Hertz On Demand, and others.

Drive a high-mileage car . . .
Think ahead at the moment you're buying a car. Just as customers buy more convertibles on sunny days, today's low fuel costs make bigger, less

fuel-efficient cars seem attractive.[33] But if you plump for a smaller, more fuel-efficient and probably cheaper car now, you not only buy built-in protection from rising gas prices and gas taxes; your maintenance, depreciation and tire costs from deteriorating roads will be lower as well.

. . . but avoid the rebound effect.

It's easy to make money-saving adjustments to your family's finances, then unconsciously throw these savings away.

A few years ago my wife and I, strong environmentalists, gave a birthday party in our driveway for our Honda Civic hybrid. It had just passed 200,000 miles; our gas mileage was in the high 40's. Over the years we had saved thousands of dollars on fuel compared to an average car. During the party, someone asked me how old the car was.

"Seven years," I said.

"So you do about 28,000 miles a year," he calculated.

"Oh no," I said, "we've always done around 20, maybe 22,000."

He raised his eyebrows and I too did the math. Whoops! Looks like we had been thinking, "At 45 miles per gallon, our cost of gas is half what it used to be, so let's go!" Without noticing, we had increased our trips and distances by over 25 percent, throwing away our gas mileage savings.

This Rebound Effect, as it's called, can hit you in many other ways as you face the costs of warming and try to become more frugal. Careful food purchases can build up to expensive binges, weatherization of your home can lead to higher thermostat choices, savings on one budget item can translate into increased spending on another. Self-awareness is the key and monitoring a family budget can help reveal where penny-pinching isn't saving dollars.

Share your own car.

If you have an underused vehicle, you could make some money by going into the car rental business yourself. Just list your car with Getaround or another car-sharing intermediary. Submit a description, your location, your hourly or daily rental rate, and other information. The company takes care of attracting renters, screening them, insuring the car for the rental, enforcing rules, and promoting etiquette.[34]

Take local transit.

Public transit may speed your commute, give you time to read, keep your travel costs down, and get you to your destination more relaxed than if you were fighting traffic. But remember, just because a city has rapid transit doesn't mean it will help a particular family get where they need to go cheaply and reliably. The Brookings Institution compared the location of jobs to the routes of public transit in 100 metropolitan areas. In Greenville, South Carolina only 40 percent of jobs are in locations reachable by transit; in Albuquerque, it's 85 percent.

Yourtown, USA

You can see these percentages by city at bit.ly/transit_access.

For some city addresses across the country, you can ask walkscore.com for their Transit Score. The website will even find apartments for rent near good public transport. But this only works for a little over 200 cities and only within city limits. It doesn't yet cover inner suburbs.

The only sure way to decide if a particular home has public-transit access to your jobs, your kids' schools and your shopping destinations is to pore over a transit map and schedule.

By the way, if you are thinking that a city with good public transport reduces automobile congestion, it doesn't work that way. For every driver who stops driving and takes transit, another driver shows up. The same thing happens when more roads are built. When you add road capacity or public transit, congestion almost never goes down.[35]

Do your errands on foot.

When we sold our house two miles from the city center and moved to a rental apartment downtown, our Walk Score improved from 13 (all errands require a car) to 92 (daily errands do not require a car).

Within half a mile we can walk to a supermarket and farmers' market, a movie theater, doctors' and dentists' offices, two bookstores and the public library, elementary and middle schools, the art and history museums, the post office and banks, plus any number of restaurants and shops. For longer journeys, our bus station is within a few blocks.

Yourtown, USA

You can see the Walk Score for any address in America at walkscore.com. Scores from 0–100 measure your ability to reach shops, banks, restaurants, libraries, doctors, and other destinations on foot.

Since we moved to our new walkable neighborhood, we drive a couple of thousand miles less each year, get more exercise, and stride past the traffic congestion.

Get around by bike.

In the right location, families can cut their transportation costs dramatically by making more trips on a bicycle, particularly if this lets your family get by with one less car. While not directly comparable, a 2012 study found that the average annual cost to operate a bicycle was $308 versus $8,220 for the average car.[36]

Cheap, healthy, ecological, and fashionable, the advantages of biking to work, school and shops are recognized in many towns. Some are building safe biking routes and traffic lanes and educating both bicyclists and motorists about how to share the road. It's tough to get around by bike where bikers have no protections on the road, or where local motorists consider bikers a nuisance. If you can find (or help to create) a town where biking is encouraged, you can do your family's budget a big favor.

Yourtown, USA

Several sources now produce annual evaluations of the "Top Bike-Friendly Cities, "US Cycling Town Winners," and so forth, including local biking statistics. Just search the web for up-to-date information.

The League of American Bicyclists rates riding conditions across the country and gives awards based on the maintenance and safety of the bike-lane network, safe routes to school, education of bicyclists and motorists, support from the police and City Hall, and other criteria. Their list of award-winning communities, businesses and universities is at bikeleague.org/bfa/awards.

WalkScore also rates towns for bikeability, but their ratings are limited to big cities. Check walkscore.com.

Share a bike.
You don't have to own, maintain and store your own bike. More and more cities now have bike pools every few blocks, such as Hubway in greater Boston. You can take a bike and return it to any rack in the city.

Yourtown, USA

A descriptive list of bike-sharing programs in some of America's largest cities and universities is available at wikipedia.org/wiki/list_of_bicycle_sharing_systems#United_States. A longer list, including programs that are 'pre-launch,' is at bikeshare.com/map.

Living in a walkable, bikeable neighborhood gives you a certain independence. It frees you from many decisions of City Hall, the State House, Capitol Hill and corporations that affect most people's costs to get where they need to go. And you cross paths, literally, with more people, helping you to make acquaintances and friends.

WHERE TO LIVE TO GET AROUND CHEAPLY
The best way to keep the various growing costs of transportation under control may be to take a big step: to move. Transportation costs are not

like food costs, interest rates or federal taxes. Both travel and infrastructure costs depend heavily on where you choose to live.

You will save on travel if you choose a no-regrets strategy, moving to a neighborhood where you can walk, bike, share cars, or take local transportation—maybe all four. You will save on taxes if you choose to live in a state and town with few weak bridges, potholed roads, low-lying airports or ocean-edge highways crying out for taxpayer money. And you will benefit where a town's financial condition makes it relatively easy to raise money for existing requirements and new ideas. We will cover this in the next chapter on state and local taxes.

The amount of repair work needed on roads varies widely by state, as do the accumulating costs from delayed maintenance and replacement. Fifty-one percent of major urban roads in California are rated in "poor" condition (Rhode Island 45 percent, New Jersey 40 percent), while only 7 percent of Florida's roads are rated in that category (Nevada 8 percent, Missouri 9 percent). If the Federal Reserve is beginning to raise interest rates, any differences in prospective construction loan costs will be magnified.

It's easy for you to discover, by state and county, what you and your fellow taxpayers are facing.

Yourtown, USA

The American Society of Civil Engineers keeps track of infrastructure deficiencies state by state, for instance bridgework needed. How many bridges, large and small, do you drive over each day? One in nine American bridges is rated "structurally deficient." More are "functionally obsolete." You can check both categories of bridge decay in your state and county on the report card created by the ASCE at infrastructurereportcard.org/states.

While you're there, check your state's grades for roads, transit, rail, ports and inland waterways as well. For roadwork needed, check, state by state, the number and percentage of miles of major roads that are rated in poor condition, plus a per-motorist cost of these deficiencies also at www.infrastructurereportcard.org/states.

You can review the latest assessments and plans from each state's Department of Transportation at bit.ly/state-trans-tools. While often technical, this may give you an idea of what infrastructure costs face your particular state and how seriously they are being taken.

You may rejoice at finding a gas station that saves you fifteen cents a gallon. But you'll be far better off finding a hometown that can save you many hundreds, perhaps thousands, of dollars a year in taxes and other transportation outlays.

Would it help to privatize roads?

You may hear proposals in your area to tackle long-delayed road and bridge maintenance by turning to the free market, through privatization of roads and other infrastructure. But so far it's been hard to find the savings.

A private company agrees to fix and maintain a road at no cost to taxpayers, fronting the money and paying themselves back with toll revenue. For a cash-strapped government, it can be tempting. In 2006, a foreign company took over the operations of the 157-mile Indiana Toll Road for 75 years. They paid the state $3.8 billion to do so.

Privatization of a road, as with a water system, means that our taxes no longer pay for the big outlays for construction and maintenance, and the company is obligated to keep things in good repair.[37] Sounds good, and these types of public-private partnerships are increasing. Between 1989 to 2013, $60 billion was spent by such partnerships on 98 projects.[38]

But there are no savings. Privatization means the road will get built or stop decaying sooner, but the costs will also hit us sooner. On roads under private control in the U.S., tolls have generally risen far more quickly than other roads. As our Congressional Budget Office points out, "revenues from the users of roads and from taxpayers are the ultimate source of money for highways, regardless of the financing mechanism chosen. The cost of financing a highway project privately is roughly equal to the cost of financing it publicly."[39]

And there are risks. In 2014 the Indiana Toll Road operator filed for bankruptcy. A major cause was a 21 percent drop in traffic since they took over, due partly to their higher tolls and partly to the Great Recession. Other bankruptcies have included San Diego's South Bay Expressway, the Southern Connector in South Carolina, and roads in Alabama and Detroit.[40] In some cases, the state and federal government provided guarantees for the private company's financings, so the public can be left paying the failed company's creditors.

Walking, biking to work, sharing rides, high-mileage cars—to many of us these still seem like fads, environmental statements, or lifestyle choices for the hip. And moving one's family to find these conditions may seem like overkill. But soon these cost-control methods could become critical for normal families, those who are not making any kind of statement, just trying to sidestep the rising costs of getting to work, the dentist or a weekend getaway.

Footnotes for this chapter, Where-To-Live Indicators for all American towns, and other tools and resources are available at savvyfamilies.org/climateproof, as well as the author's updates, your comments, and other useful information.

6 AVOID RISING STATE AND LOCAL TAXES

The typical American family is used to state and local taxes averaging 7 to 12 percent of their income, depending on where they live.[1] Increased taxes necessary to deal with the effects of warming will push these numbers up in many communities.

Facing these effects, many of our families' needs are likely to land on the steps of our State House or City Hall. There are several reasons for this:

1. As we've seen, most warming-related problems are highly local.

2. Many of those problems, though local, are not small. We can't solve them as families, only through some government or other large organization.

3. The federal government may not be much help with such local problems. The divisiveness of national politics seems likely to make it increasingly hard to tax Iowans to reengineer waterfronts in Maryland, Vermonters to create water-conservation schemes in Texas, or Arizonans to control sewage overflows in Ohio.

In the next chapter, we will look at the prospect for federal taxes and at Washington's limited abilities to protect us from the costs of warming. But here let's examine what we can expect from governments in our state and local area.

HOW OUR STATE AND LOCAL TAXES WILL GROW

Warming's impacts have at least four ways of reaching us through our state and local governments. First, there are rising taxes on property, incomes, and sales. These are in-your-face changes we'll definitely notice. Where resistance to taxes is high, the costs may arrive more subtly as new or higher service charges, fines, or fees-in-lieu-of-taxes. Each may seem a small bite, but they can add up fast. New government borrowing is another way for us to pay for the protections we need, kicking the can down the road to our children. And if taxes, fees, and borrowing aren't enough to fund the protections required to safeguard us against warming, we'll likely pay in another way with cuts in services to the community. We'll look at all four financial threats in this chapter, but first let's examine some of the specific costs our communities are facing.

Many localities will need protection from flooding.

Chances are you live in a coastal county. Fifty percent of Americans do, and sixty percent of our gross national product is generated there, so there's an even better chance you work in one. Almost five million Americans and hundreds of billions of dollars of property are located in areas less than four feet above high tide.[2]

Twenty-two states are affected by seawater flooding in a variety of ways.[3] Within the next 15 years, storms, hurricanes, and rising sea levels along the Eastern Seaboard and the Gulf of Mexico are predicted to cause losses of $32 billion to coastal property and infrastructure.[4] Beaches, even whole neighborhoods, are retreating. If the damage were evenly spread, that would be close to $200 million for residents of each coastal county along the Atlantic and Gulf coasts.

And it's not just water levels that are up; so is storm surge. Hurricanes have already increased in strength. A super-strong "hundred-year-storm," projected to have only a 1 percent chance of happening in any given year, now can happen every 3 to 20 years.[5]

Far from the center of Hurricane Sandy, the coastal municipality of Westerly, Rhode Island saw a surge of 5 feet and winds of 58 mph. The *Providence Journal* reported that "Atlantic Avenue, the main drag in Westerly, was buried in nearly 5 feet of sand. Buildings were flooded, ripped apart, some spun right off their foundations."[6]

In the aftermath of the storm, some Hoboken, New Jersey residents canoed through the streets. Almost eighty percent of the city was flooded, including fire stations, senior centers, electrical stations, and sewage treatment plants. The city has since developed a "Resist, Delay, Store, Discharge" plan to help it live with frequent overflows. It has created gardens and open spaces that will filter and delay stormwater from entering the sewer system, areas for storing excess water where possible, and a drainage plan to divert the rest. The cost: hundreds of millions of dollars to Hoboken and nearby towns.[7]

Sewage overflows soak local taxpayers.

Damage from flooding comes not just as the water washes into our communities but also as it washes out.

There used to be a bumper sticker saying "When it rains in Grand Rapids, "S***" happens." It referred to the billions of gallons of raw sewage that overflowed into the Grand River from the city's sanitary sewer pipes because they were combined with the storm runoff pipes. In 2015 the city finished separating these two systems so that stormwater can no longer force the overflow of raw sewage. The cost was about $40 million.[8]

We saw in Chapter 4 the health costs that can come from pollution, but keeping pathogens at bay can cost a lot in taxes too. In 2006, the federal EPA required the Cincinnati sewer district to upgrade their sewers. The price: $3.2 billion. Sewer rates have increased 234 percent since 2000.[9]

New York City alone has over 460 outfalls that discharge more than 27 billion gallons of raw sewage and polluted stormwater into the Hudson River and New York Harbor each year.[10] These sewers that can mix storm run-off with untreated sewage, termed a combined sewer overflow (CSO), threaten roughly 772 communities containing about 40 million people across the U.S.

When overflows occur, human pathogens including viruses, protozoa, and bacteria are released. The Great Lakes provide drinking water for an estimated 40 million people and more than 500 recreational beaches in six states and Canada.

Residents of Charleston, South Carolina, one of the lowest-lying cities in the U.S., are especially vulnerable to sea-level rise and the waves from a storm surge. But heavy rains flood the city too. Several times a year, massive pumps are called on to push rainwater into the harbor through tunnels 140 feet below ground. With extreme precipitation events on the rise, the city will have to find the money to expand an already expensive stormwater sewer system. Things are likely to get worse before they get better, thanks to another feature of Charleston: widespread disbelief in climate change. A Green Plan prepared by the city, including actions to adjust to sea-level rise, was rejected by the City Council on ideological grounds.[11]

The American Society of Civil Engineers gives America a grade of D for our wastewater infrastructure.[12] The National Association of Clean Water Agencies expects to see an average of 5 percent increases every year in sewer costs for many years.[13] At that rate, these costs will double across the country in 14 years.

Public and business structures need relocating.

Because transporting goods by water has always been cheap, and because many industrial processes require large amounts of water, factories, power plants, distribution centers, refineries and waste treatment facilities have been located on the seashore. Serving these waterfront facilities are low-lying roads, subways, shoreside airports, railroads, fuel storage tanks, and electrical distribution systems.

In New York City, 104 public schools, 85 houses of worship, and 16 hospitals are located below 6 feet in elevation. Storm surge at the Battery during Hurricane Sandy was 9 feet.[14]

To be near water for fuel delivery by ship and for cooling, nearly 300 energy facilities in the U.S. are less than 4 feet above sea level, including many of our 100+ nuclear plants.[15] As we have seen, many are now in danger from the sea. Local taxpayers and businesses face the costs of moving or abandoning them sooner or later.

Some historic sites may soon be history.

The Market House in Annapolis, Maryland was built in the 1780s and closed by flooding from Hurricane Isabel in 2003. Since then the city has relocated furnaces, water heaters, and electrical boxes to a higher floor, installed special watertight doors and windows, and reopened the market. Washington and Jefferson, who knew this building well, would probably approve of the $1 million that's been spent to preserve it.

Most of America's earliest settlements were along the coasts or rivers, with early homes clustering around the wharves and waterside markets. Thousands of America's oldest buildings are threatened by the depredations of warming. Newport, Rhode Island alone has 968 historic structures in the current floodplain. The cost of preserving America's coastal heritage, if it's even possible, will be in the billions.[16]

The costs of damage in historic districts go beyond protections and repairs paid by individual property owners or the town in general. Many of these coastal and riverfront cities are tourist destinations. If the areas begin to lose their been-like-this-for-centuries character, tourist revenues will wither.

Who is going to pay to protect your town's public facilities and historic sites? Private groups? Individual owners? Taxpayers across the country? Maybe in a few cases, but the biggest expectations and demands are going to fall on state and local governments and their taxpayers.

The same fiscal pressures arise from drought.
Flooding is not the only threat to state and town finances. Let's examine the costs of drought that will reach us through our taxes. We will look at water rates we pay as households in Chapter 8 on home costs.

Many communities are facing big expenses to combat drought, getting more water for their residents, and using their dwindling supply more efficiently. Recharging the watershed and building new reservoirs, aqueducts, and filtration plants call for big capital outlays. And plenty of smaller expenses come out of a city's everyday budget, such as policing usage, installing water meters, administering new fines and fees, and educating the public. Most of these are likely to boost the local taxes and fees that residents pay.

And these costs for new water sources and management methods come on top of others already facing taxpayers. In the queue at the cash window, warming-related needs are jostling with existing needs for long-deferred maintenance on our water systems. The American Society of Civil Engineers gives America another grade of D for its drinking water—not for its quality, which is high, but because "at the dawn of the 21st century, much of our drinking water infrastructure is nearing the end of its useful life."[17] The big challenge that keeps water utility managers awake at night is aging pipes and other equipment. At current water rates, it's two-to-one that your water utility doesn't have enough revenue to make improvements.

For example, the winter of 2013-14 was hard on the municipal water mains of the Erie County Water Authority, which estimated that an average of 3 million gallons a day were being lost from known leaks.[18] Erie County is not alone. Across the country, the EPA estimates that public water systems lose, on average, one-sixth of their water between the source and the tap. Many of these pipe leaks are undetected, and the EPA says 75 percent of that loss could be fixed.[19]

But the costs to fix or replace aging water mains, many of which date back 100 years to the early days of public water systems, will be staggering. And those outlays are already on the priority list ahead of the newer costs to deal with warming. Both costs will eventually arrive in our mail as higher tax bills or water bills.

Wildfires are more frequent.

California's Department of Forestry and Fire Protection blew through its fiscal 2015 budget in about 90 days. Costs to fight the state's wildfires have more than doubled over the past ten years, largely because of the developing drought.[20]

Fires have steadily increased in number since 1980, and the average length of the wildfire season has lengthened from five months in the 1970's to over seven months today.[21] For every 1°C increase in average temperature, the U.S. Forest Service says the area burned in the western U.S. could quadruple. If true, a 4° rise would increase the burned area by 250 times!

Wildfires are a physical danger to very few of us, but they endanger everyone's pocketbook. The costs paid by federal, state and local taxpayers just to fight wildfires has grown to over 3 billion dollars a year. And that doesn't include the costs of repairs to damaged and destroyed homes, respiratory health problems, tax revenues lost from drops in property value, and all the other expenses that appear after the smoke has cleared. These costs run from two to thirty times the cost of just fighting the fire.[22]

Drought and flooding will threaten municipal revenues.

Many of our personal costs from warming—from flooding, water shortages, health and other hazards—can be held in check if our state and municipality spend the money to protect us. But their ability to spend that money depends on local tax revenues, and those depend in turn on local prosperity.

In many drought-threatened towns, that prosperity is very much at risk. A study by the Chamber of Commerce in San Antonio, Texas claims the city will lose almost $2 billion in economic output by 2030 for lack of water, making it that much more difficult for the city to find the revenue to deal with the problem.[23]

How does this sort of economic decline come about? In the Santa Cruz survey (see Preface), residents cite many impacts on their city. With no outdoor watering, parks and playing fields will turn to dirt. The town will lose its looks. Health risks will increase. Serious conflict among neighbors and municipal government is expected. Many businesses depend on water, and when it becomes unavailable, they fail or move. The landscape industry will be the first to go. As water restrictions rise past 35 percent, restaurants will struggle to maintain health standards. Hospitals and clinics will cut services, maybe handling emergencies only. Golf courses will close and revert to rough ground. As water sources dry up, water quality can drop too, requiring investment in more expensive water treatment.[24]

It's not just a few towns; whole regions are in danger. Although southern Florida is booming today with property prices continuing to rise, *Rolling Stone*, in a 2013 article titled "Goodbye, Miami," sketched a rapid and seemingly inevitable economic decline, driven primarily by rising sea level. Author Jeff Goodell wrote, "The financial catastrophe could play out like this: As insurance rates climb, fewer are able to afford homes. Housing prices fall, which slows development, which decreases the tax base, which makes cities and towns even less able to afford the infrastructure upgrades necessary to deal with rising seas. The spiral continues downward. Beaches deteriorate, hotels sit empty, restaurants close. Because Miami's largest economies are development and tourism, it's a deadly tailspin. The threat of sea-level rise bankrupts the state even before it is wiped out by a killer storm."[25] If you want readable and reliable information about the impact of global sea-level rise, watch for Goodell's forthcoming book on the topic.

Some industries are in the crosshairs.

Does your town have a specific industry that is critical to the municipal revenue base and likely to be badly damaged? The maritime industry provided one-third of all jobs in Gloucester, Massachusetts in 2012 and, as we saw in Chapter 2 on food, the fishing industry is being badly hit.[26] Threats from warming hang over other industries such as skiing, boating, and waterside tourism. Altogether, 2.8 percent of America's GDP, 7.52 million jobs, and $1.11 trillion in travel and recreational sales are supported by tourism. And billions in state and local taxes derive from these activities.

So where will state and local authorities find the money to meet these growing needs? From us, of course—and they have at least four methods.

Potential cost #1: Taxes

If you and your neighbors can afford more taxation by state and local authorities, enough cash may be found to protect you. But tax is a dirty word to many Americans—despite what the revenues are used for—and we've built up knee-jerk resistance to tax increases.

It's Okay. They can't raise my taxes!
In many places, it's easy to think we have a defensive barrier. After all, there are laws! Some prevent the town from raising our property taxes more than a percent or two a year; others give us the ability to vote down government expenditures. And many state constitutions say the state budget must be balanced every year. That should be enough to hold off any big tax increases, right?

Maybe so, but if a community chooses not to defend against the effects of warming, it will pay the consequences in other ways. Water shortages and flooding are only two. Tax-limit propositions don't stop sewer overflows, pollution, and health problems; nor business closings and job loss; nor economic decline and falling home prices. Facing those prospects, your local authorities are likely to come at you in other ways that skirt today's tax limits.

Potential cost #2: Fees in lieu of taxes

Over forty stoplights in Rochester, New York take photos of cars running red lights. The purpose is to improve safety but the $50 ticket doesn't hurt the city's revenues either. Those 90,000 tickets bring in about $2.5 million a year.[27]

California's First Five program has received more than $3 billion so far from an added tax on cigarettes. The funds are used specifically for public preschool and child health programs. New taxes on alcohol, tobacco, betting, and the like fall more heavily on the poor and, if they actually do discourage "sin," they dwindle rather than grow over time. But they're easier to sell to the public.[28]

Lynn, Massachusetts charges stands selling Christmas trees and wreaths a $100 fee. Nearby Cambridge charges homeowners a $15 licensing fee for outdoor decorations at Christmastime.[29] An Unauthorized Substances Tax is levied in North Carolina on marijuana, cocaine, and "moonshine." That's in addition to criminal charges.[30]

New York City applies an 8-cent tax to all "altered" bagels, whether sliced, toasted or served with cream cheese or butter. Apparently, cut bagels are considered a food sold for on-premises consumption, while uncut bagels are typically sold for home consumption and are tax-exempt.[31] Anything is fair game, such as yoga and Pilates classes (Kentucky), palmistry (Massachusetts), hot air balloon rides (Kentucky), pet grooming and funeral services (Michigan), dating services (Nebraska), and comedians, clowns, jugglers, ventriloquists, petting zoos, and haunted hayrides (Maine).[32]

Other new revenue sources have included fees for vending machines, court costs, students in college towns, beach access or parking, real estate transfers, sewer use, recycling, alarm permits, police response to an auto accident, hotel occupancy, municipal application forms, vehicle registrations, and cable TV hook-ups. Taxes are being levied on soda, taxi rides, and billboards, and on homes in a fire district.

Beyond the financial pain residents feel from so many fees is the inefficiency of collecting and enforcing so many small revenue sources, plus the hassle and hostility that can be created. But as the costs from warming begin to weigh more heavily on state and local governments, such fees seem more likely.

Potential cost #3: Send the bill to our children

Bike-sharing schemes and expanded distribution for local farmers call more for imagination and leadership than for cash; they may even be self-financing. But protecting residents with seawalls, sewer overflow correction, transit services, health and housing facilities, and disaster preparedness calls for cash—and lots of it. Even if the money can be found today, states, towns, school districts, water authorities and other government entities will likely choose to spread these costs over future years—and future generations—by borrowing.

There may be pushback against this. Some Texas towns have increased their borrowing so fast that the average local debt per resident across the state is over $8,600, much of it in a form that makes low interest payments at first, but big balloon payments down the road. The state legislature is moving toward restricting how counties, cities and school districts can borrow money.[33] Such restrictions on borrowing, of course, could help the town's long-term solvency, but if we can't send the bill to our children, the onus is back on today's taxpayers to come up with the money now.

Potential cost #4: Cuts in services

"Honey, what's this payment to a Mr. Karp?"

"Oh, he's Janie's new violin teacher. You know, after the school shut down the music program this year."

When government budgets are squeezed, many town leaders will cut services rather than raise fees or taxes. There are lots to choose from. They could lay off fire and police personnel, lower pensions for public employees, freeze city wages, cut back on arts and after-school programs, fire teachers, reduce the ranks of social workers, close public health facilities, let public housing deteriorate, spend less to attract new industries to town, cut back on maintenance of parks and recreation facilities, curtail civic and cultural activities, and reduce service behind the counter at City Hall.

Your tax bill doesn't go up. But you start spending more to supplement your kids' education, join a health club instead of the public pool, maybe buy a home security system. You feel the need to contribute more to local charities. You may not be aware of the trend, but your monthly budget will point it out.

Some services will be downgraded or abandoned.

Certain expenditures may never get to the top of the pile; they'll simply be abandoned. With road maintenance costs beyond the capabilities of many budgets, 38 of Michigan's 83 counties have converted some low-traffic asphalt roads to gravel. In Wisconsin, tearing up a dilapidated paved road, pulverizing the pavement, and laying it down again mixed with gravel costs $40,000 a mile, while repaving a road with hot asphalt costs $75,000 a mile and must be done every decade or so. South Dakota has converted over 100 miles of road to gravel. Counties in Alabama and Pennsylvania have begun downgrading asphalt roads to cheaper chip-and-seal surfaces. Texas simply cannot maintain many rural roads used by heavy oil and gas equipment and is letting them deteriorate.[34]

Return-to-gravel projects are limited today to low-traffic rural roads, but they show us a future that few could imagine a while back. What if the same changes are applied to the maintenance of city streets, school properties, public parks? Today there is the occasional government official who will compare our infrastructure to a third-world country's.[35] Tomorrow, many more of us may think the same.

Warming costs come on top of other urgencies

As warming creates more costs, government bodies are already strained by a slew of existing needs. Two big ones, both caused by procrastination, loom large:

1. **Not maintaining our infrastructure.** As we saw in Chapter 5 on transportation, the maintenance and replacement needs of our roads and bridges are far outstripping our efforts to make them safe and comfortable. The longer these projects are put off, the more expensive they become. Of course, overdue maintenance is not a problem caused by warming, but it competes for funds with the work made necessary by warming.

2. **Unfunded liabilities.** As Warren Buffet put it recently, "Local and state financial problems are accelerating, in large part because public entities promised pensions they couldn't afford. Citizens and public officials typically under-appreciated the gigantic financial tapeworm that was born when promises were made that conflicted with a willingness to fund them."[36] Because

so little was put aside, many state and local governments' obligations look like they will grow forever.

The worst-funded state pension system belongs to Illinois, where unfunded liabilities stand at $100 billion. Falling credit ratings have forced Illinois residents to pay the highest state borrowing costs in the country. Political fears and threatened lawsuits have kept legislators from taking even the least painful steps, such as limiting annual cost-of-living allowances or raising the retirement age for state workers.[37]

As for cities, Charleston, West Virginia is also among the worst in the country, with only $24 in tax revenue to cover every $100 in pension obligations each year to former teachers, police, firefighters, and other city employees. The amount of money the city needs to keep those promises is increasing annually.

HOLDING YOUR STATE AND LOCAL TAXES DOWN

There is little you can do at home to hold down your local taxes and fees. Cutting your family's use of energy, transportation, healthcare, water, etc. can have tangible, immediate savings, but cutting back on your use of municipal services such as streets, schools, sewers and ambulances doesn't reduce your taxes at all. To climate-proof your personal finances from these indirect costs, you need to take actions beyond your household activities, out in the community.

You should identify and campaign hard for elected candidates who see future dangers clearly, understand the trade-offs, and will work to take serious steps towards a more secure future, while minimizing conflict. Figure out which town leaders are wearing rose-colored glasses, and educate or replace them. You may be able to help authorities come to grips with reality and to tackle problems responsibly and creatively.

Many cities, towns, counties and states across the country are beginning to take sensible actions to deal with the costs of a shifting climate. But in many towns, this will require getting more residents to see the need to climate-proof their community. You and like-minded neighbors may be able to conduct this kind of education program, perhaps through a new civic organization, a sympathetic news outlet, or a grassroots campaign or protest.

Here are some examples of the type of forward-thinking initiatives you can push for that would help control your community's costs and therefore your taxes and fees, in the long run.

Shield the watershed.
You will be better protected from water-related taxes and rates if your municipality is focused on keeping your watershed or aquifer working naturally, avoiding the need for costly new sources or purification systems.

Westminster, a Massachusetts town of around 7,000, long ago created a *Best Development Practices* guidebook that considers the effects of warming. To receive zoning approval, real estate developers must follow its principles, which include minimizing demand for irrigation water and maximizing groundwater recharge, with minimal clearing, swales and filter strips of vegetation, constructed wetlands, pervious paving, roof gardens, and rain gardens.[38]

On the downwind side of the Rockies, Denver Water is planning for a 4°F rise in temperature by 2050. That may seem high, but the state has recorded a 2° rise over the last 30 years. Whether or not warming will reduce rainfall and increase evaporation, it will certainly accelerate snowmelt, so new reservoirs are being planned. Developers must prove that a property has a source of water, such as an aquifer, that will last 100 years. The utility is working to cultivate a culture of water conservation, cutting overall water use by 22 percent from the 2001 level.[39]

An expansion of Kent Hospital in Warwick, Rhode Island, that includes more parking, driveways, and walls, was going to extend the impervious surface around the hospital, causing more runoff into streams and preventing rain and snowmelt from percolating back into the aquifer. Instead, the hospital created a rain garden that replaced a 5,000-square foot lawn. This area of low-maintenance, deep-rooting native wildflowers and grasses captures the runoff from the hospital's roof and walkways. Other advantages: the hospital no longer has the costly maintenance of a large lawn, and butterflies and songbirds now visit.[40]

Reuse water.

To protect against drought, more and more towns are reclaiming residents' wastewater. Most comes from sinks, showers, washing machines and dishwashers. After treatment, it can water golf courses, parks, and school fields, fill lakes and wetlands, fight fires, and irrigate crops and pastures. Some ski resorts use the treated water to make snow.

The international superstar of water reuse is Las Vegas. By the summer of 2014, water in Lake Mead, the country's largest man-made reservoir, had dropped to around 40 percent of capacity. But today the lake enjoys a new water source: the city of Las Vegas. About 40 percent of the water the city takes from Lake Mead is cleaned and pumped back into the lake.

What does this effort look like to residents? Water cops patrol the city watching for homes that let water from a lawn sprinkler or car-washing session, a hot tub or swimming pool drain anywhere but into a city sewer. Less than 10 percent of water used in Las Vegas homes and businesses, schools and government operations escapes to evaporate or drain into the soil. What cannot be treated to near purity is used on the city's parks and golf courses; the rest is pumped back into Lake Mead, the source of nine-tenths of the water for a city that gets less than 5 inches of precipitation a year.[41]

To cut down on water used for landscaping, the city prohibits new homes from having a front lawn and offers cash for every square foot of lawn removed by existing homes or businesses and replaced by desert plantings. The bounty comes to about $45,000 per acre and applies to golf courses as well as private homes.

Las Vegas may be at the extreme, but you could persuade your city council or State House to protect your future water and sewer costs in many other ways. Charles City, Iowa has constructed 25 blocks of porous pavement to capture runoff from streets, yards, and alleys and provide complete infiltration to the aquifer, even in big downpours. Reduction in stormwater runoff may make expensive upgrades to the existing sewers unnecessary, as heavy precipitation becomes more frequent.[42]

In 2014, Wichita Falls, Texas declared a drought emergency and began to send reclaimed water back to residents' taps. So far there are no ill effects. Although few towns have begun supplying treated water as drinking water, plenty of water authorities from Florida to Minnesota to California are finding uses for reclaimed water that would otherwise just flow away in rivers to the sea.[43]

The board of the Water District in Portland, Maine recently voted unanimously to buy more conservation easements in its rapidly developing watershed. Although Portland enjoys a high-quality water source, the city is looking far ahead to maintain its high standards and avoid treatment costs by securing its watershed against development.

Raleigh, North Carolina has allocated $7.5 million since 2005 for strategic land conservation to help address declining water quality in its primary reservoir. Land trusts, landowners, municipalities and other government agencies have used voluntary measures to protect from development more than 6,000 priority acres along 63 miles of stream in Raleigh's watershed. The future savings are expected to be many times the cost.

More than 100 drinkable, swimmable, and fishable waterways across the country have appointed a Waterkeeper, Riverkeeper, or Coastkeeper to keep the water clean and avoid the costs of new treatment plants. The Waterkeeper Alliance uses publicity, lobbying, and legal action to protect bodies of water around the world and rally local support for the regulations and activities needed to do so.[44]

Stop development in flood-prone areas.
Because of the infrastructure maintenance, disaster preparedness, relief, and repair costs to the state and its municipalities, North Carolina no longer allows homes to be built on a shoreline that is likely to erode within the next 30-60 years. In Maine, Rhode Island, South Carolina and Texas, you can build, but only on the condition that you agree to remove the structure if it's threatened by the disappearing shoreline.

To secure a no-regrets future, it may be important for your town to revise its building codes to prevent development in flood-prone areas. Owners of low-lying land fight these regulations based on "property rights," but the new rules are designed to protect the rest of the community from long-term expenses caused by these owners, and they have usually been upheld in court.[45]

Push for true-cost flood insurance.
Underpriced federal flood insurance can sock local taxpayers with big costs. Low premiums disguise the true cost of ownership and encourage

building and rebuilding in flood-prone areas. These repeatedly damaged properties hurt those communities, adding to what local taxpayers pay for disaster and emergency costs, plus repairs to municipal property, like sewers and roads near the damaged homes. Where a town lacks the money to repair this damage, neighborhoods can be left in bad shape for years—a sad sight, and a depressing influence on nearby home values.

One solution: push your representatives in Washington to raise flood insurance premiums more rapidly to reflect the true risk of flooding, and to deny repeat claims. The sooner this happens, the sooner flood-prone homeowners will have an additional incentive to make decisions that are good for the town's budget, not just for their own.

In Chapter 8 we will look at this question from the homeowner's angle.

Buy and demolish repeatedly damaged properties.

From 1993 through 1995, Missouri was hit by repetitive flooding. damaging many properties over and over again. Each time, the owner was entitled to claim from the national flood insurance program. Adopting a new tactic, FEMA and the state of Missouri paid roughly $75 million from 1995 to 2008 to purchase and demolish 4,045 repetitive-loss properties across eight counties. FEMA pays three-quarters of market value, and the state or municipality pays the rest.[46]

A 2009 study of 885 purchased properties showed that FEMA and Missouri saved nearly $97 million in losses during 14 subsequent flood disasters. That represents a 212 percent return on investment for the public funds that had been invested in those particular buyouts.

New York and New Jersey have sophisticated homebuying programs, with incentives for sellers to move within the community. FEMA lists over 7,500 properties bought between late 2003 and late 2014 at an average price of $59,000. Similar programs have been carried out in Iowa, Georgia, and Kentucky, with good returns on the purchase outlays.[47]

Pulling down houses in your town may be hard to imagine today, but the next big storm, even in a distant coastal area, could persuade municipal governments, with a little push from taxpayers like you, to begin cutting long-term costs with buyouts.

Support local businesses.

Want your town, county, and state to have more revenues? Attract and support locally-owned businesses.

Studies by economists at Harvard and Penn State have found that regional economic growth, including tax revenues, "is highly correlated with the presence of many small, entrepreneurial employers—not a few big ones."[48] Locally-owned business owners not only pay local and state income taxes. They hire within the community, mentor and train residents, participate in local volunteer projects, and work with schools. Their owners serve on boards and donate to local charities. They stay in town when the going gets rough. The same is not as true for large companies or national chains.

Hire forward-thinking town officials.

City officials are a different breed from state and federal bureaucrats. They often have stronger connections with the people they serve, since we can pound the counter at City Hall more easily than at the State House or a federal office. Perhaps because running a city calls for pragmatism, city officials are usually less encumbered with ideology and red-blue partisanship.

City officials also quickly copy ideas from other cities. They're not captive to The Centerville Way or Springfield Exceptionalism, as national politics is often hostage to jingoistic concepts and state government to States' Rights.

Take an extreme example of forward thinking. Aspen, Colorado is a resort community—skiing in winter, white-water rafting in summer—and is totally dependent on temperatures and water flows. In 2005, leaders in this resort and town started the Aspen Canary Initiative, viewing Aspen as an early-warning example of possible devastation from atmospheric warming.

The study they commissioned projected that less snow would cut skiers in Aspen by 5-20 percent by 2030, causing $16-56 million in lost personal income to the area. And those losses do not include the likely far bigger losses in property value in what is one of the country's priciest real estate markets. The result has been an extensive strategic plan by the city, the county and the resort aimed at creating a diversifying economy, preventing wildfires and flooding, maintaining water availability and biodiversity, and creating resilient buildings.[49]

Although few are as endangered as Aspen, more than one city has started serious planning. Many have created the post of Chief Resilience Officer. The CRO in Boulder, Colorado is making sure that all city departments are doing their planning based on the same climate predictions and has created climate boot camps, which many city officials are required to attend. These focus on the particular effects predicted for Boulder, cross-department impacts, and the need for cooperation in planning, budgeting, and action.[50]

Even when farsighted, unbiased town leaders are chosen, you may still need to support citizens' committees, collect signatures for voter referenda, stage rallies and protests, and otherwise speak out. Some bureaucracies are going to need a lot more pressure than others. For instance, the state of Florida has prohibited state officials from even using the words "climate change" or "global warming" in government discussions, documents and statements.[51]

And you don't just need a forward-looking Governor or Mayor or enlightened city council members. A lot of lesser positions will become increasingly involved with protecting residents from specific effects of climate shifts. In most towns, for instance, elected water and zoning boards used to be pretty ho-hum committees, with little imagination or initiative required. That's changing fast, and it will pay you to make sure there are thoughtful people on those committees.

To protect your personal finances, at your next city council meeting you should stand up and say, "But what are you doing about the such-and-such effect of warming?" Or better yet, join or form a local organization to create awareness and raise these questions throughout your town, county or state. Some towns will take early steps to dodge big warming-related expenses down the road. Others will find themselves making excuses to future residents for high taxes, limited services, and a declining economy. The difference may depend on what you and your neighbors are demanding today.

Make sure officials are producing real action plans.

A community is much more likely to work its way past current constraints and be ready for future pressures if it has a definite plan.

When it comes to the effects of warming, most state legislatures and town councils are not there yet. In many towns, there has been no wake-up call. In some, the dominant ideology doesn't permit acknowledging problems from warming. In others, taxes needed to protect the town are not looked upon as payment for services but as some kind of theft.

Many jurisdictions are thinking about how to reduce their city's carbon emissions—a good thing for the planet—but not how to create protections from the consequences and costs of warming. When you evaluate your town's plans, be sure to distinguish between the two types of actions.

New Jersey, for instance, has any number of initiatives to reduce emissions: the Global Warming Response Act, Clean Car Program, Renewable Portfolio Standard, Clean Energy Program, Consolidated Energy Savings Program, Cool Cities Initiative, Executive Order to Promote Energy Efficiency, Green Homes Office. In addition, the state has classified CO_2 as a pollutant and joined the Regional Greenhouse Gas Initiative, a multi-state carbon tax. Impressive! But, like most states, by mid-2016 New Jersey had not yet published a plan for actually helping to protect its residents from the consequences of warming.

The U.S. Conference of Mayors claims that four in ten cities are developing a climate adaptation plan, and the same percentage is "undertaking assessments or creating community-wide responses to predicted climate impacts."[52] But few of these plans are actually written yet. Probably the best way to see whether a particular county or municipal government is planning to protect you is to spend a few minutes on its website, searching for *warming, climate, adaptation,* and maybe *sustainability*.

Upgrade the skills of municipal leaders and employees.

State and municipal managers are going to require some new skills to keep residents safe in the face of climate shifts. Traditional abilities will always be important, but we'll be better off if we can encourage our civic leaders to improve their abilities to plan, educate the public, handle cross-border issues, and be sensitive to the effects of warming on the poor.

The North Carolina Local Government Commission set up the School of Government at the University of North Carolina. The state urges, and sometimes requires, municipal employees to upgrade their professional skills there. Similar programs are increasingly available. Have any officials in your area attended?

Value new thinking.

With plenty of other cities and states running experiments to improve their finances, their services, and their residents' lives, it will pay to live where your leaders are receptive to these outside ideas.

Most of us are aware of cost and revenue tactics cities are taking to improve their budgets: adopting LED street and traffic lights, buying hybrid and natural gas-powered vehicles, selling advertising on park benches, public trash bins, even street signs. Hundreds of new ideas are in the works.

New York Mayor Bloomberg's 2014 attempt to prohibit the sale of large sugary soft drinks within the city was shot down by the courts. But it's a model of serious cost cutting. The rise in obesity has been a growing public health cost to virtually all cities. In New York City, the medical and social costs of diseases caused by obesity are estimated at $4 billion a year.[53]

Landfills in Warren County, New Jersey capture methane gas and burn it to create 20 megawatts of electricity. Other landfill authorities have followed suit.[54]

Allentown and Bethlehem, Pennsylvania have introduced split-rate property taxation, where buildings are taxed at lower rates than the underlying land. This sends a message to landowners: improving your property now costs less. The aim is to increase housing supplies, dampen the rise in housing prices and rents, rehabilitate homes, stores, and offices, attract new private investment to central business districts, and encourage the development of urban lots and under-used buildings, producing higher density and lower sprawl. Added benefits have been to reduce taxes on most owner-occupied and rental homes and to leave more suburban tracts in a condition to capture and percolate rainwater into groundwater. It seems to work. Sixteen Pennsylvania cities have tried it. Allentown started taxing land separately in 1996. Nearby Bethlehem has not done so. Allentown's new construction and renovation grew 54 percent faster than Bethlehem's.[55]

Consider privatized water services. Carefully.

If your town is like many others, it faces long-overdue capital improvements to the water system, even before it copes with the effects of climate shocks. With other growing demands on local tax revenues, you may be asked to approve turning all or some water functions over to a private company willing to make the investment in return for selling the water to residents. Over 2,000 water facilities across the country are privately owned.

When a private utility takes over, you can expect water rates to go up— not a bad thing if the increase actually covers improvements, competent long-term-oriented management, and a modest profit. A new rate structure can also include incentives for water conservation throughout the town.[56]

In 2011, Indianapolis, Indiana sold its aging, leaky water supply and wastewater systems for $1.9 billion, not to a private company but to a local charitable trust, the Citizens Energy Group. The new group has raised water rates and begun spending millions to replace 100-year-old pipes (700 breaks a year). While there have been complaints about executive salaries, billing practices, and call center response, and Moody's has lowered some of the company's bond ratings, the arrangement is still considered to be working. And it freed up a whole lot of cash for the city to spend on other needs![57]

Privatizing may be the only financial option for some communities, and it may be a good idea in others where old-school town managers insist that low rates, low maintenance costs, and decaying infrastructure are "all we can afford." But risks arise when the private company has the wrong incentives or supervision. Between 2000 and 2014, 59 U.S. cities "re-municipalized" their water and sanitation services.[58] In 2010, Gary, Indiana canceled its 10-year contract with the private operator of their water system. The company had exceeded discharge limits dozens of times, had failed to maintain equipment, was not giving proper reports to the city, and was late on deadlines. There are quite a few other horror stories about the privatization of water and other municipal services.

Resist undue optimism.

As you evaluate your town and state's ability to protect you from warming, watch for the over-optimism many officials and local interest groups put on when they face these issues.

In 2010, a North Carolina state agency predicted the seas around the barrier-island community of Nags Head will rise 39 inches by 2100, dooming many homes. Just the prospect of such damage could trash the island economy, which is based on beach houses and vacation tourism. Local officials, Realtors, homebuilders and other interest groups jumped into action to save their island economy. Their solution: stop looking ahead. A bill that would prohibit state agencies from planning for sea-level rise was strongly supported in Raleigh. It failed, but official predictions are now restricted to no more than 30 years, at which point sea-level rise is predicted to reach 8 inches.[59]

The actions you take to keep your property value healthy and your state and local costs under control are very different from those that cut your family's energy or food bill. It takes time and a certain aggressiveness to persuade your public officials to protect you. Not all of us are comfortable speaking at public hearings or canvassing neighbors on an issue. But even if you want to stay out of the limelight, there are behind-the-scenes roles you can play: sending mailings, creating posters, organizing meetings, and more. All these efforts can help persuade your town, county and state officials to start taking action to climate-proof your community. In doing so, they will also be helping to climate-proof your personal finances.

WHERE TO FIND LOWER STATE & LOCAL TAXES

Not every town can be climate-proofed. Drought, flooding or respiratory problems are hard to prevent. Fiscal and leadership weaknesses are hard to change. As new environmental costs loom, you may wonder why you should stick around to watch the problems grow, and your state and local taxes and fees grow with them. You may conclude it's a no-brainer to move away to a better-funded, better-managed town.

On the other hand, you may think it cowardly or selfish to leave behind a city's unfunded liabilities, falling revenues, and needed infrastructure projects—all the more so if the exodus shrinks the population, hence the tax base and the community's pool of capable leaders.

But look carefully; moving may be the only way to avoid sacrificing your family's finances. Moving is an American tradition anyway. Only 25 percent of those living in Nevada were born there. It's 36 percent for Florida and 38 percent for Arizona. America may have grown in population according to the 2010 Census, but a whole lot of cities shrank, some by more than 5% over the decade.[60]

As you consider relocating to dodge some of the threats caused by warming, it makes sense to add state and municipal finances to your checklist. Does a particular city and state have the fiscal strength, management skills, and civic attitude to protect you from even modest dangers?

Yourtown, USA

The Natural Resources Defense Council rates state governments according to their climate preparedness planning (to cope with problems from warming as distinct from preventing warming) as it relates to water issues. Nine states are considered the best prepared with twelve others on the list of largely unprepared. Check bit.ly/NRDC_water_readiness for the state ratings.

Look for low taxes and fees.
In many communities, you can walk into Town Hall and come out with one or more printed lists of municipal fees and taxes. But that doesn't tell you how the town compares to others.

Yourtown, USA

Comparative state and average local tax "burdens" within each state are calculated by the Tax Foundation. Check how your state ranks at http://taxfoundation.org/article/state-local-tax-burden-rankings-fy-

2012 (Jan 2016) with updates at taxfoundation.org/ sites/taxfoundation.org/files/docs/TFD%20Map.png.

Remember, however, that low taxes don't necessarily mean good fiscal conditions in a town. They may be low because local and state government is underspending on the place's future.

Look for strong municipal credit.

It takes time and skill to assess the financial strength of a city by yourself, but it's easy to find out what the investment community thinks. Municipal credit ratings are indicators of general financial health. A good score usually means that median income is higher than average, the community is not dependent on one or two employers, population growth is not booming or crashing, the average net worth of residents is above average, tax revenues come from stable sources, and no particular economic challenges loom on the horizon.

A city with these advantages should have little trouble maintaining its revenues and service levels. What's more, it can borrow money at favorable rates if it decides to undertake some big projects to protect the community from the impacts of warming.

The most-used measures of government health are bond ratings. Many municipalities have issued municipal bonds in the past, often several times, to finance projects. The ratings agencies give each bond issue a score to help bond buyers know which are currently considered a good investment and which are in danger of not being repaid. A bond rating is similar to your personal credit rating, which tells investors such as mortgage companies how likely you are to repay your debt.

Moody's, Standard & Poor's, and Fitch provide municipal bond ratings based on many local economic factors. You can go to one or more of them, get an idea of a town's credit risk, and use that as an indicator of the likelihood that the town will be financially capable of protecting its residents from any big costs of warming.

Yourtown, USA

To find your town's municipal credit ratings, go to moodys.com, standardandpoors.com, or fitchratings.com. Register with your email address, choose a password, and enter a municipality and state. If the city has one or more outstanding bond issues, you will see the ratings, from AAA on down, for each issue. Ratings can be also found in at SavvyFamilies.org/Where-To-Live-Indicators.

A few caveats:

1. **Ratings are for specific securities, not for the town as a whole.** Normally a city's overall financial condition is most closely mirrored by the ratings of their general obligation (GO) bonds. Other bonds may have different ratings if they are tied to a particular revenue source, such as water rates, road tolls, or electricity billings.

2. **Ratings consider business as usual.** A city with a AA+ (high grade) rating today, may be facing much bigger costs from drought, flooding or other consequences of warming than a city with a B+ (highly speculative) rating. The rating agencies have not considered many of those risks yet.

3. **The ratings agencies were asleep at the switch when subprime mortgages, collateralized debt obligations, and derivative products began to deteriorate before the crash in 2008.** Securities worth hundreds of billions of dollars were rated triple-A, then suddenly downgraded to junk status just before and during the crash.

Find the best information about future problems.

If you are to dodge warming-induced boosts to taxes, fees and other municipal costs, learning what is ahead for your town is critical. This may take a bit of research. Certain dangers are not yet discussed by politicians in some City Halls and State Houses. But even if elected officials and the local press won't talk about the effects of warming, behind the scenes in planning offices and committee rooms, professional staff and citizen groups are likely to be working hard on how to cope. Poke around a little among the state and local government departments, sub-committees, commissions, and consulting contracts. You could find studies and plans not yet publicized which may indicate that your family's finances have a good chance—or not—of being protected by the authorities.

Footnotes for this chapter, Where-To-Live Indicators for all American towns, and other tools and resources are available at savvyfamilies.org/climateproof, as well as the author's updates, your comments, and other useful information.

7 PROTECT AGAINST RISING FEDERAL TAXES

Former Treasury Secretary Robert Rubin, put it best. "Future federal spending to deal with climate change is likely to be enormous and should be included in fiscal projections . . . If nothing is done to prevent climate-related crises, the federal government will be forced to deal with them later. These huge risks are not currently in official future estimates or federal budget plans. To cover those costs, we will have to increase the deficit, raise taxes, or significantly cut spending."[1]

To every new Congress, the Government Accountability Office presents a High Risk List calling attention to federal agencies and programs that present high "fiscal exposure." Since 2011 the GAO has included risks from climate change, pointing out that Washington is a huge property owner, insurance underwriter, and provider of technical assistance and disaster aid—domestic and foreign. In these capacities, the federal government will require far more funding than Washington's business-as-usual budget provides.[2]

But Congress is strongly divided on the issue, with the majority of lawmakers preferring not to acknowledge the coming costs throughout the government. For instance, in May 2014, the House of Representatives passed an amendment prohibiting the Department of Defense from even considering the effects of climate shifts on America's national security. No consideration of sea levels on naval bases. No disaster planning for climate events. No instability scenarios based on climate-driven drought or flooding.[3]

The provision did not become law, and the Pentagon and other federal departments continue to create some of the most detailed scenarios and projections for costs of climate disruption.[4] Referring to the new security, geopolitical and human issues that are growing as warming makes the Arctic Sea navigable, Rear Adm. (ret) David Titley said, "The ice doesn't care about politics or Democrats and Republicans; it just melts."[5]

HOW OUR FEDERAL TAXES WILL INCREASE

If Congress continues to appropriate little or nothing to protect the country from the effects of warming, our family budgets may not be affected by rising federal taxes. But for the moment, let's look at what costs we taxpayers are likely to feel if Washington does take Rubin's and the GOA's advice and begins to cope with the effects of warming on its own operations, and also tries to help citizens, towns, states, and the rest of the world. Here are some of the problems Rubin, the GAO and others think that the federal government—and the American taxpayer—should begin to tackle.

Government property is at risk.

The *Quadrennial Defense Review* from the Pentagon tells us: "As greenhouse gas emissions increase, sea levels are rising, average global temperatures are increasing, and severe weather patterns are accelerating. These changes . . . will devastate homes, land, and infrastructure."[6] As the seas rise, for instance, replacement bases will need to be found for our huge low-lying installations on Diego Garcia and Guam, central to our military presence in the Indian Ocean and the Western Pacific.

Beyond our defense infrastructure Americans, through our federal government, own billions of dollars worth of non-military property and equipment that face the same threats. The number of federal buildings and facilities at risk from the effects of warming are likely to be in the hundreds of thousands, with replacement value in the tens of billions of dollars.[7]

Government insurance and disaster relief are growing fast.

In 2015, there were 10 weather- and climate-disaster events—droughts, floods, severe storms, and wildfires—with losses exceeding $1 billion each across the U.S. The average since 1980 was 5.2 events but that has jumped to 10.8 events since 2011. Not everyone knows it, but only a quarter of these costs were covered by commercial insurance. Most were paid by you and me as taxpayers, through our federal government's various insurance programs, including the Federal Emergency Management Agency (FEMA), the National Flood Insurance Program (NFIP), The Federal Crop Insurance Program (FCIP), and others.[8]

The NFIP is running a $20+ billion deficit because premiums are low and don't cover claims.[9] In 2012, Congress passed a flood insurance reform act that boosted premiums a lot closer to costs. This lasted only as long as it took for waterside property owners to start screaming. Congress quickly dropped the new realistic premiums. Instead, premiums will now rise gradually over time toward the real underwriting costs. In the meantime, federal taxpayers continue to absorb the difference.[10] (Federal taxpayer costs for suppressing wildfires have already risen substantially from a few hundred million dollars in the 1980s and 1990's to more than $3 billion in recent years.[11])

Looking more broadly, a measure called 'Federal Climate Disruption Costs' compiled by the National Resources Defense Council indicates that 16 percent of our government's non-defense discretionary expenditures were related to the effects of warming, exceeding any other single category such as education or transportation.[12] In recent years programs designed to reduce the long-term costs of warming—environmental enforcement, energy efficiency, clean energy vehicle research, and advanced energy research—were all cut by a Congress worried about budget deficits.[13] These cuts merely postpone and multiply the outlays the American government and its citizens will have to make to deal with these costs.

Military and security costs will grow quickly.

The Pentagon has been building predictive models and scenarios that forecast, country by country, what flooding, drought, and famine will do to force migration, erode public health and threaten political stability. Our military's big missions may move from the invasions in recent decades to a future of extensive humanitarian aid delivery, stabilization of weak but friendly governments, and peacekeeping.[14] In addition, they stress the need to prepare for increased patrol operations in the Arctic, soon to be open to navigation.

There have been hopes that American taxpayers might be able to spend less on our armed forces, now that we are mostly out of Iraq and Afghanistan. But taxes to support our military seem just as likely to rise as new missions in new theaters are thrust upon us, thanks to accelerating climate shifts. The retired Admirals and Generals who prepared the 2014 report *National Security and the Accelerating Risks of Climate Change* emphasized the "profusion of demands for military support resulting from climate and weather–related conditions and events . . . and the limitations on readiness accompanying climate changes."[15]

Conflict and unrest are growing.

While Syria's devastating civil war has a number of causes, recent research has unearthed the hidden roles that warming, extreme weather events and a water crisis have played. Between 2006 and 2011, up to 60 percent of Syria experienced one of the worst long-term droughts in modern history. Together with the mismanagement of water resources, this drought led to total crop failure for 75 percent of farmers, forcing their migration and increasing tensions in urban cities that were already experiencing economic insecurity and political instability.[16]

Closer to home, drought in Venezuela has reduced hydroelectric power generation, caused frequent power and water cuts, and seriously degraded the healthcare system.[17] Warming is only one of many factors in that country's economic paralysis, which has resulted in serious civil unrest. But it may be the factor that is hardest to reverse.

Pollution and pandemics, internal conflict over resources, food riots, mass demonstrations, and other conflicts are likely results of climate disruption. *U.S. News and World Report, Fox News,* and *Al Jazeera* are only a few places where we read headlines such as "The Wars of the Future Will Be Fought Over Water." Areas predicted to be hit hardest by climate shocks are mostly where governments are less stable. The Bangladesh scenario, for instance, gets complicated real fast: hundreds of thousands of refugees stream from Bangladesh into neighboring India after a massive flood, religious conflict grows, contagious diseases spread, and infrastructure in both countries is damaged.

Overseas problems from warming likely to hit U.S. taxpayers are not limited to local natural disasters such as flooding, drought, or storms. Many can have distant, complex and roundabout causes. Follow this sequence: In 2010, drought caused by global warming was responsible for unusually severe wildfires in Russia. Twenty percent of the country's wheat crop was destroyed. Russia stopped exporting wheat, causing a shortage in many parts of the world. About the same time, Australia, Canada, and the U.S. were experiencing flooding, also the result of climate anomalies. This killed parts of their wheat crops and further reduced global supplies. Because of the growing scarcity, some wheat importing countries started hoarding wheat as a safety measure against famine, further raising world prices.

The result was a doubling of international wheat prices, which were already historically high. This affected the food security of people in wheat-importing countries, contributing to the riots in Tahrir Square, Cairo, to social unrest in other countries in the region, and to the Arab Spring uprisings.[18] Stated simply, warming is a major cause of the current Middle East instability.

Mass migrations forced by drought or flood look to be inevitable. Even if these develop slowly, with food and shelter provided along the route, where do millions of migrants go, and how are they greeted when they arrive? We have only to look at the Hindus and Moslems during Partition in India, the Israelis and Palestinians, or the Syrians trying to get into Europe today to see the level of conflict and misery such moves can cause—and the international costs of helping out.

Perhaps the biggest powder keg is the Indus River, which flows through China, Pakistan, and India and is threatened by disappearing glaciers at its source. Each country is dependent on the river, and all have large armies and as well as nuclear weapons.

Attacks on America may grow.

As floods cover big portions of Bangladesh, as the Himalayan snowpack disappears, and as southern and northern Africa dries, the affected peoples will be reminded of who caused their misery. That would be us. Rich countries have emitted the great majority of greenhouse gasses blanketing the globe.

America may be able to peacefully buy its way out of some of this blame with reparations (see below). But even if we can mollify some traumatized populations with financial and humanitarian aid, others may seek some form of revenge.

Literally billions of young people around the world will grow up learning that 20th-century emissions by America and other rich nations caused the growing misery and costs in their lives. Each effect from climate change, whether it's a discreet event like a storm or a creeping menace like sea-level rise, will likely be used as a rallying cry by anti-American militant preachers, politicians, and militia leaders.

Antagonism toward America seems a permanent feature in many groups around the Muslim world, waiting to be exacerbated by warming. Dr. Paul Smith, who teaches Security Strategies at the U.S. Naval War college, says, "The collective feelings of alienation and estrangement which radical Islam draws upon are unlikely to dissipate until the Muslim world again appears to be more fully integrated into the world economy. However, climate change may stifle, delay or completely derail this integration."[19]

Other countries' affection and respect for America have ebbed and flowed over the decades, but when non-state terrorists hit the Twin Towers in New York, America woke up to the potential costs here at home from hostile groups around the world. We have already grown the federal budget for homeland security functions from $16 billion before 9/11 to over $70 billion today. How much more will taxpayers need to pay if organized attacks on America—or our citizens and property here and abroad—start to ramp up?

Beyond dollars, Jim Hansen, head of the NASA Goddard Institute for Space Studies, testified before Congress about two other dimensions to America's responsibility for climate change. "As indigenous people must abandon their land to rising seas or shifting climatic zones, they will be well aware of the principal source of the problem. Thus if we continue on this course, failing to effectively address climate change, we will leave a heavy moral burden, and perhaps a legal burden, for our children."[20]

This global blame could take at least one very practical form. It may seem impossible today, but pressures to allow many more immigrants into the U.S. could grow to become irresistible. Today's political climate suggests this would increase security and justice challenges here in the U.S.

Pressures to boost non-military aid will mount.

Protests and negotiations by poor countries have so far resulted in the creation of the UN's Green Climate Fund. At the Copenhagen Climate Summit in 2009, world leaders promised to provide funding to help poor countries adjust to a changing climate and to reduce their emissions. As a sort of advance reparations, these funds would help developing countries prevent or cope with threats from climate damage.

America's current pledge of $3 billion to this fund is a tiny price for us to pay to help the world cope with climate change, but the plan is for this climate finance, available at low cost to affected countries, to grow to $100 billion a year by 2020.[21] Much of this funding is supposed to come from private investors with government guarantees and rate buy-downs. Whether they are grants from Washington or complex financing schemes from Wall Street, $100 billion a year will likely cost American taxpayers significantly.

Since the aftermath of World War II, America has not spent a lot of money to help other countries. While we spend a higher dollar amount on development assistance than any other country, as a percentage of Gross National Income we are 20th, just behind Portugal.[22] In 2013 we spent just under two-tenths of one percent, and since 2011 a large bloc of House Republicans have called for defunding of the U.S. Agency for International Development completely. While dragging our feet on contributing might save America money, it is very likely to increase resentment in places where the funding is needed, raising long-term military or homeland security costs.

As foreign disasters grow, so will humanitarian assistance.

America has always used its military to help other countries recover from natural disasters. In 2011, following the massive earthquake, tsunami and nuclear disaster in Fukushima, Japan, U.S. Marines were among the first to reach the Sendai airport (by parachute), helping to reopen it by clearing away hundreds of jumbled vehicles.[23]

After the 2010 earthquake hit Haiti, the U.S. military deployed roughly 22,200 personnel, 33 U.S. Navy and Coast Guard vessels, and more than 300 aircraft.[24]

In 1991 Cyclone Marian sent a storm surge 20 feet high across the coast of Bangladesh, leaving over 130,000 bodies. Ten million were left homeless. The storm destroyed crops on 75,000 acres of land, with 300,000 more acres of cropland damaged. American relief efforts involved over 4,000 Marines and 3,000 Navy personnel.[25]

Natural disasters caused by warming around the globe are likely to become more widespread and complicated. Several central African countries are predicted to become virtually uninhabitable thanks to increased warming and drought, forcing mass migrations.[26] A straw in the wind: only a few years ago in 2011, 920,000 refugees from Somalia fled to Kenya and Ethiopia to escape drought-induced famine.[27] The U.S. will likely provide supplies and logistical help in an increasing number of these crises.

The list of American rescue and supply efforts is already long, but most are just that: localized rescue and supply, costing a tiny fraction of the Pentagon's budget. Delivery of food, water, tents and medicine will be just the beginning. It remains to be seen whether new technologies and equipment our armed forces will need to deal with humanitarian missions are as expensive as what we needed for combat missions of the past. We can imagine moveable desalination plants, tanker and hospital ships, rescue aircraft, hydroponics houses, instant refugee camps, and other gear for humanitarian disasters. And those items are generally much lower in sophistication than fighter planes and cruise missiles.

On the other hand, the equipment, delivery methods, and command and control needed for these missions may be less developed within the military, requiring a heavy investment in design and training. And humanitarian aid is likely to call for far more front-line troops than modern warfare does.[28]

One other aspect of world food supplies should be considered. Accepted by American farmers and consumers, genetically-engineered (GE or GMO) seeds account for over 80 percent of the corn and cotton, and almost 90 percent of soybeans in the U.S. By contrast, most GE foods are banned throughout Europe, based on a variety of fears about long-term effects.

In Africa, a huge market where raising yields could stave off hunger and famine, GE foods are banned in almost all countries. The problem was dramatically illustrated in 2002 when Zambia's president refused to allow American food aid to be distributed to starving Zambians. European environmental groups had convinced him that genetically-engineered corn provided through the World Food Programme, the corn Americans eat every day, was poisonous.[29]

As Stewart Brand tells us, "I daresay the environmental movement has done more harm with its opposition to genetic engineering than with any other thing we've been wrong about."[30] To reduce American taxpayers' outlays for famine relief around the globe, we should push for acceptance of GE agricultural products within those countries.

A federal carbon tax would raise most other costs.

America may come to believe, as most other developed nations already do, that the more we burn carbon the more we warm the world and the more we store up future costs for ourselves. If so, our country may eventually accept some form of federal carbon tax as an artificial incentive to switch our energy sources away from carbon.

We've discussed how a carbon tax works and affects our fuel and electricity purchases in the chapters on energy and transportation. But, of course, those are not the only ways our family finances will be affected. Virtually all the other products and services we buy—groceries, clothing, lawn care, medical testing—are created using energy from fossil fuels and would feel the knock-on effect from the new federal tax. Until the don't-burn-carbon incentive has worked its magic and consumers and businesses have moved to new energy sources because they are cheaper, the tax will permeate the economy and subtly increase the cost of everything.

The earlier we pay a carbon tax, with all its knock-on costs throughout the economy, the less we will pay for the long-term economic effects of warming and its even greater knock-on costs over the coming decades. Thus, although this book is about how to dodge many of the financial penalties warming will bring, a carbon tax is not a penalty we should try to dodge. Rather, we should welcome the chance to pay it now, to avoid paying a whole lot more later.

GETTING THE MOST FROM YOUR FEDERAL TAXES

This is a short section. Few tactics fit this heading. We can't dodge federal taxes by moving within the United States. Even if we move to another country, as U.S. citizens we are still subject to federal income taxes.

But here are a few ideas.

Cut influences in Washington against climate-proofing.

If you are concerned about the effects of warming on your personal finances, cutting your federal taxes should not be your goal. There are many ways the federal government could spend your tax money to shelter you and your community from the personal expenses of warming. Some of these protections only Washington can provide, and only if they have the tax revenues to cover them. Your goal should probably be to make sure more and more of your federal tax payments, perhaps even new taxes, go toward programs to adequately protect you, your community, and the nation.

Think for a moment of the federal government as just another vendor, one who in return for our tax payments supplies many of the needs we can't buy elsewhere. If Washington doesn't implement—and ask you to pay more for—federal flood-control, drought-prevention, health-protection, and other programs to fight the effects of warming, your tax savings will be offset—or more than offset—by the impacts on your bank account described elsewhere in this book. As the country warms, we will have plenty of needs for new and increased federal services. We should make sure they are supplied efficiently and equitably, not blindly resist paying for them.

Of course, many rich campaign donors and big-company lobbyists show little interest in seeing the federal government help us dodge the long-term costs from warming. Big oil, utilities, and anti-tax groups are among the most influential, but plenty of other special interests argue against public transport, watershed protections, feed-in electricity credits, fisheries rehabilitation, R&D funding, and other federal actions to deal with warming.

Your voice, concerned and well-reasoned, can offset thousands of campaign dollars, but only if your legislator hears you. A phone call is most influential, followed by a handwritten letter, a custom email, a form email, and a petition signature, in that order. If you aren't pushing to have the politicians in Washington take more steps to protect your family from warming, you have little cause for complaint when they sit on their hands.

Prepare for a federal carbon tax.

If a carbon tax law is passed, not every family will be positioned to respond, dodging the resulting higher prices and embracing new lower-cost alternatives. It will pay to look ahead. Take your choice of a home, for instance. A carbon tax will raise the price of heating oil and natural gas, but not the cost of hydronic solar heating, solar-driven geothermal pumps, passive solar and other alternative ways to heat your home. If you are thinking of buying a house in the next few years, you could save big in the long run by choosing a house suitable for conversion to these technologies, not locked out of them by its orientation (solar) or lot size (geothermal).

If big RV's and jet planes, with no fuel substitute, are destined to become more expensive thanks to market forces or a carbon tax, or both, you may want to alter your family vacation habits and expectations. A cabin in the woods instead of a distant resort, sailing instead of sport fishing, hiking instead of traveling by RV could all be part of a no-regrets lifestyle plan.

Things don't seem bad today. The weight of U.S. business and political interests against dealing with warming makes it likely that any carbon tax introduced will be tame at the outset. However, if the country begins to panic about the effects of warming, taxation of fossil fuels could accelerate. Even if the federal government is paralyzed over a carbon tax, some states have already taken the initiative. Wherever the tax comes from, it will pay you not to be committed to a fuel-guzzling lifestyle.

WHERE TO LIVE FOR LOW FEDERAL INCOME TAX

Federal tax rates are the same for everyone, right? So how could your federal taxes be lower if you lived somewhere else?

Consider this example. You and your recent classmate are both nurses. You have roughly the same experience, the same duties. You make $94,000. He makes $61,000. Is that unfair?

Not in the direction you may think. Your classmate works at Mercy Medical Center in Des Moines. You are at Santa Clara Valley Medical Center in San Jose. Your rent is $1,538/mo; his is $586 for a similar apartment and neighborhood. Yes, you earn 54 percent more than he does, but you pay nearly three times as much for housing.

Your monthly energy costs are $280; his are $145. An electrician's visit costs $218 in San Jose; $65 in Des Moines. You get the idea. When everything is counted up, you would need to earn $105,000, not $94,000, to afford the same life your classmate in Des Moines can have for $61,000. He's better off than you.

And here's the kicker: because your earnings are higher and push you into a higher tax bracket, you make payments to the IRS of $17,099 while he sends in $8,849. For the same lifestyle! Most U.S. taxpayers don't understand that where they live affects how much they pay. But now you do, and you can take this into account along with the many other where-to-live factors discussed in this book.

Yourtown, USA

If you want to check the costs of living in a particular area, a good place to start is at bit.ly/moving_costs. These figures are averages for big U.S. metro areas, and costs vary widely within each area.

Wage data by area and occupation are available at bls.gov/bls/blswage.htm.

Moving because you want lower costs is a big step, and you may have to give up something else you value. But moving could be your single most important no-regrets tactic to take pressure off your family budget in the face of new costs from warming.

Footnotes for this chapter, Where-To-Live Indicators for all American towns, and other tools and resources are available at savvyfamilies.org/climateproof, as well as the author's updates, your comments, and other useful information.

PART II

PROSPER AS YOUR SURROUNDINGS WARM

8 KEEP HOME COSTS DOWN, YOUR HOME'S VALUE UP

Sea-level rise will wash the value out of many homes around the edges of America. When the federal government released updated flood maps for the New York City region in 2013, residents were shocked to find that the flood zone had expanded to include double the number of houses and businesses since the maps were produced less than twenty years ago.[1]

A 90-year-old house on Brownell Street in New Haven has never been flooded, but recently the owner's flood insurance bill jumped 30 percent, reflecting the threat from a changing climate. FEMA's new flood maps show potential flooding based not only on local history but also on what happened elsewhere during recent big storms. Parts of New Haven that have never been flooded are suddenly considered to be in the new Sandy- and Irene-inspired floodplain.[2]

HOW HOUSING COSTS WILL RISE AND HOME VALUES WILL FALL

Housing costs already take the single biggest slice of the typical American's budget, at over 30 percent; and the growth of home costs is faster than our total outlays.[3] The effects of warming are driving these growing costs. Here are some that are pushing directly into our homes.

Subsidence and wildfires may be dramatic.

Land subsidence is a growing danger. A 60-foot sinkhole opened in Seffner, Florida under the bedroom of a Florida man, and he fell through the floor to his death. In Dunedin, Florida, a larger sinkhole swallowed a swimming pool and boat and collapsed two houses.[4]

Dramatic scenes like these, although rare, remind us that pumping out groundwater leaves space underground.[5] Fortunately, the collapse of aquifer areas will be mostly gradual. Thanks to the drought produced by warming, pumping from aquifers is so intense in California that parts of the Central Valley are sinking about a foot a year.[6] There have been no collapses, but growing cracks in homes, driveways, and underground pipes are costly.

Wildfires have been a threat to relatively few homes, but that is changing. Before 1995, America saw an average of less than one megafire per year (larger than 100,000 acres). Between 2005 and 2014, with higher temperatures and lower rainfall caused by warming, the average increased to almost ten a year.[7] In late 2015, a California fire destroyed 400 homes. Thousands fled the area.

But wind and flood damage are the big threats.

While dramatic subsidence and forest fires affect relatively few of us, storms find far more victims. Well below the hurricane level by the time it reached Long Island, Sandy still destroyed or severely damaged around 100,000 homes and left over 2,000 uninhabitable. Much of this damage was not covered by insurance.[8]

Combining storm surge with sea-level rise makes everything more dangerous. A 27 percent increase in wave height doubles the force.[9] If the sea level in San Francisco Bay rises by just 6 inches, the fairly common storm that residents anticipate once in ten years would produce as much damage to the same shoreline as a far more serious hundred-year storm today.[10]

A hurricane doesn't care whether you own or rent. Depending on how exposed your house or apartment is, wind and storm surge can pose physical dangers to your family members and possessions. And if a storm or flood damages your rented home, it's not just the landlord's problem. Your lease may legally trap you in a damp, moldy, damaged home, and you may find yourself fixing or coping with problems the landlord is slow to deal with.

Today about 6.6 million homes along the Atlantic and Gulf Coasts, plus many more on other coasts and riverbanks, are at risk of storm surge.[11] Those growing risks from sea-level rise and greater storm intensity operate even when no physical damage occurs, because the mere threat of storms can erode house values for millions of Americans.

Even without storms or sea-level rise, flooding will become more common. Warmer air holds more moisture than cool air; so warming brings more rain in a rainstorm, more snow in a snowstorm. Between 1958 and 2012, the amount of precipitation falling in very heavy events (the heaviest 1 percent) has increased hardly at all in the Southwest, 12 percent in the Northwest, 16 percent in the Great Plains states, 27 percent in the South, 37 percent in the Midwest, and 71 percent in the Northeast.[12]

High insurance rates devalue property.

Homeowners insurance companies are beginning to tell us in no uncertain terms how the effects of climate shifts have been pushing up claims. In June 2014 Illinois Farmers Insurance filed nine class-action lawsuits against cities and counties around Chicago, claiming that officials were aware that climate change is causing heavier rainfalls but failed to prevent costly sewage backups in more than 600 homes.[13]

Thanks in part to the various effects of warming, from 2001 to 2006 the premiums for homeowners' insurance in nine states jumped between 42 percent (Alabama) and 77 percent (Florida). Premiums jumped 500 percent in Miami. In many Gulf Coast states, Allstate says climate change has prompted it to cancel or not renew policies.[14] Rising claims from severe weather are a prime reason for recent premium increases.[15]

After huge snow and ice storms buried Boston in early 2015, the property insurance industry asked for a 9 percent increase, a much bigger annual jump than usual.[16] The Massachusetts Division of Insurance said okay.

As rates rise, house affordability goes down. Mortgage banks look at a buyer's ability to pay principal, interest, property taxes and insurance. For existing owners, the subsidy of flood insurance premiums will go away slowly; but new owners must pay the full premium from Day 1—a likely increase of several thousand dollars a year. This higher cost will make it that much harder for buyers to get a mortgage, pressuring sellers to lower the price of their properties.

Rising domestic water costs

Relatively few of us will actually see water flooding into our living rooms. But most of us will see a higher price for water coming in through our water mains or wells.

Water rates are rising fast.

The water table under Cape May, New Jersey has dropped about 100 feet. Seawater seeping into the aquifer has made many wells supplying the area unusable, and a desalinization plant was built in 1997. It cost $5 million to build and is expensive to run.[17] Salt-water intrusion problems confront coastal aquifers under South Carolina, Georgia, northern Florida, Louisiana, the Napa-Sonoma Valley in California and other coastal areas.[18] The cause in most areas is depletion of the coastal aquifer, reducing its pressure and ability to resist the intrusion of seawater. For many coastal aquifers, rising sea level alone is predicted to increase that intrusive pressure, whether or not the aquifer is being depleted.

Many water authorities are totally unprepared for the additional costs from warming, which will find their way inevitably into our water rates. Authorities already have to raise the prices for water for other reasons, before they even begin to deal with drought, sea-level rise, or a falling water table. *USA Today* surveyed 100 cities in 2012. Over the previous 12 years, charges for delivering and disposing of water in 29 of those cities had doubled or more. Atlanta's charges were up 233 percent, San Francisco's 211 percent, Wilmington's 200 percent, and New York's 151 percent.[19]

The Great Lakes contain one-fifth of the world's fresh surface water, but many nearby residents struggle to afford it. In January 2014, the Detroit-area human services agency Wayne Metro received 10,000 calls from residents asking for help paying their water bills. Less than 10 percent received aid before the agency's funding ran out. The average water bill in the city is $75 per month for a family of four, nearly twice the U.S. average. Rates are rising rapidly. The water department, caught between falling sales and its high fixed costs, shut off water to more than 90,000 customers, hoping that would force them to pay their bills.[20]

Today's water rate increases go almost entirely to maintain the *current* aging and neglected systems. Factors caused by warming, such as less precipitation on watersheds, relocation of pipes required by rising sea levels, growing pollution, or dropping aquifers caused by overuse, are not yet considered. The costs to upgrade, expand or move water delivery infrastructure to cope with drought and other effects of a shifting climate are also not yet finding their way into water rates. When the water authorities get around to confronting these effects, rates are bound to jump further.

Some water authorities are considering another justification for raising rates aggressively: to provide an incentive for residents to reduce water use. But it's hard to find a win-win. Where residents have been persuaded to use less water, their good intentions have caused problems for the water utilities. In Austin, Texas the utility is losing millions in revenues as customers install low-flow toilets, showerheads and washing machines, drip-irrigation for their flowerbeds, and other water-saving devices. The better its customers become at conserving water, the more the utility is squeezed between falling revenues and fixed costs. A water rate hike of over 10 percent was approved in mid-2014. The city also considered an additional "drought fee," a surcharge that kicks in during periods when water restrictions are in effect—a double whammy for customers.[21]

The free-market price of water is skyrocketing.

Underground water, like underground oil and gas, can be privately owned. Even the rain belongs to those who own a lake or watershed. The laws affecting water rights, even private wells, are complex and vary by location. With so many factors pushing the price of water up, investors have been moving quickly to buy up water sources not already owned by the public and sell their contents at the highest price they can get.[22]

In a private water auction, Santa Barbara, which needs additional water for the domestic use of residents, lost the bidding to farmers, who can recoup their higher water costs by increasing food prices.[23]

We will discuss the private water business in Chapter 9 on investments.

Well-water is becoming more expensive.

More than 15 million homeowners get their water from a well on their property or nearby. Where groundwater levels are dropping, the costs of drilling deeper and filtering increased pollution are adding to their cost of water.[24]

SAFEGUARDING YOUR HOME AND ITS VALUE

Let's start with flood dangers. If you choose to live in or near a flood-prone area, here are ways to climate-proof your home.

Buy flood insurance.

When flash floods on the Texas' Blanco River killed 17 people and destroyed hundreds of houses in 2015, many owners did not have flood insurance. This risky choice is widespread. The number of policies has actually declined in some states in recent years.[25]

If you live in a floodplain and have a mortgage, you are required to have flood insurance. But if your property is just outside today's floodplain you would do well to buy the insurance anyway, since we're learning that many homes outside official floodplains are endangered by this century's storms. And even if below-market flood insurance premiums are painful for federal taxpayers or municipal governments, they are a bargain for you, the homeowner, thanks to that continuing government subsidy.

Note to renters: Flood insurance is not just for building owners. If you rent where there is moderate to low risk from flooding, you can buy a tenant's version of FEMA flood insurance to protect your possessions at a lower premium than your landlord pays to cover the building.[26]

Improve your drainage.

The FEMA Flood Maps, detailed as they are, can't be accurate predictors of damage home-by-home. In particular, good or bad drainage is not taken into account. In a storm one family may be up to their ankles on their lawn, another up to their knees in the basement, while a third neighbor's property drains perfectly. Their costs from stormwater flooding can range from simply sweeping debris off the driveway to major restoration of walls and furniture. If you are purchasing a home, you can sidestep these costs by making sure the home has good drainage and an always-dry basement. A home inspector can usually tell you.

Armor your shoreline.

For decades, shorefront property owners, private or municipal, have been building seawalls, bulkheads, riprap, groynes, and other fixed structures to keep the sea from eroding their land or damaging their buildings.

Sometimes these are joint projects with multiple neighbors joining in. By and large they don't work, at least not for any length of time. Hydrology is complex and every property is different, but most of these physical defenses wind up delaying the damage for less time than anticipated, scrubbing away the beach in front of them, and deflecting the damage elsewhere to unanticipated places.[27]

That doesn't mean you can't protect your shoreline in other ways. Flexible, non-fixed features, such as renewed wetlands, envelopes of sand, helical anchoring, drift fences, tubes filled with sand, marine mattresses, artificial reefs, or coir logs can be more effective than boulders and reinforced concrete.

Rhode Island isn't called ""The Ocean State for nothing. With a long coastline fringing the country's smallest state, Rhode Island is ahead of most others in planning for the effects of sea-level rise. The state has created an elaborate Special Area Management Plan for shoreline change and has been educating home and business owners about sea-level rise. The *Rhode Island Coastal Property Guide*, available online, covers many of the topics above. No matter what portion of America's seashore you live on, this guide is a good compendium of ideas for safeguarding your property.[28]

To help home or business owners learn their risks and available defenses, a Rhode Island legislative commission has recommended offering flood audits, similar to the energy audits available to the public for many years. A consultant would visit the property or business, perform a flood risk assessment, and provide the owner with an evaluation of flood risk and preparedness, along with a list of appropriate resiliency measures available. As with energy inspections, the property owner could be eligible for financing to help implement the recommendations.[29]

Independent engineering advice is a fast-growing industry serving endangered waterfront property owners who want to protect the biggest piece of their net worth. The owners of a home sitting 25 yards from a coastal bluff in Little Compton, Rhode Island were watching a 15 to 20-foot cliff being eroded back about six inches a year. They asked a specialist firm, Natural Resource Services, for a Climate Change Checkup. From the many armoring methods available, the engineers recommended re-grading the slope and installing logs made of coconut fiber. This will allow deep-rooted shrubs to reestablish on the bank, making the bluff slower to weather from storms and sea-level rise.[30]

Raise your house.

Many new homes in flood-prone areas are built with the living quarters raised, leaving an open area under the house. For existing homes, there are several ways to lift the living quarters above flood level. Houses can be detached from their foundations, raised with hydraulic jacks, and held there while piers, columns, pilings, or whole new foundations are inserted underneath. The new lower level can be made of columns with breakaway walls between them.[31]

There are cheaper methods of flood-proofing, including creating holes into the existing basement or crawlspace under your house, allowing floodwaters to enter. This equalizes the water pressure on your walls and foundation and makes it less likely that the house will be pushed or floated off its foundations. Alternatively, an additional story can be built and all living quarters moved up one floor, leaving the original ground floor to accept floodwaters when necessary.

Other methods are described in detailed text and illustrations in FEMA's *Homeowners' Guide to Retrofitting: Six Ways to Protect Your House from Flooding.*[32]

Float your home.

A different approach to surviving repetitive inland flooding without much damage is to own a home that rises with a flood. Houses have been created that sit on riverbanks but are designed to float when raised by the river in flood stage.[33] Large blocks of foam flotation are placed under the home, secured to multiple tall guideposts to keep the home in place as it rises with the flood. When the water recedes, the house settles back onto the ground, right where it was before.

The concept has been put into practice in Canada and the Netherlands and is being considered in prototype for some homes being rebuilt around New Orleans after Hurricane Katrina.[34] It's hard to see this as a widespread solution, but it might work for some households in some locations.

Another approach is to live in a permanently floating home that allows you to live on the waterfront but be safe from very high tides. Although many residents of Sausalito, across the Golden Gate Bridge from San Francisco, live on the steep hills, the downtown and shorefront industrial areas were built on marshland and will flood as the sea rises. Nevertheless, a 65-year-old community of over 400 custom houseboats is expected to be safe. It may be necessary to raise the docks and adjust the anchoring, but the city thinks that even a ten-foot rise in San Francisco Bay would allow the houseboats to remain as they are.[35]

Similar communities exist in Seattle,[36] Portland,[37] on the Great Lakes and on other sheltered bodies of water, with new floating communities being developed.[38] If you are becoming leery of waterfront homes, check out watertop homes with an online search for images of *community floating homes*.

Install a waterproof fence.

With record spring floods threatening to overflow the Iowa River, the University of Iowa in Des Moines installed "invisible flood walls" to protect a dormitory and several arts buildings. From a company called Flood Control America operating nationwide, the walls consist of a permanent concrete foundation at ground level that accepts steel posts slotted to hold removable aluminum planks. The posts and planks can be stored until floods threaten, then quickly erected. When the water recedes, planks and posts are removed for storage; nothing visible remains above ground to mar the view or hinder traffic.[39]

The wall base can hold out several feet of water. Rubber gaskets keep leakage to a minimum. Other installations surround the Verizon Building in downtown New York City and run for thousands of feet along the riverbank in Coralville, Iowa.[40]

Move your house.

Across the country, nearly 5 million people live in 2.6 million homes that are less than 4 feet above high tide. Many more live in an inland floodplain. Some have actually picked up their homes and moved them to higher ground. Yes, the chance is remote that you have such a home, that it can be picked up, and that there's a nearby lot out of flood danger. However, if you need to move from a threatened location, want to stay nearby, and can't bear to leave the house you love, jacking up a home and moving it a few blocks uphill may be a possibility. Indeed, for some owners, it may be the only alternative to losing a threatened and unsaleable house.

Find out if you can rebuild.

Finally, check to see if your home could be insured again after being flooded. For most of its history, the NFIP has paid flood claims over and over again for the same property. Owners take the money, repair their places, wait for the next flood, and then claim again. These claims account for only 1 percent of policies but over 33 percent of the dollar claims.[41] NFIP is now changing its rules about "repetitive losses," making it harder to renew insurance or rebuild or both.

FEMA and some state agencies enforce special building codes for repairing substantial flood damage. In some cases, rebuilding is too expensive to be worthwhile or is prohibited altogether regardless of flood insurance availability. Check the regulations in your area.

Learn to need less domestic water.

When you consider that the average American uses 80-100 gallons of water per day at home, it would seem there's room for cutbacks without much deprivation. Remember those days you spent in a campground, cabin or boat when you used only a few gallons a day and didn't feel deprived?

There are plenty of books, government pamphlets, and home products to help you use less water, from low-flow showerheads to drip irrigation in the garden to new household habits.

Meadow grass or wildflower covers may be the biggest bang for the buck. They require much less watering, only occasional mowing, and no fertilizing. These grasses, along with wildflower mixes, can make your yard look more interesting than a run-of-the-mill lawn. The right choice is very location-dependent, so check with a local garden-supply company or landscaping firm.

Xeriscaping is the name for a more complex approach to beautifying your yard and saving water at the same time. It involves adding drought-resistant shrubs and plants, rocks and tiles, and other elements that need little water and even less maintenance. Although the kids can't play soccer on it, the result can be more visually interesting than a lawn, with less upkeep expense.

Water rates may not seem like a big part of operating your home, but they are likely to grow faster than most other expenditures. Learning now to live with less water will make adjustment easier when there is a shortage. Making changes voluntarily now, for instance replacing your turf lawn with dry landscaping, is easier than having to do so in a water emergency.

Collect, store and reuse water.

In addition to reducing your use of water, you may be able to augment your supply. Whether you catch rainwater from your roof or fill tanks with tap water from your water utility, water storage can help you get through restrictions during dry times. There are several methods.

1. **Downspout barrels** can supply your garden hose during dry patches. A few 50-gallon plastic barrels in the basement can be filled from a tap or roof downspout. When it's dry, they can be pumped into the pressure water system of your house or used through a separate tap.

2. **Stored tap water** may be safe for all uses, but water from the roof or other sources needs to be filtered or confined to toilets, lawn, garden, and other uses that don't involve human consumption.

3. **Stored shower and bath water** can be used on the lawn if you use benign soaps and shampoos.

4. **A water garden or simple swales** hold water in the soil and prevent runoff, reducing your sprinkler needs.

Destruction of value caused by warming

In addition to the rising out-of-pocket costs to protect against flooding, buy water, drill a new well or plant a drought-resistant lawn, the price of your home may be declining because these needs are becoming obvious to potential buyers.

Even if hardy residents in a town like Santa Cruz can grin and bear the water cutbacks, their town will become less competitive against other towns not so badly affected by drought. Diners, patients, and golfers will find more accommodating places to go. Potential homebuyers will think twice. Business investors will see the costs and risks. All these contributors to the local economy will begin to spend their money elsewhere.

The National Association of Realtors acknowledges sea-level rise, also water scarcity and other warming effects, and their downward pull on home prices.[42] Not all real estate brokers, however, are willing to discuss these downward pressures on the value of their listings, or the long-term price risks they bring to certain communities. Awareness could grow suddenly when the next storm or drought comes along, or when the popular media notice that waterfront property prices are declining and make it a hot topic.

Declining neighborhood values can raise your taxes.

Homeowners in the same town who are safe from flooding, face a different danger. We've talked about the effects of warming on state and local taxes in Chapter 6, but this is probably a good place to point out the dangerous relationship among warming, home prices, and property taxes. Here's an example based on ocean or river flooding; the same principles apply to towns where home values are dragged down by drought or other threats from climate shifts.

Say a family decides to sell their million-dollar waterfront home. They quickly find that the value of their exposed property has dropped. There's been no actual damage, but news about storms elsewhere has hurt the attraction of water frontage in the area.

After nine months on the market and several price drops, this home begins to get nibbles at $650,000. Fed up with their high property taxes, they walk into City Hall and ask for a reassessment. There are quite a few similar appeals that year, so the assessor does a city-wide reassessment. Their property is revalued at $700,000. All the homes in the high-priced district by the water (a fifth of the town's total valuation) get about a 30 percent reduction. Assessments elsewhere in the city are unchanged.

So what happens when 20 percent of a town's assessed valuation is cut by 30 percent? Obviously, the town knocks millions of dollars from its tax base. But the costs of schools, police and other town services don't change. The assessor must still spread the town's budget over the town's total assessed value. To make up for the drop in value of those waterfront properties, everyone else's property taxes have to go up by 6.4 percent to raise the same money as last year. That's on top of normal budget and tax increases planned for the year, including any new costs to fight the effects of warming. And because *total* taxes didn't rise, individual homeowners whose property tax did jump are not protected by property tax-cap laws.

How likely is this? In Satellite Beach, Florida, which is typical of many communities on barrier islands in Florida, Georgia, and the Carolinas, roughly 30 percent of the city's property-tax base has been built along the sandy beach, within 300 feet of the Atlantic waves.[43] In Norfolk, Virgina more than 17,000 properties, amounting to 34 percent of the tax base, are in the high-risk floodplain.[44] Not only oceanfront areas are threatened. In Cape Vincent, New York, at the entrance to the St. Lawrence River from Lake Erie, lakefront landowners make up 75 percent of the town's tax base.[45]

And increased taxes are just the beginning. When a family on a "safe" property hit by those tax increases tries to sell their house, those higher taxes could deter buyers, thus lowering its price. The same is true for a town's commercial properties.

Of course, this process may play out slowly, almost invisibly. And towns with an eroding tax base may choose not to jack up the tax rate, cutting public services instead. But it seems inevitable that, if warming damages even a relatively few expensive homes over the coming years, that will affect not only home values in vulnerable neighborhoods but also asset values throughout the community.

Yourtown, USA

Do you know a real estate agent personally? You might ask if she or he sees any signs of reduced demand in neighborhoods with some sort of water or drought risk—flooding, dropping well water, oceanfront. Although most agents don't acknowledge this trend yet, I have talked to several who admit it's already happening.

Mortgage payments are likely to rise.

The standard length of a home loan has been 30 years. A 30-year term means the lender believes the collateral will retain its value that long. As real estate markets wake up to the various threats detailed in this book, mortgage lenders may stop taking this for granted.[46]

To reduce their risks, lenders could begin to insist on 15-year mortgages, meaning homeowners will need to sign up for higher monthly payments. (This has nothing to do with interest rates but with repaying the principal over fewer years.) True, many financial experts actually recommend we choose the shortest mortgage we can afford since that will dramatically cut the total interest we'll pay over the life of the loan. But a 15-year requirement hurts buyers, since the higher principal payment each month will reduce the amount they qualify to borrow from a mortgage lender, based on an affordability formula. So they wind up with less house than with a 30-year mortgage. And whatever hurts the buyer hurts the seller. Higher principal payments, just like higher insurance rates, mean more people who like your house find they can't afford it.

Understanding your home's investment value

As expenses grow, thanks to warming, you may want to reconsider whether you really want to own your own home. There are certainly advantages—the home-as-castle satisfaction, the enforced savings inherent in mortgage payments, and the freedom from rent increases. But the popular idea that renting is throwing money down the drain is simply not true. There are strong but little-known reasons why renting may be a better financial strategy than owning.

Most homes are very low-return investments.

First, most of us think of buying a home as a financial investment, but it's usually one of the worst we can make. When you factor in mortgage interest, insurance, property taxes, maintenance and your opportunity to invest the down-payment elsewhere, buying a home usually has a lower financial return than renting one.

Robert Shiller, the Nobel Prize-winning economist specializing in housing, has calculated the average appreciation of U.S. homes from 1890 to 1990. Turns out it was almost exactly the rate of inflation. That means no real increase in value at all. We know there are home price booms here and there, so if the average U.S. home gained nothing over that period, a whole lot of homes in other places must have lost value.

"So, why is [home ownership] considered an investment?" Shiller asks. "That was a fad. That was an idea that took hold in the early 2000's. And I don't expect it to come back. Not with the same force. So people might just decide, 'Yeah, I'll diversify my portfolio. I'll live in a rental.' That is a very sensible thing for many people to do."[47]

Many of us have learned this lesson during the past decade. In 2003, the wealth of the median U.S. household was at $87,992. Ten years later, in 2013, it was down to $56,335.[48] Much of this huge drop was caused by the fall in home values in 2008 and the following years. When you add this drop to the decline in middle-class incomes over those ten years, it's no wonder the American middle class is no longer the most affluent in the world.[49]

Considering the downward pressures on the value of many homes from warming, it may make sense to sell and move into a rental. You will transfer to a landlord such potential problems as physical damage, declining property values, rising flood insurance premiums, and higher property taxes.

Of course, renting has risks too.
Rents across the country have been rising and are projected to continue upward. They increased 6 percent over the twelve years from 2000 to 2012. In a town whose advantages are growing, home prices and rents will also rise, with rents quickly spiking. In such a community, it may be financially better to buy than rent, if you're sure you want to be around for a while.

A second disadvantage of renting: an owned home is a piggy bank into which you put principal payments each month. The act of selling and moving to a rental breaks the piggy bank. If you're not disciplined, that cash can run through your fingers pretty fast. If renting is to have advantages, you need an impulse-proof plan for saving and investing the difference. (Of course, investing need not be in the stock market; more education or a career switch can have high returns too.)

If you are wedded to the idea that property ownership is a good investment, remember that you don't need to invest where you live. You could sell your house in a threatened town, stay there in a rental, and put the proceeds into a building plot or income property in a community that's likely to attract climate migrants over the coming years. You're still a property owner, but you've chosen a more promising location for your investment.

WHERE TO LIVE TO PROTECT YOUR PROPERTY VALUE

Is it worth a move for more reliable water?

When you look ahead at increasing costs for tap water, restrictions on watering a lawn or vegetable garden, plus the state and municipal taxes needed to deal with these highly local problems, the no-regrets approach may be to find a hometown where water supplies are predicted to remain reliable.

Yes, you might succeed in using a lot less water around your current house, but if a decline is setting in all around your particular town, frugal water habits won't protect you from that economic slide. Rising costs and loss of value in a town may come slowly, but they could come suddenly. The loss of a big employer or a sudden awakening in the real estate market might be all it takes to start a rapid drop in your town's wealth. Any long-term investment—a career, business or home—in one of these towns could become a disappointment.

To dodge these long-term threats, what areas of the country should you consider? It's easy to get an overall evaluation of the water situation in your town.

Yourtown, USA

To find out if a town has a drought problem ahead of it, you can look up the NRDC Water Supply Sustainability rating mentioned in Chapter 2 on food. It's at bit.ly/NRDC_water_sustainability_report and covers most counties in the U.S.

Color-coded maps showing counties in each state are provided, so you need to know the county for each town whose rating you want to see. Here are a few unexpected findings.

Columbus, OH (Franklin County)	Extreme Risk
Globe, AZ (Gila County)	Moderate Risk
Bridgeport, CA (Mono County)	Low risk
Osceola, AR (Mississippi County)	Extreme Risk

If you don't want to deal with counties, you can find drought ratings on the scorecards for most American towns and Zip Codes among the Indicator Scorecards at SavvyFamilies.org/Where-To-Live-Indicators.

Over the coming months and years, you will see plenty of magazine articles titled something like "The Ten Worst Cities for Drought." Some of these will be based on drought predictions that consider global warming; most will not.[50]

As with health, transportation and other problems confronting your community, you may be able to get a look at what's being planned to deal with drought, flooding and other threats to your home from warming. Your town or county probably has one or more plans. Start by looking through the town's website. You can also use the search string *site:anytown.gov drought OR water OR flooding* to let your search engine find relevant pages on a town's website.

Then check in person at Town Hall for studies or plans that may be in draft but aren't up on the town's website. Don't waste your time on reports or plans older than five years; a lot has changed in both the urgency of the problem and the variety of solutions. And don't spend an evening trying to get through one of those professional-planner documents (full of phrases like "strategic framework," "template," "planning process," and "program capabilities"). Look for documents that clearly identify hazards and vulnerabilities, and the specific actions, policies, and budget needed to counter them. Look for words like "timetable," "funding sources," "household," "2020," and "2050."

And remember to differentiate between plans for weathering "seasonal" drought and those for coping with long-term intensifying drought caused by warming. Some towns react intelligently to the one but ignore the other.

Ask whether the town has a Watershed, Groundwater, Waterfront, Beach or Flooding Committee that includes knowledgeable citizens. If you find there is a Citizens' Group, learn if it's representing only a few special interests. But don't reject them for this; reports written or commissioned by the Chamber of Commerce or similar groups will often predict the impact of the town's coming problems more vividly—perhaps more accurately—than official studies.

Is it worth moving to avoid flooding?
We've discussed plenty of reasons why you may want your home to be somewhere else. Potential flooding is another. Today, 9.6 million homes in the U.S. are located within designated FEMA flood zones. That number is increasing each month, as FEMA remaps affected areas.[51]

There are two places where you can see how your town and your property rate for different kinds of flood risk.

Yourtown, USA – ocean flooding

Climate Central has created a tool that lets you look up, by Zip Code, town, county, and state, what infrastructure in your area is vulnerable to coastal flooding and sea-level rise. It operates from a database of airports, roads, schools, hospitals, wastewater treatment plants, and 100 other elements of your local infrastructure, with the elevation of each.

The same organization publishes an interactive map that lets you see which areas of America's coastline (down to the street level) will be submerged by rising sea levels (from 1 to 10 feet).[52] Think of it as a flood map for a future date. It's at sealevel.climatecentral.org. Another source is NOAA at coast.noaa.gov/digitalcoast/tools/slr. Some states have more detailed maps and other tools, such as Rhode Island's beachsamp.org/resources.

There are many similar maps made by state and local officials. You can find them with an image search, such as *Yourtown sea-level rise map*, or by contacting your planning board.

Yourtown, USA – property-by-property flood risk

FEMA's floodplain maps are used by banks, zoning boards, insurance companies and others to determine if a particular home is likely to be flooded. These are available at msc.fema.gov/portal and can also be found on many municipalities' websites. You can zoom to individual properties.

In light of recent storms and flooding, the floodplain is being remapped. Consult floodsmart.gov to see if your area is soon to be remapped.[53]

Yourtown, USA – flood risk by town and county

When you look over a flood map, be sure to assess the danger to the whole town, not just one property. As discussed above, even if river or ocean water never comes within a mile of your house, you will suffer along with the town residents who are flooded. Nearby devastation can be a big downer, both to your spirits and to the local economy, and flooding can do a number on your municipality's budget. Think emergency services, clean-up, the protection and repair of public property, and the possibility of property tax reapportionment, raising your share of town property taxes discussed above.

Another way to gauge the risk from flooding is to see the flood insurance claims from a particular town over recent years. The dollar amount of payments from FEMA to residents is available at bsa.nfipstat.fema.gov/reports/1040.htm. Click on the state name to see losses by county and town.

You can get an even better idea of risk by comparing the dollar premium for insurance against the dollar amount of insurance in force. The higher the premium for a given amount of insurance, the riskier FEMA thinks the area is. You can look at these figures at bsa.nfipstat.fema.gov/reports/1011.htm.

Moving to greater physical and financial safety is an option you should at least consider. If your town is subject to flooding, municipal water cost rises, damage to the fresh water supply, threats to the historic neighborhoods you love, or health hazards from overflows, a move could pay off big-time for your personal finances in coming years.

Footnotes for this chapter, Where-To-Live Indicators for all American towns, and other tools and resources are available at savvyfamilies.org/climateproof, as well as the author's updates, your comments, and other useful information.

9 CHOOSE FINANCIAL INVESTMENTS PRUDENTLY

Not all of us have financial assets or investment income. Only 55 percent of Americans today own stocks, a lower percentage than before 2008.[1] As we saw in Chapter 1, many are living from paycheck to paycheck and can't find cash for emergencies, let alone savings. With expenses going up and middle-class incomes flat so far this century, it may be increasingly difficult for American families who don't already have some savings to start creating them.

But it's worth the effort. Stock prices have more than doubled from 2009 to 2016, while paychecks have scarcely risen at all. Being an investor beat being a worker by a wide margin. If we can manage to save enough to gain even a small stake in the investment markets, that could help our personal finances over the long term by supplementing our slower-growing job income.

We will discuss other advantages of saving in Chapter 12 on attitudes. But first let's examine some of the investments we might want to own in the future, with the strict understanding that predicting which industries and stocks are going to do well is generally a fool's errand. After all, eighty percent of professional mutual fund managers can't pick investments that beat the average stock market return. And even if you pick a growing, healthy company or industry, it may already be overbought by other investors.

That said, let's look at some future developments being touted today.

HOW WARMING WILL AFFECT ASSETS

Any portfolio of decent investments can make you more resilient in the face of financial pressures. Here, however, we will discuss those whose prospects may be directly affected by warming.

Investments with recognized upsides

If warming across America is going to add heavy costs to the economy, the not-very-exciting economic growth we see today could easily decline. Consumers will have less to spend, and many companies will struggle against anemic demand. For the moment, however, let's assume that the government and the private sector decide to fight the damage from warming with initiatives such as construction, repowering, vertical farming, health services, and many others. The result could actually be an employment and technology boom in certain sectors and localities. Which industries are likely to reinvent themselves as they face a slow death from warming? Which industries will curl up and die?

As of mid-2016 here are a few sectors that seem like beneficiaries as our climate shifts. Note that the title of this section refers to 'recognized upsides.' That means they may already be overbought. No doubt by the time you read this there will be a slew of new ideas being discussed. If you are an investor, vigilance and perception will be really important as changes from warming accelerate.

Water rights

The rush has been on to buy water for a while now. Taking advantage of the complex laws and agreements governing who gets to use what water across America, many private companies are buying up land for its water, or simply buying water rights separate from the land.

Many water utilities are already owned by for-profit investors. Aqua America, a publicly traded firm, is the largest U.S.-based water and wastewater utility holding company. In the twenty years up to 2003, the company bought 300 local water operations. It now serves more than 2.5 million residents in 13 states from Illinois to Texas to Florida to Maine.

You can buy mutual funds, ETF's and hedge funds that invest in water companies. Search online for *"water rights" investments* (with the quotation marks).[2] You should be aware that the privatization of water is creating conflicts with those who believe that access to fresh water is a basic human right.[3] As water problems become more severe, public acceptance of free-market water firms may wane as communities rebel against paying profit-making companies for one of nature's most basic commodities.

Desalination and purification

Real improvements to water purification technology will be hugely valuable. Investments are available both in operating companies removing salt from water which is then sold to local authorities and in technology companies that are creating new ways for doing this.

The market is growing. The South Florida region operates 35 desalination plants, and seven more are being built. But there are risks. If the costs to build and operate a huge Carlsbad, California project turn out as projected, it may validate the desalinization industry and create similar investment attractions. At the moment, however, Carlsbad is planning to raise most of its funds through bond issues, and these have been rated just above junk status because of the perceived financial risks.[4]

There's a need for desalination not just near the oceans but inland where groundwater is brackish. Because today's techniques require such large amounts of energy to push water through the membrane filters, a technical breakthrough could be a financial gold mine. But even if desalinization becomes cheaper, there's the question of where to put the salt. It's lethal to most plants and animals. Coastal units can pump the brine way out to sea, but inland units need to put it underground, another big cost.

The reuse of wastewater, whether in the home or throughout a town, is certain to grow. That means new systems that make this cheap and safe will be in demand. The same will be true for technologies that remotely detect and plug leaks in water or gas mains.

Water transport

Around the world there are huge stores of fresh water just there for the taking. Businesses have been formed to use supertankers to transport water from Alaska and Iceland where it's just draining into the sea to dry places, such as California and Israel. The costs are high, and no company has started to do this commercially.[5] So far desalination is cheaper, but as demand for water rises, there are firms positioning themselves to carry water long distances.

Other water-related businesses

There are plenty of mutual funds and ETFs that invest in private water utilities that treat and pipe water; technology companies working on purification or disinfection methods; firms collecting, treating, and disposing of industrial liquid wastes; and water-related consulting and engineering services.

The water industry is large enough that S&P Dow Jones created a Global Water Index. It contains 50 stocks of firms building water infrastructure and creating water equipment & materials. Another index, the NASDAQ OMX Global Water Index, concentrates on technology companies creating products that purify water and reduce its use in homes, businesses, and industries or developing water-efficiency techniques for agriculture. There are index funds geared to these indices.

Water funds and the S&P's water index haven't performed quite as well as the broader S&P Index over the past five years, but that could change as water prices rise and affect profits in agriculture and industry. If you're interested, search for *water investments* or talk to a financial advisor.

Clean energy

There are many ways to place financial bets on renewable energy. A research firm has developed the Clean Edge Index, tracking the performance of companies that make, develop, distribute, or install renewable-energy technologies.[6] There's an index ETF that mirrors this, also dozens of other ETFs and mutual funds that claim to invest in "green" energy. It's worthwhile delving beyond the fund name. Some may not mirror your idea of the kinds of energy production or use that will survive the many effects of warming discussed above.

Solar energy

The cost of a photovoltaic panel has dropped by more than 80 percent in the past five years. That's definitely good news, both for electricity users and for companies. In the UK big-box retailer Ikea has started selling solar panels as DIY appliances. If consumers respond, Ikea may someday do the same in their U.S. stores.[7]

New solar power utilities—the multi-acre collection of mirrors that heat fluid into steam that turns a turbine—are promising.[8] Covering four times more land than New York's Central Park, Ivanpah Solar Electric's array of 347,000 mirrors tracks the sun and, unlike the solar-trough designs mentioned in Chapter 3, reflects that energy into boilers atop 450-foot towers. The world's largest concentrating solar thermal power plant produces enough power for 140,000 homes without producing any CO_2. The water needed to cool the boilers is 100 percent recycled, so the only water lost is in washing the mirrors periodically.

There is speculation that big oil and gas companies will conclude they must try to dominate solar energy too. If their efforts cause dramatic growth in the industry, that could be very good for the price and availability of electricity, and therefore for companies that use lots of power. But the potential entry of Big Oil makes the market more dangerous for smaller solar companies and their investors.

Nuclear energy

Nuclear energy, along with tobacco and casinos, may be excluded from mutual funds appealing to socially responsible investors. But as discussed in Chapter 3, nuclear power might just be the key to meeting the demand to reduce carbon emissions, a social responsibility, while keeping our air conditioners humming. If the industry, particularly lower-priced less dangerous thorium-based technology begins to tip the scales of public approval, plant makers may be unable to cope with the flood of orders.

A specialized stock index, DAXglobal Nuclear Energy Index, tracks the stock value of many large uranium mining, enrichment, and storage companies, builders of nuclear power plants, and fuel transportation and equipment companies. There is at least one exchange-traded fund, the Market Vectors Uranium+Nuclear Energy ETF, that tracks this index. Other mutual funds specialize in nuclear energy investments.

Infrastructure repair and replacement

As mentioned in Chapter 5 on transportation, the long-deferred costs to repair our dilapidated roads, bridges, and sewer systems, to name just a few of America's overdue maintenance projects, have become huge. Add in projects to repair damage from climate shocks, plus new building projects—desalination plants, solar and wind generator farms, and seawater flood barriers, to name a few—and you have an endless stream of construction projects just waiting for funding.

New York City's climate plan, spurred by Hurricane Sandy which flooded the subway and threatened other infrastructure, calls for $19.5 billion in extra spending over the coming years to protect the metropolitan area from sea-level rise and storms. The plan includes surge barriers, bulkheads, and levees along the 520 miles of city coastline, plus a new elevated community on the Lower East Side, called Seaport City. Almost all of New York's power utilities would be moved or raised. Healthcare facilities and telecommunications gear would be moved or protected. In all, the plan proposes one of the largest construction programs in history.

Across the country, billions of dollars worth of construction is being planned to protect other cities and towns against climate effects. And that's just in America. Similar construction opportunities are growing in dozens of foreign countries, and many will provide work for U.S. companies.

Opportunities for companies supporting the construction industries, such as cement and metal manufacturers, inventors of new construction methods, new materials and technologies, and providers of engineering skills and financing, are huge. Construction finance is likely to be a major bottleneck and therefore an opportunity for creative investors.

Medicine

The aging of Americans is already expanding the need for healthcare. Recently the World Health Organization announced that the impacts of climate change and variability on human health have increased considerably in recent years.[9]

Beyond malnutrition, growing needs discussed in Chapter 4 include methods of dealing with heat itself, along with the allergies and asthma from changing vegetation and increased ozone. Microbes and parasites in sewer overflows and other water pollution, along with virus- and bacteria-carrying animals and insects finding habitat farther north, will call for protective solutions.

The health dangers from warming should add value to investments in therapeutic and diagnostic systems, hospitals, and other parts of the healthcare industry. In the case of the pharmaceuticals industry, there is already huge unmet demand overseas, particularly in the poorer nations, for drugs to combat existing health risks that are being compounded by warming. This is a challenge to drug company profits: third-world markets are huge in volume but cannot pay first-world prices.

Biotechnology

Drug research may hold the key to keeping down costs from allergies, asthma, heat stroke and other dangers exacerbated by warming, but it's likely in agriculture and other areas where biotech's big contributions will come. We discussed the need to create hybridized crop varieties that will thrive in drier and hotter conditions. This may be particularly important in the world's poor countries.

Overseas markets, however, are iffy. As we saw in Chapter 7 on federal taxes, the biggest challenge to getting real value from genetically-engineered foods in the rest of the world is not the science; it's public attitudes. As with drug companies, there's another barrier to agtech profits. The greatest need is likely to be in countries that haven't the means to pay for them, and pressure may mount on GE seed companies to give away their products for humanitarian purposes or sell to relief agencies at greatly reduced prices.

In addition to food there are, of course, dozens of ways that biotechnology is expected to help consumers cope with pressures to reduce energy use and carbon emissions—from bleaching, dyeing and laundering textiles to making bioplastics, converting timber into paper, tanning leather, and making biofuels that don't compete with the food supply.

Robotics

Robots, artificial intelligence, software, remote sensors, big data, and related technologies will be helping us cope with effects of warming. Swarms of remote-operating gizmos are being developed to fight forest fires, remove CO_2 from the ocean and pollution from our waters, and find, even rescue, survivors after natural disasters.[10] New applications are being announced every month.

As data gets cheaper and energy more expensive, networking of devices in our homes, business, fields, and infrastructure can lead to major efficiencies in electricity use and distribution, fuel-saving, food production, free-flowing transportation, and other areas. Using massive analytical databases and real-time sensors, these systems offer opportunities for data and software firms.

In addition, of course, AI and robotics are poised to obsolete many jobs. Today's technologies appear capable of performing both high wage jobs in narrow fields like medical diagnosis or analytical research, and also to replace widely-held lower-paying jobs such as food service and retail. If this is true, Harvard professor Richard B. Freeman points out, first, the investment upside of this development, "Income will increasingly come from ownership of robots and the income they produce, rather than from human labor" and, second, the societal downside, "We should worry less about the potential displacement of human labor by robots than about how to share fairly across society the prosperity that the robots produce."[11]

Not only does robotics give us another reason to choose our careers carefully, it's an illustration of why saving in order to build our investment earnings may help us become owners, not victims.

Other technology opportunities

There are those who think that the threats from warming can be largely met with technical solutions beyond robotics. Capturing carbon, building safe cheap nuclear generators, controlling water, reusing and recycling, mapping dangers and, perhaps the most useful, storing energy are all touted as opportunities for American technology firms.

If there are attractive opportunities, American corporations are hoarding about $1.7 trillion in cash, some of it waiting to be invested in high-return businesses when they can be identified.[12] Let's hope that much of that cash can support the rapid expansion of new technologies and services that will protect people from the effects of warming.

Moveable structures

States and towns are beginning to prevent new construction on land threatened by sea-level rise unless the building owner agrees to remove it when shoreline erosion threatens it. Innovative designs that can be easily disassembled and trucked to a new location may make these agreements financially practicable. Companies with innovative designs may find a good niche.

Minerals

Buried under sheets of ice, the land surfaces of Antarctica and Greenland have been inaccessible for mining, but that is about to change. The race to secure mineral rights is already on, and large and easily accessible deposits of iron ore, copper, manganese, molybdenum, uranium, titanium—not to mention gold and silver—will certainly make many fortunes when these minerals are uncovered by receding icecaps. There are many ways to invest in minerals via the stock market or commodity trading.

Agricultural commodities

Given steadily rising food prices around the world and the predicted impact of changing weather patterns on agricultural output, it's tempting to place financial bets on future food prices. In addition to wheat, corn and soybean meal, you can bet on the value of other growing things, like wool, palm oil, rubber, and timber. Playing the commodities markets as an amateur is, of course, a tried-and-true way to lose your shirt. That said, there are plenty of professionally-managed funds investing in agricultural commodities.

Broader commodities

Throughout the 20th century, the prices of a range of mineral and agricultural commodities dropped 70 percent on average. But from 2002 to 2011, the GMO Commodity Index shows this decline was entirely erased. The past decade has seen a bigger rise than any other period, including World War II and the Oil Crisis in the 1970's.[13]

The S&P Goldman Sachs Commodity Index shows the same thing, a six-fold growth in commodity prices since 1969. Yes, there was a dramatic drop in 2008 when the Great Recession hit, but prices today have climbed back close to their longer-term trend.

From Malthus in 1798 to the Club of Rome in 1972 to others today, many futurists have predicted that a growing human population will exhaust the resources of our planet. The stuff we rely on every day—aluminum, coal, coconut oil, coffee, copper, corn, cotton, diammonium phosphate, flaxseed, gold, iron ore, jute, lard, lead, natural gas, nickel, oil, palladium, palm oil, pepper, platinum, plywood, rubber, silver, sorghum, soybeans, sugar, tin, tobacco, uranium, wheat, wool, zinc—it will all be used up. If scarcity of these commodities is in the offing—or if other investors believe so—a long-term bet on their prices could pay off.[14]

Beyond betting on the future price of a physical commodity that could be affected by weather, it's now possible for you to simply bet on the weather itself. Investors can win or lose depending on how temperatures, frost, hurricane damage or snowfall deviate from the monthly or seasonal average in a particular city or region. Hurricane-specific investment products rise or fall depending on how much damage a hurricane causes compared to standard predictions.[15]

Property insurance underwriting

The insurance business is probably becoming riskier. Claims for damage to property and crops from warming-induced fire, drought, wind, and other risks have increased dramatically. Munich Reinsurance, the backer of many property policies, reports that the number of natural disasters in the U.S. has increased more than 400 percent since 1990, with the fastest-growing sector labeled climatological and including temperature extremes, drought, and wildfire. Despite the resulting rate hikes, high-profile global warming events have pushed up demand for insurance and provided justification for higher, sometimes panic-level, premiums. Insurance companies whose actuaries can accurately gauge these risks stand to make big profits as warming-driven disasters increasingly spook property owners and businesses.

Other businesses dealing with fire and flood are seeing demand grow. Chemical fire-retardant spray services are sold to well-to-do homeowners and businesses in wildfire country. There's a huge private ambulance industry, with private firefighting or flood protection services available as well.[16]

Regardless of what type of insurance market they are in, most property insurance companies are facing a triple threat from warming: higher damage claims, rising liability settlements as the world begins to go to court over damages, and dangers to their investment assets, for instance potential stranded assets among energy stocks.

Today's products and services re-imagined

At the Liberty Mountain Resort in Virginia, you can ski down an outdoor slope on what this facility calls its *Snowflex* system. They've padded their hill with a durable Astroturf that is kept moist to simulate real snow.[17] At Liberty Mountain, you ski under the sky, but indoor ski areas are also growing. The Netherlands now has about fifty stand-alone indoor ski and snowboard centers with revolving slopes. Just as on a treadmill, you never run out of slope.

With ski resorts being hurt by warmer winters, will a new industry spring up? City workers taking a few runs on their lunch hour? Ski Moms driving kids to slalom practice. Ski chains could spring up across the country, looking for start-up investors, IPO buyers, or mutual funds to hold their publicly traded stock?

With foresight and imagination, there should be lots of entrepreneurial opportunities to substitute something new for something threatened by warming.

Social enterprises

A strong distinction has always been drawn between businesses and non-profits. For one thing, they usually have different goals. Recently, however, the concept of the social entrepreneur—operating a profit-making business for the purpose of doing good—has grown. Long-time examples include the museum shop whose profits support museum activities, companies formed to employ the handicapped, and Newman's Own, which gives its profits to charity.

A new corporate entity, the B Corporation, has been developed and approved by 27 states to accommodate these mixed purposes. In pursuing its social goals the B Corp needs to make money, rather than getting it from donors or foundations, but shareholders cannot expect profit-maximization to be management's primary duty, as for-profit company shareholders can.[18]

Social enterprises are not usually touted as investments, but unlike their near and distant cousins such as the co-op, mutual organization, and non-profits, they can perform socially useful services in your community and provide outside owners a return on their investment as well.

Climate bonds

Also called green bonds and touted as a new asset class, climate bonds are issued to raise money for 'green' projects. Anticipated uses include energy-efficient industrial retrofits, bicycle-renting schemes, water treatment and recycling, low-emission vehicles, storm surge protection and methane capture.

To attract funds for these uses, many climate bonds have found they need to be issued or guaranteed by international or national government agencies, so they may be reasonably safe investments.[19]

Other investments with long-term downsides

Nicholas Stern called climate change "the greatest and widest-ranging market failure ever seen," in his report *The Economics of Climate Change*.[20] Market failure happens when the price we pay for something today does not include all of its costs, particularly those that affect others or which will come due in the future. Examples include home pricing that ignores the future chances of flooding, energy pricing that leaves out tomorrow's costs from pollution, and business valuations that ignore environmental challenges or future resource scarcities.

Such assets are overpriced and will eventually have the costs of warming deducted from their market value.

Some big assets are endangered.

Publicly-traded companies are expected to disclose information that could have negative impacts on their future earnings and asset values. Some do, some don't. Firms that are going public or issuing new securities, however, often take disclosure more seriously, listing all the risks they can see, no matter how remote, in a section of their public offering document called Risk Factors. (The massive Alibaba IPO in 2014 had more than 40 pages describing risks.) Existing public companies must disclose new risks in their quarterly statements and reflect those risks in their financial statements. Checking this section of a company's latest prospectus may help you see risks from warming that are not revealed by the company anywhere else.

Even if a company's earnings look good today, its assets may not, and its stock and bond prices can be modified with the stroke of an accountant's pen. Companies may begin to reduce the expected life of assets, for instance structures in a floodplain, land subject to drought, or mineral reserves that may never be exploited. These are often called stranded assets. Writing off assets and creating reserves for long-term negative possibilities are responsible ways of expressing new risks in a company's financial statements. Although the risks may relate to events in the distant future, they reduce the company's "book" value today, which can reduce its value in the stock market.

If you are investing in individual companies, it pays to look beyond earnings projections to find out whether they have already done a thorough examination of where their assets are vulnerable to the anticipated costs from warming. If not, are they likely to get around to it—right after you've bought their stock?

The Coca-Cola Company is taking warming very seriously. After all, Coke is 90 percent water; Diet Coke is 99 percent water; and many of Coke's operations are facing an existential threat from warming, the loss of a good water supply. As part of the company's planning, each bottling plant around the world has prepared a *Source Water Vulnerability Assessment* and implemented a *Source Water Protection Plan*,[21] an indication the firm is both addressing and disclosing its risks.

Carbon-based energy may take a write-down.

Many such risks are in the fossil fuels industry. How they resolve themselves will create investment opportunities and disappointments.

Scientists and economists tell us that to have a reasonable chance of stopping global warming at 2 degrees Celsius only 20 percent of the world's proven oil and gas reserves can be burned. We must leave the rest in the ground.[22] Carbon assets on companies' books total in the tens of trillions of dollars today. If their owners can't eventually sell a high percentage of those assets, this means a drop in profits in the future, a prospect that reduces the true value of energy stocks today.[23]

New government constraints, such as emissions policies or a carbon tax, will make carbon fuels and the energy they supply more expensive. This would hurt the value of today's utility, coal mining, and oil and gas stocks as their customers are incentivized to find other sources of energy. You may not hold individual stocks in any oil and gas companies or utilities, but check to see if they are a big part of your retirement plan or mutual funds.

There are other forces too working to depress the market value of oil and gas companies. One of these is the divestment movement. Shunning stocks of companies that did business with South Africa may have helped bring on the demise of apartheid, but there is little evidence that divestment efforts against carbon-based energy have so far had any effect on the companies' behavior or stock prices.[24] This could change if the New York State's attorney general prosecutes Exxon Mobil for misleading its investors about the causes and ramifications of climate change.[25]

On the other hand, there may be valuable innovations, even in the coal and petroleum industries. Some investment advisors say there's more money to be made investing in technologies that cut emissions, even a tiny bit, than in backing wind, solar, and other technologies that eliminate them.

Some property companies are overvalued.

At this point in the book, I don't need to discuss the effect of warming on the value of land, homes, and commercial properties. Investment in a resort chain with large beachfront holdings, a real estate investment trust (REIT) in drought-threatened areas, or commercial/industrial properties sited in the floodplain seem worth careful review. Even where a property is not threatened physically, migration out of the area or general economic decline could hurt area property values generally.

Municipal bonds have growing risks.

Municipal bond funds may not be a good place to keep your money. As we discussed in Chapter 6 on local taxes, the budgets of many (but not all) states and towns are likely to be pummeled by the effects of warming.

After Hurricane Sandy, Governor Cuomo of New York decided that these effects should be listed as risks in the offering statements for state bond issues, along with other standard risks such as unsatisfactory union negotiations or cuts in federal spending. The financial world has been slow to applaud, with some observers seeing the new wording as a political statement. Bond rating agencies and the SEC are not yet highlighting these risks, but that may change.[26] Until they do, you should be aware that there are new and growing risks to municipal bondholders, many of them discussed in Chapter 6 on municipal taxes.

False hype abounds.

For years, companies have been telling consumers that their products are 'green' and therefore worth buying. More companies are going to tell investors that their business model is 'climate-proof' and therefore worth investing in.

In retail it didn't take long for consumers to understand that many of these claims were *greenwashing*, marketing descriptions only. The same is beginning to be true in the corporate stock market. Look behind the climate-proof investing claims to see if these businesses really have a strategy aimed at dodging business risks from warming.

The problem of false business claims about how good they are on climate issues has led a group, the Asset Owners Disclosure Project, that creates a Hypocrisy Index. It's meant to identify big investment fund managers who are paying lip service to climate action but not translating words into urgent action, falsely claiming their investments help prevent global warming.[27]

When you read financial commentary and company claims, remember there may be little connection between how green a company claims to be or even how genuinely it is helping to save the planet through emissions-reduction and other actions, and how vulnerable its own profits are to the effects of warming.

Information as key to investing well

You don't find a lot of personal investment advisors or business journalists talking today about protecting portfolios or homes from the effects of warming. Try an online search for the phrase: *"global warming" OR "climate change" "financial planner" OR "realtor."* As of July 2016, you get just about nothing useful to home buyers or sellers.

Similarly, mutual fund managers seem reluctant to spend time evaluating the climate risks of what they buy. Why? Because climate poses long-term risks, while investment managers are rewarded on short-term performance.

Climate-proof investing might suddenly become first a fad, then a commonplace. But until that time, you could reduce your investment risks somewhat by finding one of the few advisers who can answer the question, "What are some of the impacts that climate change could have on such-and-such company's stock price?" Ideally, you should find one who knows more than you do.[28]

Company data about warming are becoming available.

How can we research how much exposure a particular company, industry or mutual fund has to weird weather and other effects of warming? There is beginning to be some analyst chatter and behind-the-scenes research identifying the risks and opportunities being created by global warming. You may be able to tap into this if you search or ask for it.

And pressure is growing to require investment managers to calculate and describe the climate-change risks to the funds and portfolios they manage. Unlike the divestment movement, these surveys are about the risks our fund managers are causing to our investments rather than to our planet. Such disclosure is still considered optional by the Securities and Exchange Commission, but pressure is growing.

You might want to keep an eye on the Asset Owners Disclosure Project, mentioned above. Starting in 2012 they have conducted a yearly assessment of the largest asset owners around the world, looking at how they manage the risks and opportunities of climate change. In the U.S. in 2016, only CalPERS, California's public employee pension fund, and the New York State Common Retirement Fund received a rating of AAA. TIAA-CREF got a BBB, up from CCC the year before. MetLife, the Harvard, Yale and Stanford endowments, Prudential plans, and others got D ratings from this group. Dozens of companies received X ratings, meaning they provided no information about how they are managing climate risk.[29]

Quietly over the last decade, the Investor Network on Climate Risk, another group of investment managers, has been pushing to identify and drop climate-risky and energy-inefficient investments from their own portfolios. They are advocating that other professional investors do the same, that decisions about hiring an investment manager should include considerations about climate attitudes, and that investors should lobby investment regulators for more climate-sensitive policies.[30]

Timing is always important.
Spying an overvalued or undervalued asset is a key to good investing, and warming is going to change a lot of values. But just because we see a change coming doesn't mean we can make money on it. Others may have seen it and bid the price down or up already.

Defensive investing

It's not a given that damage from warming on Main Street will trash the markets on Wall Street. Since the Great Recession, median household income has been essentially flat but the value of the U.S. stock market has more than doubled.[31] If new industries, jobs, and investment opportunities start to appear in the fight against the many different threats from warming, the market could thrive even as those threats do their damage. After all, when we fight catastrophes, repair damage, or wage wars we raise national income, employment, and corporate revenues just as much as when we build something safe, healthy and peaceful.

But if the effects of warming are going to be negative overall for U.S. businesses and the investment markets—and that's a real possibility—normal broad-based investments in American businesses will be the wrong place to keep our savings over the coming years. So where to put those savings if we expect a long-term bear market? In addition to some of the promising industries mentioned above, there are the usual bolt holes for defensive investing—low-risk bonds, money-market funds, maybe some short selling. And there are plenty of investment advisors to help choose among them. It's even possible that some bear market funds will spring up specifically to take advantage of value destruction caused by warming.

Invest in necessities.
When there's trouble predicted, such as a storm likely to create power outages or icy roads, what do you do? You stock up on necessities: food that doesn't need heating, bottled water, diapers, batteries and candles, a few good books. You're going to get all of these things sooner or later anyway; you've just accelerated the timing of the purchases.

It may be wise to think of the growing costs caused by warming as an approaching storm. Protections you can buy now and dangers you can get rid of will either increase your income or reduce your expenses in the future enough to give you a solid return. Spending money today to learn skills that will earn or save money later is one investment worth considering. Whether it's for one of the occupations suggested in the next chapter on jobs, or simply learning to operate an efficient home garden, the money you invest in skills can provide a return if your current occupation is endangered or your expenses rise. If you make a commitment to these new skills, you may also want to invest in the plot of land or start-up business that makes them truly productive.

Another investment that could pay off better than Wall Street is in your own solar panels or a wind turbine. Like many investments, these are up-front purchases that earn back their cost over years. Even if it takes 7 years to cover the purchase and begin getting truly free electricity, that's a 9 percent return, better than the historical rise in stocks. And your payback is in cash (or cash not expended) while you own that investment, not just on paper until you sell it.

Some other investments with a payback based on dodging the long-term costs of warming might include the cost of moving to a more climate-proof and low-cost hometown. If you can't do that, you might invest in the extra costs to send your children to college in a more climate-proof region; the payback comes because they're more likely to settle in that area, not in the threatened part of the country where they are now. Putting your money into these strategies could earn a payback that far exceeds what you can get in the investment markets, especially if the costs of warming start to seriously damage the American economy.

WHERE TO LIVE FOR BETTER INVESTMENTS

Throughout this book, we've seen that many of the threats from warming vary from location to location, profession to profession or lifestyle to lifestyle. This makes it easier to find a no-regrets approach to dodging these dangers. However, when it comes to investment vehicles, such as

Index funds, international ETFs, or municipal bonds, it's hard to see that where we live matters.

But just as you should consider a more climate-proof location for your home and your children's future lives, you should think about that same location as a place to invest in businesses that are likely to be more climate-proof. In-migration may be the biggest play here. It doesn't take a huge increase in families moving into town before real estate developers, building companies, retailers, and consumer services begin to expand. With early research and a watchful eye, over time you could identify the location and the timing for one or more profitable local investments. A good place to start learning about local investment techniques is with Michael Shuman's book mentioned in Chapter 2.[32]

Alternatives include starting a business, investing in someone else's company, getting in on the IPO of a regional company, or putting money into a mutual fund that specializes in a particular state or region. The funds from Mairs & Powers are examples. They invest in Midwest companies, particularly those headquartered in Minnesota. Local investor's clubs or chapters of the American Association of Individual Investors are likely to be a source of ideas about ways to invest in the region.[33]

Footnotes for this chapter, **Where-To-Live Indicators** *for all American towns, and other tools and resources are available at savvyfamilies.org/climateproof, as well as the author's updates, your comments, and other useful information.*

10 WORK IN A GOOD JOB MARKET

Given all the ways our lives and communities will be changing, you might think new jobs would be springing up left and right. And it's true that there are already lots of new job titles related to warming. In late 2015, the biggest online job board, Indeed.com, showed 19,448 jobs containing the word "sustainability" in their titles or job descriptions. Another 5,191 contained "resilience." Sustainability consultant, resilience engineer, campus sustainability director, corporate sustainability manager, green building workers and professionals, and water, food, or energy scientists—the list goes on, and it can sound like a cornucopia of new jobs.

Job descriptions are more important.
If, however, you look closely at the actual job duties and skills under these new titles, you will see that most are pretty much the same as before their titles changed. Don't confuse a job description that has green buzzwords sprinkled through it with one that actually meets a growing need caused by warming. Such jobs should have staying power and increasing value as the effects of warming grow. They are likely to be for crane operators, allergists, foundation contractors, agronomists, sanitary engineers, and clinic managers—and most ads for these positions won't use new catchy job titles.

CHOOSING CAREERS IN THE FACE OF WARMING

Choose a growing industry.
Yes, warming will create or expand jobs. To find one with a healthy long-term demand for your skills, it's better to search, not by title or job description, but by industry. And location. In declining industries there may still be work to be done, but for how long? And in declining towns, even good business can die.

Firms like Flood Control America, mentioned in Chapter 8 on our homes, are producing local jobs with products that help protect local communities. There will be many such innovative products and services in construction, healthcare, transportation, energy, and other industries that could provide a more climate-proof career. We will discuss some potential winners and losers below.

Of course, you may also want to look for sectors that are relatively safe, not so much from warming, but from recession. Remember, the general prosperity of the nation—even in the healthiest regions—is likely to be as big a factor in our career and earnings as our choice of industry or location. The costs of adjusting to warming could throw America into a prolonged recession. If so, it may be safer to find work with one of the economy's recession-resistant sectors than with a great new warming-related product or service no one has the money to buy. Healthcare, law enforcement, and certain IT sectors are relatively recession-proof.

Do employment forecasts help?

It would be nice to find well-thought-out predictions, telling us which jobs are more climate-proof and which not so much. There are surprisingly few long-term employment forecasts available to guide us. Current government projections for 2022 do not consider any effects from warming.[1] And when you come across one of the few studies relating in some way to climate change, you have to consider the source. As you might imagine, the American Solar Energy Society sees rapid job growth if America will increase incentives for photovoltaic installations.[2] On the other hand, the conservative Heritage Foundation predicts that curbing CO_2 emissions will cost over half a million manufacturing jobs.[3]

International organizations have been more inclined to take climate shifts into account in their projections, and they tend to reach sweeping conclusions such as "Wholesale changes in the way economies are structured" are on the way.[4] That's great, but it's hard to find answers to the obvious questions that confront individuals: should I be worried about my field, my skills, or my location over the next decade? And even if the outlook is good for that timeframe, what about longer-term? What would a no-regrets choice of career involve? What skill and location trends will benefit my children and grandchildren?

Until serious predictions are published, we need to do our own employment forecasting. Let's start with a few of the negative possibilities to consider: our present industry could be decaying, our region of the country going downhill, or our skill set losing its value.

Industries likely to wither

Some industries are hostage to temperature. We've looked at devastation in the seafood industry—lobstering, offshore fishing and shellfish—caused by warming and ocean acidification. Fine wines have heavenly years and so-so years, and warming could tip the mix toward the so-so. Ranching has been hurting badly as heat kills herds. Skiing and dairy likewise depend on the right temperature.

Still others will be affected by the indirect effects of higher temperatures. For instance, coastal tourism is predicted to suffer as beaches are eroded and seaside buildings threatened.

And, of course, the oil, gas, coal and property industries discussed in the previous chapter may eventually come under increasing pressure to downsize. Given their tremendous capital bases, however, they may be able to update their companies, morphing their businesses into something unrecognizable today and providing lots of new jobs.

What's called "creative destruction" of industries, trades, and companies is touted as a positive force in *laissez-faire* economics. Where change destroys jobs, new industries spring up and entrepreneurs take advantage of those changes. While this can be true for the country as a whole, if your career is in one of the destruction zones, the country's progress could come at the expense of your family's finances.

Serious studies of the prospects for specific industries in the face of warming are beginning to be published. The Cambridge Institute for Sustainability Leadership[5] in the UK leads the way with its series that includes "Implications for Agriculture," "Implications for Extractive Industries," "Implications for Tourism" and more. You should search for this sort of analysis on your own industry.

And check the prospects for other industries in your area, whether or not you work in them. When a particular industry suffers, nearby businesses are affected. When a plant closes, local businesses from restaurants to dry cleaners, car dealerships to cable companies feel the pinch and cut back on their hiring. We will discuss the relationship between jobs and geography below. In the meantime, let's look at industries that may increase hiring as their surroundings warm.

Industries predicted to hire

It pays to be where jobs are appearing, and to be qualified for them. Here are a few that appear poised for expansion, thanks to the effects of warming.

Construction

Much of what many communities need to do to protect themselves involves building stuff.[6] The heavy construction industry, whether paid by government or businesses, could take on hundreds of thousands of workers to increase storm drain capacities, repair coastal erosion, build barriers to protect river and seaside cities from flooding, and move power and sewage plants to higher elevations. In light construction, the number of workers needed to install solar panels, lay drip irrigation systems and insulate houses and businesses could also be very large.

We saw this over the past ten years in New Orleans. After Hurricane Katrina, the federal government appropriated $14 billion to construct or improve 133 miles of levees, floodwalls, floodgates and pump stations around the city. Thousands of jobs were created. Multi-year employment opportunities like these may become more common as flood risks and damage climb around our coasts.[7]

Hurricane Sandy called for less cleanup than Katrina, but by hitting the New York area, it has set in motion huge future expenditures to protect parts of the city. Almost before the winds died down New York City had created a $20 billion plan to build sea walls in certain areas of the city. And that's just the first phase.[8]

Before any construction project begins, related industries will get a lot of business. Work done by engineering and consulting firms—assessment, risk analysis, modeling, and planning—will likely rise quickly. In addition to the big projects, many innovative private companies will create niches for themselves alongside the rebar-and-cement mixer firms.

At the building-by-building level, if the price of energy rises—whether from a carbon tax or other factors—many property owners will again think about making their homes more energy-efficient. The payback times on buying insulation, passive solar elements, green roofs, or high-efficiency cooling and heating would improve, and demand for local contractors to do this work would grow. The timing of these building-by-building construction projects depends on when owners find themselves paying too much for energy, thanks to either rising energy prices or rising temperatures.

Local and state regulations on environmental impact, carbon emissions, and other dangers seem likely to expand in many places. This could dampen construction jobs somewhat, but it could also increase demand for the engineering, legal and consulting services needed to create and comply with these regulations.

Remember that construction-related jobs, no matter how plentiful, have drawbacks:

1. **They're nomadic.** Once you've built a seawall, your construction team needs to move many miles to its next job.

2. **They're not permanent.** Once our farm fields are covered with water-saving irrigation and our rooftops with solar panels, they're covered.

3. **Projects often depend on government funding.** Even if private contractors do all the work, hiring plans can be jerked around by quixotic lawmakers and administrators.

Real estate developers, agents, and long-distance movers

As families across America begin to understand that where they live will endanger their personal finances and wellbeing, many will pull up stakes and move to less threatened parts of the country. That suggests the need for additional housing to accommodate these migrants, which creates the need for additional business buildings nearby. New buildings increase opportunities for movers, real estate agents, home inspectors, and related service people.

Warming, while it will make many of today's ski, beach and desert golf resorts less attractive, probably won't dampen Americans' vacation urges. The incentive for vacationers to find new playgrounds away from the summer shoreline and winter mountains will create jobs in new leisure destinations and activities.

House movers

There are customers who are going to want to move, not their belongings, but their whole house. In Chapter 8 we noted that 2.6 million American homes are threatened by sea-level rise and strong storm surge.[9] The cost of moving a structure, if there is room on the roads and a safer lot nearby, is far lower than building or buying a home. House-moving, which takes skill and experience, could be a growing business.[10]

Going one step further, speculative buying of upland lots ready to accommodate nearby threatened shorefront homes could be financially lucrative as well. House-moving is a tiny unknown industry now with possible explosive growth ahead.

Solar and wind

Renewable-source electricity and energy conservation have been touted for a long time as big new industries, offering a cascade of products, services and jobs similar to what grew from semiconductors over recent decades. From 2011 to 2015, solar jobs nearly doubled nationally to more than 200,000 workers, mostly in installation.[11] While employment may be growing, the industry employs about the same number of workers as shoe stores, dairy farms, or chiropractic offices.[12] Not exactly a big industry yet. And with fossil fuel prices down, investment in renewable energy has been dropping both worldwide and in the U.S. for the past few years.[13]

Likewise, the on-again, off-again history of government subsidies for solar installation has made the industry a bumpy one. In recent years, entrepreneurs started domestic solar, wind-turbine and permeable-driveway businesses to get on board ahead of the rush, create skills, and build a reputation. Today many of them have gone back to their previous roofing or engineering or landscaping jobs.

What happened? The market developed very slowly. Unlike Germany and other countries that resolved to create healthy solar industries, government subsidies in the U.S. stopped and started and stopped again. State regulations to protect consumers added costs. But mostly, fracking happened. The arrival of low-cost natural gas slowed the growth in the price of electricity from some U.S. utilities. Electricity from wind and solar had to be as cheap to compete. Fracking put grid parity, as it's called, further into the future in many areas, and we wait for technical breakthroughs to drop the price of solar panels or wind turbines or for the fracked gas sources to peter out and become more expensive.

In the long-term, renewable energy sources and related businesses seem like sure winners, but so far they have been lessons in uncertainty and disappointment.

Consulting and advice

None of the decisions I discuss in this book—moving to a more advantaged hometown, changing your career, changing your financial thinking, or becoming more self-reliant for energy or food—is an easy one. There's research to do, attitudes to change, and long-term plans to be made. A range of advisory sources seems likely to develop, from high-priced business consulting to advice columns in the popular press.

Home advisory services, do-it-yourself products, and how-to videos are already showing signs of growth, along with relocation advisors, outreach and marketing organizations for specific towns, and stepped-up advice and marketing for mobile-home vehicles and parks. Clients' questions could be many:

- What specific dangers are we facing where and how we live today?

- Would it be best for our family or our business to put down new roots? If so, where?

- Which careers will grow long-term while suiting our skills?

- In what new ways should we invest our savings?

- How do we make these transitions?

New services from financial planners and investment advisors, relocation consultants, business planning experts, practitioners in stress management and wellbeing, and many new areas of expertise should see increased demand. You may find that your skills suit the growing need for specialized advice, and this type of work provides steady employment for the foreseeable future.

Law, mediation, expert witness, and work-out experts

One of the industries likely to grow as the country warms is the legal profession, with all the paralegal, investigative, expert-witness, and other jobs associated with it. A little thought will suggest the many issues just waiting to be litigated or mediated.[14]

Property owners versus lenders Where sea-level rise pushes the values of vulnerable homes below their mortgage debt, a lot more homeowners will likely end up—uh—underwater. Unlike the real estate collapse in 2008, neither the owner nor the mortgage holder will expect the price of a flood-prone property to recover. Widespread bankruptcies seem likely in some areas.

Developers versus towns Municipalities have an interest in preventing development in areas that are in danger. Sensitive watersheds, aquifer recharge areas, and districts subject to increased flooding are examples where a city's public works and water departments argue that limiting investment today will reduce future costs. On the other side of the debate are real estate, retail, tourism, and other interests that will suffer if development is curtailed or building codes changed.

Citizens versus governments We've mentioned the many who-pays disputes that lie ahead, and we will discuss them further in Chapter 11 on conflict. Lawyers will be busy for decades on tort claims as citizens, towns, counties, states and the federal government—not to mention economic interest groups—fight over how to share the costs of helping one another, or the pain of not doing so.

Civil rights Because the costs we are discussing are so geographically specific, "redlining" (discriminating by location, which often means by race or income level) to reduce risk may grow. This is illegal now, but banks and insurance companies, and perhaps governments themselves, may find this kind of cost control irresistible. In addition to "discrimination," the phrases "act of God," "private property," "impossibility of performance," "malpractice," "endangered" and "proper disclosure" are all likely to be used in new contexts, perhaps with new meanings.

Government versus contractors The costs of maintaining infrastructure and public services in the face of climate shocks is projected to be so huge that many governments are likely to turn some of these functions over to public-private partnerships, or to entirely private suppliers. Custom structuring of these entities to balance incentives for private investors while protecting the public is likely to become an expanding area of legal and managerial practice.

Municipal bankruptcies There are fears that many municipalities or their agencies, such as water, sanitation, or schools, are sliding toward insolvency, pressured by labor contracts, retirement obligations, or debt. The emergency-manager skills needed to prevent or navigate bankruptcy may see increased demand, not just from governments and their agencies and suppliers, but from property companies and other organizations whose finances are in the direct path of warming threats.

Liability avoidance Insurance companies are concerned that they will find themselves covering newly-acknowledged liability risks. Lloyd's of London has noted "an increasing possibility of attributing weather-related losses to man-made climate change factors. This opens the possibility of courts assigning liability and compensation for claims of damage."[15]

Legal structures and investment products Financial and regulatory innovation will be needed. For instance, new forms of home mortgages, debt protection, or debt insurance are already being discussed. Municipalities are beginning to consider special zoning areas or tax districts to control development. Sea Level Rise Relocation Accounts, tax-free like IRAs or Health Savings Accounts, are being proposed.[16] Likewise, the creation and marketing of new financial instruments (think "sea-level futures," "climate bonds derivatives") are being considered. This work is, of course, likely to be in localities where the threats are greatest.

Other promising industries

Here are some industries being discussed in the business and consumer press.

Where there's increasing heat and drought:

- Air conditioning.

- Collection and reuse of wastewater. Pollution control.
- Domestic equipment: reverse-osmosis water makers, rainwater catchment, filtration, wastewater reuse, etc.
- Water-main repair and replacement.
- Replacement of center-pivot irrigation with drip-feed systems.
- Land-use planning, pollution control, other engineering consulting.
- Hydroponic farming.

In areas of likely flooding:

- Constructing barriers to hold rising seawater at bay.
- Raising water, sewer, electricity transmission, and fire suppressions systems to avoid immersion.
- Raising and fortifying low-lying or waterfront homes.

In places facing changing energy options:

- Installing domestic, commercial or community solar and wind systems.
- Building distributed energy systems.
- Increasing energy and water efficiency in buildings.
- Retrofitting insulation and efficient air conditioning.

Almost anywhere

- Restoring wetlands and other ecosystem cleaning.
- Carbon markets management and trading.
- Aquaculture.
- Project finance and management.
- Manufacture of energy-efficient appliances, desalinization equipment, carbon sequestration, biofuels.
- Insurance and risk management.
- Healthcare specialties.

Developing the right skills

Check the list above to see the variety of skills likely to be needed in the near future, and keep your antennae up for others just beginning to be discussed. Narrow specialties in which you can develop strong credentials may offer job safety. Take salt ponds as an obscure example. With their huge acreage and the number of interests likely to clash over these threatened shoreside areas—property owners, shellfishermen, environmentalists, municipalities, leisure businesses, construction projects—it's not hard to predict the need for specialized expertise.

Beyond specific vocations, there are a few more general factors to consider.

Avoid jobs that a computer or robot can soon do.

One of the biggest causes of stagnant wages is the growing ability of businesses to substitute their software for your brain. When you consider that computers can do a better job of diagnosing your medical complaint than a physician, and may soon do a better job of driving your car than you can, it's obvious that even complex skills are in danger.[17] It makes sense to look ahead and imagine which jobs are most likely to be computerized.

Your field

Researchers have been examining this question and have created a tote board, giving the chances that certain jobs will be replaced by automation over the next decade.[18]

Among the ten fastest-growing jobs today, administrative assistants are said to have a 96 percent chance of losing their job because of computers. It's 92 percent for food prep and serving workers and retail salespeople. Other endangered jobs may surprise you. Check the list compiled by Atlantic Magazine at bit.ly/fastest-growing-jobs.

Sharpen widely valued skills.

We will talk below about maintaining the mobility to easily move to where a new job awaits. The same advantage goes to those who can easily apply their skills to a new career. If, thanks to warming, the U.S. job market is going to see big changes over the coming decades—less predictable and more sweeping than in the recent past—how can you stay marketable as jobs change?

Becoming a specialist in, say, hydrology, energy efficiency or asthma treatment is not the only way to increase your chances of retaining your job. If you are good at supervising teams, managing deadlines, persuading customers, resolving conflict, boosting morale, or controlling costs, you have skills that are demanded by many industries. Developing these talents should be part of a good no-regrets career plan.

Develop remote-working skills.

We will discuss the importance of location for good jobs below, but there is one general skill that can help you get a job while at the same time choosing to live in a low-cost hometown where you're likely to dodge many of the effects of warming. That's the ability to work from anywhere, using the Internet. Several factors must converge to make this likely. Census statistics show that it helps to have

- computer, engineering or science skills,
- junior- or middle-management duties, maybe with financial responsibilities,
- higher-than-average education, and
- an employer in a western state.[19]

Another factor in getting and keeping a job in the cloud is personality. If you are naturally a team player, a frequent communicator, a goal- and schedule-oriented producer with a non-threatening attitude, you are more likely to enjoy, and be valued in. a remote working arrangement.

Demand for old-fashioned skills may grow.

As warming squeezes certain job markets, it's likely to force many families to live more simply. This may seem like a hippie dream, but the value of low-tech skills could climb, as families slow their buying of consumer products, keep their existing stuff longer, and seek second-hand items. Personal services and products such as crafts, repair shops, and resale outlets may see increased demand. Teachers of craft skills such as clothes making and repair, vegetable gardening, fishing, cooking with basic ingredients, bicycle repair, home insulation and repair, and passive solar heating may be more in demand.

For many of us, these vocations would supplement, not replace, traditional employment.

Try not to play catch-up.

I advocate for a no-regrets approach. When you make career decisions in your family, think hard about leapfrogging ahead to an entirely new career rather than hoping to get there incrementally. As potential job-killers play out, you don't want to find yourself saying, "Hey, I was learning, looking around, waiting for a good path out of my industry, but now it's gone. How did I let that happen?"

Shifting job markets can become very competitive. Not only does it pay to look ahead, but also to act ahead of the crowd. If you're going to move, acquire skills and gain experience to make you attractive in a prosperous safer industry, that preparation takes time.

Helping to create local jobs

Most of what was discussed above has been in terms of individual employees, you or me. But we benefit greatly from our neighbors' jobs too, and we can help retain and expand those in several ways.

Buy local.

When we spend a dollar with a local business, unlike a national chain, much more of that money circulates locally.[20] The business owner spends a large portion to employ local residents, to buy stuff from other local businesses, and to make local charity donations, keeping the money circulating within the community. This is called "the multiplier effect."

Stacy Mitchell of The Institute for Local Self-Reliance has conducted studies that tell us the multiplier effect is far greater when we buy goods and services from local organizations than from national chains.[21] Others have done similar studies. A typical finding: each $100 spent at local independents generated $45 of secondary local spending, compared to

$14 for a big-box chain.[22] And, of course, a dollar spent with remote vendors via mail order or the Internet brings even less to the local community.

The more money that flows within our local economy, the more likely we and our neighbors are to have jobs, wealth, property, and a community that feels good and attracts others. It's hard to pay $5 more for something at the local store when we could save that at Walmart. But if we can create or support local businesses with a campaign to "buy local," the long-term financial and community benefits to us can outweigh the short-term savings.

Beyond just our purchase decisions, there are other ways to promote local businesses. For instance, the residents of Jamaica Plain, the particularly forward-looking suburb of Boston, have created a New Economy Enterprise Hub, with the purpose of promoting local jobs. It includes efforts to help entrepreneurs with advice and capital and to incubate their start-ups; to encourage big local employers to hire locally; to help preserve non-growth businesses; to encourage consumers to buy locally; and to develop grassroots influence on government policies.[23]

Join a cooperative.

Taking things one step further, some local communities have established cooperatives for a variety of business purposes. In a poor neighborhood of Cleveland, a collection of worker-owned local businesses called Evergreen Cooperatives operates a laundry, a solar panel installation business, a local newspaper, and hydroponic vegetable production, among other businesses. Workers at Evergreen are thriving in a part of the city with high unemployment.[24]

National cooperatives that maintain major brands, such as dairy products from Organic Valley and Ocean Spray cranberry products,[25] strengthen local producers. Buying from a cooperative has the same advantages for the community as buying local, plus the profits stay with the workers, thus strengthening the working and middle class more than if the profits all flowed to a few business owners.

Encourage the bartering of skills.

Although work done within a time bank does not bring you cash, it creates credits for free services you would otherwise pay for. And it creates jobs for you and others nearby. Timebanking will be discussed when we talk about modes of cooperation in Chapter 12 on attitudes.

WHERE TO LIVE FOR BETTER JOB OPTIONS

In many places throughout this book, we have seen that the impacts of warming will be highly local. This means that infrastructure projects to protect communities, industrial plants, utilities, roads and water sources will vary widely from city to city. While a place that needs a lot of protection or repair may not be a good hometown in the long term, if the funding is available it could be the place to find a good job, at least temporarily.

Yourtown, USA

Data and projections from the Bureau of Labor Statistics have been used to forecast how fast each metro area across the U.S. will grow by 2022. These growth numbers are further divided among low-wage, low-skill "service class" jobs; high-wage knowledge-intensive "creative class" jobs; and "working class" jobs largely in factory production, construction, and transportation.

Depending on your skills—or those you intend to acquire—the maps will show you which areas are most likely to grow new jobs that would suit you. You can peruse them at bit.ly/jobs-10yrs-hence.

Of course, these projections do not consider the effects of a shifting climate. In particular, they probably understate the number of new construction jobs, and they may also overstate job growth in the cities in the South and Southwest that will suffer from drought and heat. You can take these city-by-city projections and mentally overlay your thoughts about the effects of warming. Unfortunately, no such warming-conscious analysis has been done yet.

Not everyone can move to a job-growth city. The Great Recession was exacerbated by the inability of workers to move to job opportunities because they couldn't sell their homes. When you don't own your home, you are a lot more nimble; you can go to where the jobs are. This is particularly advantageous in a troubled economy, which may shrink both job opportunities and the ability to sell a house. It's going to be increasingly important to be mobile, to keep all options open as opportunities ebb and flow around the country—to be where people are arriving, not leaving.

Be where it's easy to start a business.

Over the past couple of decades, it is very young businesses that have accounted for nearly all net new job creation in the U.S. Not small businesses, not big businesses, but new companies—companies less than five years old.[26]

Be near a college town.

College towns are generally more recession-proof than others.[27] If not a college town, at least choose a better-educated population. A Brookings Institution study of the Great Recession concluded, "Metro areas with highly educated populations experienced more modest declines in employment during the recession than others. Among the 20 metro areas with the highest rates of bachelor's degree attainment, only four registered declines in their overall employment-to-population ratio that exceeded the national average."[28]

If there is going to be significant migration among Americans, going to college where you're likely to want to live has another advantage: you get there ahead of other people who go to school elsewhere and who discover your town's attractions only later in life. It's hard to see this when writing college applications in high school, but there's something to be said for encouraging your children's college criteria to include the likelihood that a college town will attract them as a place to live and work after graduation.

Work near high-earning workers.

It's not just college-educated workers who benefit in innovation-oriented cities; less-educated workers benefit too. The Brookings study says,

"Employment for workers without a high school diploma was less impacted in these highly educated metro areas than in other markets."[29]

Cities with a heavy concentration of knowledge-based jobs somehow create an atmosphere of high pay, compared to cities with fewer 'creative class' jobs. The differences are huge and growing: an average college graduate in the Boston area earns $75,000; in Brownsville, Texas only $44,000. High school graduates earn over $100,000 in Stamford, Connecticut, under $30,000 in Danville, Virginia.[30]

Of course, the downside of trying to work in a knowledge center when you are not a knowledge-worker yourself can be the cost of living. As we saw in Chapter 7 on federal taxes, a higher cost of living can more than erase the gains of a higher income.

Stay light on your feet.
In Chapter 12 on attitudes, we'll cover the importance of flexibility. This is particularly true for the economic and employment picture as the country warms. Both in geography and skill set, the ability to move to tomorrow's opportunity and not be anchored in yesterday's is a no-regrets approach that will help if opportunities begin to erode.

Footnotes for this chapter, Where-To-Live Indicators for all American towns, and other tools and resources are available at savvyfamilies.org/climateproof, as well as the author's updates, your comments, and other useful information.

11 UNDERSTAND HOW MUCH PLACE MATTERS

For millions of Americans, the biggest factor in climate-proofing our lives will be where we live. The last section in each preceding chapter has tried to emphasize this. Let's review.

It is easy for us to see places suffering from the effects of warming. Aerial shots show the house swallowed by a sinkhole in Dunedin, Florida, the thousand homes burned in Lake County, California, and the five thousand homes badly damaged in New Jersey by Hurricane Sandy. But those photos show only physical damage. Many of us would look at them and say, "Not a problem for me. I live nearby, but I'm on solid ground. Or out of the forest. Or 200 feet above the shore."

Wrong. We might be out of physical danger, but so long as we live in the same tax district, job market or real estate market as our physically damaged neighbors, our personal finances are in danger from those events. Here's one scenario.

A hurricane destroys a nearby family's home. Yes, their pain and loss are great, but at least they can move on. They can take the insurance money and rebuild their lives in a more climate-proof town. In the meantime, we lucky neighbors who escaped with no damage get to stay and help pay, through our local and state taxes, for the clean-up, the municipal engineering studies, the new erosion control and stormwater overflow structures, the relocation of shoreside infrastructure, the construction of dykes, and all manner of other efforts to protect residents and businesses from the next disaster.

We endure a squeeze on municipal services—education, police and fire, parks and recreation, trash collection, street maintenance—that comes when the town's revenues need to be spent on disaster cleanup and new protections for parts of our town. Furthermore, those who stay become spectators or participants in the bickering and politicking among residents of the town, county and state over what should be spent, who should benefit, and who should pay.

Before long we get a postcard from the family whose home was destroyed. Forced to become mobile, they now live in one of the many U.S. towns where they don't face dangers or big shared costs from flood, storm or drought.

Which towns are those?

As we've seen throughout this book, some places will be hit much harder than others by the costs from warming. After Hurricane Sandy, residents of Monmouth County, New Jersey at the mouth of the Hudson River, were ten days without power; 16 percent of homes filed insurance claims; 14 of every 1,000 residents were served at a shelter.[1] These risks are growing all along our coasts, and half of Americans live in a coastal county.[2]

Baca County, Colorado hasn't had normal amounts of rain since the blizzards of 2007. Pastures have dried up or are covered by drifts of sand. Tumbleweed collects against fences, homes, and barns. Dust storms steal topsoil making it almost impossible to grow the county's normal crops.[3]

Sullivan County, Pennsylvana and hundreds of other counties are rated low in their ability to deal with and bounce back from disasters like those that warming will cause. The University of South Carolina calculates a Social Vulnerability Index for every U.S. county. It's based on the strong effects that things like family structure, language barriers, vehicle availability, medical disabilities, healthcare access and other variables strongly have on a locality's preparation for and response to disasters.[4]

Yourtown, USA

To check the Social Vulnerability Index of your county, go to http://svi.cdc.gov/.

In Jefferson County, Alabama, mandated repairs to its municipal sewer system became the costs that broke the camel's back, pushing the county into bankruptcy in 2011.[5]

Other dangers from warming are equally place-centered. Certain counties will suffer from river and lake flooding caused by the increasingly intense rainstorms predicted. Others will be untouched. Growing asthma, declining job markets, and the rising use of energy for air conditioning will affect some regions but not others. And, at the extreme, as agriculture shifts northward, as towns are abandoned for lack of water, and as industries like coal gradually die out, in some places communities will be abandoned or destroyed, people scattered, and centuries-old ways of life snuffed out.

Even before warming is considered, the costs and dangers in American towns already vary widely—some wildly. Hartford's drought risk is rated "Negligible." Sacramento's is "Extreme." The average cost per patient day in a South Dakota hospital was recently $985. In Washington State it was $2,696. Amarillo, Texas doesn't really have enough wind to generate low-cost electricity, but Port Angeles, Washington has plenty. In Hoboken, New Jersey most daily needs are within walking distance. Residents of Jackson, Mississippi are car-dependent.[6]

All this says that, by moving to a more climate-proof location, many Americans will be able to safeguard their personal finances in the face of warming. And how nice that when you move, you can more comfortably choose to downsize, because you are leaving your neighbors' expectations, and some of your own, behind. A big benefit of combining a lifestyle change with a move is that you have fewer friends and acquaintances who expect an explanation of your newfound frugality. And if you choose a town with a significantly lower cost of living, you may not have to cut down on your toys and pleasures. For instance, a home just like that lovely million-dollar house in Brookline, Massachusetts is available in Shaker Heights, Ohio for $300,000.

The risks in your hometown, and others

Scientists, journalists, and data-gatherers love to rate and rank the places we live, and many of these ratings and rankings reflect the threats discussed in this book. There are many little-known sources for these measurements, indicators, and other hard data about localities across America. In previous chapters, I have pointed out in the Yourtown, USA boxes how you can easily find information about predicted risks to your personal finances town by town.

By using these sources, you are only a click away from maps, tables and lists detailing which localities are threatened by drought, flooding, energy needs, sea-level rise, job losses, allergen increases, and various other disasters or deterioration caused by warming.

Checking each of these sources separately can get to be a big project, especially if you're looking at multiple localities. That's why I have compiled them into town-by-town reports, available free online. (See sample on page vi, above.) Savvy Families' *Where-to-Live Indicators* include measures for many of the strengths and weaknesses discussed in this book. The data sources are the same as those in the Yourtown boxes in this book, but I've tried to make them easier to locate, navigate and understand. For instance, we have labeled them all by town name and Zip Code so you don't need to know your county or the name of your hospital service area or nearest weather station. We have also made it easy to compare multiple towns at a glance.

What data are available?

After studying the many warming-related indicators mentioned in this book, you will be able to answer questions about important attributes of some towns better than most people, perhaps even better than the town's planners or its chambers of commerce. Here are a few questions we have covered.

- What is a town's long-term risk of drought?

- What is the projected risk of flooding in a community and the local level of disaster preparedness?

- If driving is to become more expensive, does a town provide useful local transit, easy walking or safe biking around town?

- With fiscal pressures expected to rise dramatically, does a town have a low tax burden and good borrowing capacity? Do local roads, bridges and other infrastructure already need heavy funding for delayed maintenance? Is the community out of danger but nonetheless likely to be taxed to help neighbors in the same coastal county or state?

- What is the area's need for heating or cooling? How much sunlight is available for solar energy? How much wind for wind power? How favorable is the local utility's net metering policy?

- When it comes to health factors, how good is the local air quality now? What increase in pollen is expected from warming? If warming does affect your family's health, what are the local healthcare costs? How does your community rate for quality of healthcare?

- Does a town have local sources and distribution of food? Does it own its water source?

There are other rankings and reports.

Bert Sperling's *Best Places* website (bestplaces.net) and his book, *Cities Ranked and Rated*, are useful sources of data on 400 cities in the U.S. and Canada. Although they write about more popular topics such as America's manliest, most romantic or most playful cities, you can also find information about drought risk, cost of living, teleworking, hurricane risk, respiratory problems, and other geographic rankings relevant to the challenges discussed in this book. There is no indication, however, that these ratings yet take into account any future changes from warming.

The best estimates of a community's costs and risks from warming may come from local sources. Some American towns have already started thinking about how they can not only protect themselves but also how they can track improvements in their preparations and declines in their risks.

Jamaica Plain, Massachusetts, Boston's inner suburb discussed above, has an unusually active group working to improve their town's resistance to "expected shocks of oil shortages, climate change, and economic downturns." To help understand what constitutes "community resilience," they drew up a list of measurements. The JP Resiliency Measures Project tracked local food production, public transportation usage, local employment, rent/home prices, water supply, measures of local networking, and other metrics. The thought-provoking report that resulted was distributed through the community for discussion and feedback. If you are thinking about ways your town can protect itself from the consequences of warming, this report is a great place to start.[7]

Some broader organizations offer research and commentary on resilience and vulnerability. Although mostly focused on crisis management for such disasters as hurricanes, oil spills and pandemics, the Community and Regional Resilience Institute is creating specific measures of the resilience of a city's transportation, energy, health service, and communications systems. The institute also highlights some non-physical vulnerabilities, such as growing bureaucracies, unrealistic expectations of governments, and community leadership. Their website, resilientus.org/category/blog-archives, though somewhat ideological, is thought-provoking for those interested in measuring community risks and preparedness.

Some localities are sleepers.

When we look around for a safer hometown, we should consider areas that might not otherwise catch our eye—or the eye of a *Best Cities* writer. James Howard Kunstler, author of *The Long Emergency*, has a region in mind: "My corner of upstate New York includes both the upper Hudson and the Mohawk River valleys. They were dotted by what used to be a series of vibrant manufacturing towns—places like Hudson Falls, Fort Edward, Glens Falls, Amsterdam, Johnstown, also small cities such as Troy, Schenectady, Utica, and Syracuse. . . Today these places stand gutted, half-vacant, idle, hopeless. Paradoxically, they may be the kinds of places that have the strongest chance of surviving the challenges of the Long Emergency. . . These towns are located on rivers and, in the case of the Hudson Valley, with its rugged topography, they have many potential sites for local hydropower generation. They are surrounded by good farmland that remains substantially intact. The downtowns and old residential neighborhoods are laid out along the lines of pre-cheap oil urbanism: compact, dense, and walkable."[8]

Paul and Hazel Delcourt, authors of *Living Well in the Age of Global Warming*, started early thinking about where to live as America gets hotter. One of their stories: a neighbor on the Upper Peninsula in Michigan who arrived amid the regional heat wave of 1999: "As he slowly eased into a lawn chair, intentionally half-submerged at the cooling water's edge, our friend described the scene he had left behind in Grand Rapids . . . 'a hundred and five in the shade. It's never been this hot before!' With the cooling breeze off Lake Michigan, a fast expanse of shimmering blue water steps away, our neighbor felt he had finally arrived at a safe site."[9]

Some of us may look abroad. Lots of Americans move overseas at retirement or earlier in their lives. Costa Rica, Ecuador, Panama, and many other countries contain U.S. expatriate retirement communities, interesting surroundings, fast Skype connections, and dramatically lower costs. *International Living* magazine's website is a good place to get the flavor and facts surrounding this lifestyle. But moving outside the U.S. may not climate-proof your life as securely as finding a safer hometown here in North America, particularly if you move to a warm country to escape the effects of warming.

North America! Many who begin to look north within the U.S. for a cooler safer hometown will wonder, why stop at the border? Giles Slade, who has written *American Exodus*, the best book about North American migrations, past and imminent, says "Canada, of course, is the obvious destination for Americans suffering from the increasingly "hot, flat and crowded" conditions of the United States in the 21st century."[10]

Climate-proofing is not the only consideration.

The *Where-To-Live Indicators* do not, of course, tell the whole story. In fact, they give a fairly narrow view, concentrating on the predicted threats to the economic, social and physical aspects of American hometowns. Indicators rate hometowns primarily on how likely they are to insulate residents from the costs and dangers from warming over the coming decades. They don't measure the other attractions of a place.

There are plenty of sources out there to help you find "America's Ten Best Places To Retire" or "Great Places To Raise Children." Criteria for these usually focus on amenities (art galleries, sports and recreation facilities), children's resources (schools, activities), ambiance (riverside bike paths, sidewalk cafes), and history and heritage (beautiful buildings, historic districts). But don't expect them to include many of the factors discussed in this book.

How accurate are predictive data?

I have not been able to test the forecasting value of the *Where-To-Live Indicators*. Does using them raise your chances of actually dodging the future costs of warming? We won't know for years. Looking for parallels, the experience of 'business climate' indexes created for various localities is not encouraging. These claim they predict the economic growth potential of a state or city and its businesses. Included are measures of fiscal policy, competitiveness, business taxes, labor market, "economic freedom," and others. In practice they explain only about 5 percent of actual growth! Basically useless as predictors, they're used mostly as political philosophy weapons or business recruiting tools.[11] I suggest you use Savvy Families *Where-To-Live Indicators* as just what we call them— indicators of places you should evaluate much more deeply on your own.

In any research you do about places to live, be prepared for a lot of rumor, propaganda, and misinformation as municipalities, real estate agents and others with local vested interests make their marketing pitch.

Trade-offs can be paralyzing.

Even with reliable indicators, trying to evaluate your town for the many risks discussed in this book can become a cumbersome research project. The job really gets big when you start to evaluate multiple places you might choose to go.

There are so many trade-offs. A town safe from flooding may be threatened by drought. One where the pollen count is not expected to rise may sit on top of a threatened aquifer. A city whose taxpayers face expensive construction costs may offer lots of related jobs. And of course a town that looks good by the criteria discussed in this book may turn you off for other reasons.

The online *Where-To-Live Indicators* let you compare any number of towns on a grid showing the grades for each indicator. If you are seriously looking for a more climate-proof hometown, I suggest you create your own more extensive checklist or spreadsheet to collect and compare information.

A good place to live: one last indicator

Beyond those discussed so far, there's one more effect of warming that could have serious implications for your personal finances—maybe serious enough to influence your choice of hometown. That's conflict.

The financial strains building up within state, municipal and family budgets lay bare natural clashes of interests. Most of these conflicts will be local, will cause extra expense and unpleasantness, and could be overcome by compromise and an understanding that "We're all in this together."

It makes sense to look for a town that's likely to face its problems with a spirit of cooperation. What indicators suggest a town will use teamwork and mutual understanding to find solutions to protect the finances of our family and our neighbors? First, let's examine a few likely causes of conflict and their effects on our personal finances.

There are different reasons to push and shove.

One combative issue is the question of who pays—them or us? Recently eleven towns in Northeast Ohio Regional Sewer District sued to prevent the district from imposing a stormwater fee. The fee was levied on homeowners for stormwater control (reducing erosion and sediment, removing debris, cleaning ditches, preventing overflows, restoring wetlands, fixing dams, and upgrading sewers). The eleven litigants, facing fewer problems than the average town, didn't want to pay to fix their neighbors' difficulties.[12]

In 2013 eleven counties in a section of Colorado considered whether to secede and form a 51st state, partly because the state imposed higher renewable energy standards on electricity cooperatives to help reduce CO_2 emissions. For some voters, the added costs to their electricity bills caused pain; for others the idea of mandatory renewable energy caused outrage. The result: five counties voted to pick up and leave the state.[13]

Don't be deceived by such headlines as: "Poll finds U.S. support for adaptation to climate change." Read more closely. Yes, polls find that over 80 percent of Americans favor policies to help coastal areas increase their defenses against rising waters and extreme weather. But what those people actually support are no-cost-to-me measures, like stricter building codes and bans on construction in risky areas, policies that place the burden on the threatened communities. When asked about spending public money to build expensive sea walls or replenish beaches, two-thirds said no, arguing that the families and businesses that lie in harm's way should bear the costs of defending themselves against the effects of warming.[14]

Another issue will be who gets access to natural resources. Laws in Texas give control of underground water to the water conservation district above it. But private properties near Wimberley, Texas, which don't fall into a district, are drawing and selling huge amounts of water to nearby Austin suburbs. The rural families in the district, ranchers and farmers, could run dry as the aquifer under their land is pumped down by their out-of-district neighbors.[15]

Halfway through 2014, Sacramento, with heavy water restrictions, had received more than 6,000 reports from residents calling its water-waste hotline. That's up by a factor of 20 from the previous year. Many reports were about surreptitious watering of lawns and gardens at night. Encouraging residents to tattle on their neighbors was a decision the city made when water warnings and restrictions had little effect by themselves.[16]

It's not just water. Who knew there'd be a tug-of-war over a truckload of sand? But sand has become more and more valued for its use in protecting oceanfront property. Shoreside residents in Salisbury, Massachusetts have asked their town to spend $300,000 on sand and other components to protect their homes, encountering growing pushback from other residents.[17]

As more people begin to move, there's the question of who got here first. Today about 7 million Americans move across state boundaries each year (mostly south).[18] That's around 2 percent of us. But what will happen as the effects of warming begin to trash some communities while making others seem safe by comparison? How many of us will try to move (mostly north)? Five percent? Ten percent after a few disasters?

Migration may be the best thing that could happen to the economy of destination towns, as it brings new housing construction, revives neighborhoods, expands local businesses and adds taxpayers. But current residents might also react to unfamiliar faces and accents, the transformation of the familiar landscape, also the shifts in voter blocks and power groups. Rapid change, especially when caused by someone we can blame, has always been a spur to conflict. It's easy to imagine long-time residents and new arrivals at each other's throats over dozens of issues from zoning and growth controls to taxes, schools and other services. Beyond legal and political issues are attitudes towards things like historic preservation, property rights, aesthetics, treatment of natural resources, and loyalty to the community.[19]

When power bases shift rapidly, it's not always democracy that triumphs. As Kunstler observes in *The Long Emergency,* "People desperate for legitimate authority to assist them in organizing their survival will probably accept more starkly hierarchical social relations in general and disdain democracy as a waste of effort. They will be easily led and easily pushed around. . . Do not expect more social equality—expect much less."[20]

And then there's the potential for strife if it becomes obvious that the burdens from warming are falling disproportionately on the poor. With inequality and social justice issues increasingly highlighted in the news, it's reasonable to worry that the effects of warming could add fuel to the discontent and violence. We will examine why the poor are so vulnerable in Chapter 12 on attitudes.

Conflict adds two big costs.

Conflict is stress, and stress can create animosity—even violence—in the community. Sixty separate studies have looked at local violent crime and domestic violence, and more broadly at civil war, expulsion of minorities, political instability, cross-border conflicts, and the collapse of order. They find strong evidence that climatic events increase human conflict. Overall for each unit of change in climate toward warmer temperatures or more extreme rainfall, interpersonal violence rises 4 percent and intergroup conflict rises 14 percent.[21]

The second cost comes in the form of the decision paralysis that conflict can cause. How will a town protect its water source, reduce flooding, improve schools, or expand low-cost transportation if conflicting interests cannot reach a compromise?

Find a cooperative community.

When you look at a new home, you ask yourself, am I going to be happy with the number of bedrooms, the quality of local schools, and the attractiveness of the neighborhood? Add another question: are my fellow residents likely to agree with one other, and with me, on how to protect our community against the costs of warming?

Communities are more likely to cooperate, avoiding or resolving conflicts, if they have already shown a help-thy-neighbor attitude, have enough natural resources to go around, are unlikely to see heavy in-migration, and have fairly homogeneous income levels. Here are a few other indicators to look for.

Is there broad citizen involvement early? Long Beach Island, on the coast of New Jersey, is densely developed with small houses. The Environmental Protection Agency examined the costs of gradually raising the island by adding sand to beaches and building lots, engineering a slow retreat that would eventually connect the island with the mainland by building a levee to surround it.

Beyond the engineering challenges, the EPA looked at the potential for strife and court challenges around the necessary decisions. "Picture the public hearings that might take place on the island," they reported. Different residents would benefit from different solutions. Most would prefer the low-tax solution, best or not. Outside pressure groups such as "federal agencies that encourage risky development, state agencies that discourage it, residents who feel entitled to subsidized coastal protection, and environmentalists insensitive to constitutional property rights" could all be expected to join the fray.[22]

Based on this study, the EPA concluded that it's best to establish citizens' committees early, and get them to mull the what-if and how-do-we questions well in advance. This can be key to dealing amicably with the inevitable choices that so many communities across the country will face, thanks to the effects of warming.

Is local government non-politicized? When considering a hometown, there is one source of information that tracks conflict closely. That's the local news media. A few hours spent in the local library or online searching through local papers, radio stations, local cable news, or websites like Patch.com should give you a sense of how well, or not, the community has handled divisive issues, collisions of interest, and long-standing antagonisms.[23] On what issues has the local government "agreed" or been "divided?" What measures had "strong support" or passed "unanimously?" Have local leaders been finding balanced solutions? Or do they consider, as in Washington, that compromise is a form of treason?

Agreement and cooperation, of course, don't tell the whole story. In many localities, politicians work well together because they all share the same ideology. However, for some groups, that common ideology is unanimously *against* taking actions and finding money to protect residents against the effects of warming.

Yourtown, USA

If you want to know what percentage of a locality's residents believe warming is taking place, how much it worries them, and what policies they support to slow warming, you can see estimates by county at http://environment.yale.edu/poe/v2014/. Remember, however, that these data are about actions to slow warming, and tell us little about how easily county residents will agree on protecting against its costs.

Yourtown, USA

If you believe that living in a heavily Democratic or Republican district might be an important factor in reducing conflict, you can check the red-blue voting record of any U.S. county. The sources change election by election. The 2012 Presidential election results are at http://www.theguardian.com/news/datablog/2012/nov/07/us-2012-election-county-results-download#data. Again these red-blue distinctions at the local level tell us little about the how a particular town will actually deal with the underlying conflicts discussed above. Presumably the 2016 election results will be available on the same website.

Is conflict resolution taught in local schools? When we recall that most of the impacts from warming will fall on our children and grandchildren, it makes sense to find out how well their hometown is preparing them and their peers to cooperate in protecting one another. The principles of conflict resolution are proven and, in many places, taught with positive results, particularly if the purpose of the local program goes beyond simple violence-avoidance. A comprehensive conflict-resolution course in the local school curriculum, after-school program, or church and civic organization is one indicator that the town's future leaders may be able to cooperate, resolve disputes, and mediate among the divergent interests that warming will likely create.

For most of us, place matters a lot. Our hometown provides a team to root for, a sense of belonging, familiar surroundings, and a world of memories. With nearby family, old friends, and work colleagues, our social and business networks give us security and pleasure. But we need to see that these surroundings are changing. Thousands of dollars per year are at risk, and warming is raising those stakes. Choosing your hometown carefully and keeping your options to move open are probably the epitome of no-regrets thinking and the tactics most likely to help you dodge the growing costs from warming.

Footnotes for this chapter, **Where-To-Live Indicators** *for all American towns, and other tools and resources are available at savvyfamilies.org/climateproof, as well as the author's updates, your comments, and other useful information.*

PART III

DEVELOP A CLIMATE-PROOF MINDSET

12 ADOPT ATTITUDES THAT PROTECT YOU

Charles Darwin said, "It's not the strongest of the species that survives, nor the most intelligent that survives. It is the one that is the most adaptable to change."

Adaptation is hard. Even if we've taken no-regrets measures to deal with the dangers we face, the costs and disruptions from warming will likely take a psychological toll on us. Maintaining our family's morale can be as important as maintaining our earnings and assets, especially for those of us who have already been watching ourselves "come down in the world" because of stagnant wages and declining economic mobility over the past two decades.

Attitudes that will help maintain our self-esteem and good spirits over the coming years may be different from those we've held before. They may also be different from what's promoted today by leaders in politics, religion, and the media.

Here are eight ways of thinking about your life and your personal finances that seem especially useful. But be warned: even if you've been nodding your head in agreement over other portions of this book, in this chapter you might find yourself saying, "Whoa, we're not going to have to go that far!" or "You're talking about changing the real me, my personality, my character. No way!" A natural reaction today, perhaps, but you may want to revisit this chapter if the burdens from warming do begin to sap your family's spirits.

Think mobile.

Being willing to move means your family can be where incomes are growing, costs are under control, and your family's health and lifestyle can be sustained. And as changes flow across America, it may take multiple moves over several years or decades to maintain a family's comfort and safety.

We Don't Move The Way We Used To.

It used to be that families in the U.S., more than in other countries, would pick up and relocate for better prospects. Immigrants arrived in big coastal cities and moved inland to find or start communities. Later generations spread across America looking for better land and opportunity. With mechanization, young people moved off the farms. Kids went away to college and stayed. Sixty years ago, 20 percent of Americans moved each year. During the Great Recession only 11 percent of us moved, an all-time low.[1]

Many trends depress mobility. Our homeowner equity has almost recovered from the 2008 debacle, but it's still lower than that in the last century. And it's always harder to move when our mortgage is big, almost impossible if it exceeds our property value—a problem that remains for more than 8 percent of U.S. homeowners.[2]

The American population is now older, and older people tend to move less. Many of us are in two-income families, so a move means finding two new jobs, not one.

For decades, industrial jobs were in relatively few locations—Pittsburgh, Detroit, and a few dozen other cities. People moved to them. Today most jobs are service jobs, with the same retailers, food chains, financial businesses, and other services found in most towns. There's less need to move to find a particular industry, and today fewer localized industries boom and draw job seekers from other parts of the country.

It could also be, as commentators note and polls confirm, that we've lost some of that American self-confidence and faith in our free-market, anyone-can-get-ahead, land-of-opportunity, rags-to-riches confidence that sent so many in previous generations off to seek their fortune.[3]

Whatever the reasons fewer Americans have been pulling up stakes over the past decades, that could change. The effects of warming are today bringing the new problems we've discussed to many hometowns, giving us new reasons to move.

Evading these problems will be a lot easier if we and our family are not just logistically and financially free to relocate, but also emotionally okay with the idea.

Lower the emotional barriers to moving.

Relocating today is easier than it was for families in the 1960s. The logistics are well developed, with real estate agents, moving companies, rental trucks and self-storage in abundance. Getting comfortable with the idea of pulling up stakes is the hard part.

Many things immobilize us: love of place, relatives, family history, a job, a circle of friends. And anxiety about making new friends, walking into a new school, or settling into a new job can be daunting. Then, think about rooting for the Cowboys when you're now surrounded by Vikings fans!

If your mind votes to relocate but your emotions are against it, here are a few tips that may make a decision to pick up and move easier.

Try to see a new place through its residents' eyes. Connecting with locals can give you a much more intimate and favorable picture of a potential hometown. It's worth reconnecting with old friends who live there and asking about their community. When my wife and I were thinking of moving 20 years ago, we researched half a dozen small cities, then spent a day or two in each, driving and walking around, checking out the attractions, getting a feel for the place. When we got down the list to Newport, Rhode Island, I recalled that a high school friend lived there. I found him in the phone book, and Dale and his wife Joanne drove us around their city for two hours. Not only did they point out the sights, they talked about people they'd introduce us to, an organization they thought we'd enjoy, the character of several neighborhoods they recommended, and their experience with the schools in the area. Need I say where we decided to settle?

Participate in some activities. Find the town's online calendar and choose a few events to attend: maybe a city council meeting if you're interested in municipal issues; perhaps a school play, an exhibit opening, a religious service, or a ball game. Choose an event where you can get talking with people. Spending time with locals, even superficially, can make that unknown town seem friendlier, or it can turn a community that looks good on paper into a no-thank-you. Take your children to meet kids in another town for a short while—through a volunteer project, for instance, or a church or school exchange, a tournament, even a short vacation. Kids have strong instincts about a place and, with a little exposure, they may be able to see the good or the bad awaiting the family more clearly than you can.

Rent in transition. This can be a particularly useful tactic in connection with a move. Say you've made the decision to leave town, but the moment is not right. Selling your house, putting some stuff into storage, and moving into a nearby rental for a year or two could be a good idea. You can sell while the market is high, yet stay in the neighborhood until there's a better moment to move away from friends, schools, jobs, and other ties or obligations. You are mobile! And uncoupling house-selling frustrations from the anxieties of moving to a new town could make life a lot less stressful.

Or, let's say you've decided on your new hometown. Choosing a rental as your first home there lets you get to know the area and the people, the schools and the city management, while watching for the right house to come on the market, all before you commit. If, while renting, you discover you've made a mistake and really should be somewhere else—well, you haven't made the plunge into home ownership.

Many of us can't move easily—or at all. Obligations trap us in place. Bey they logistical or psychological barriers, we just can't get past them. But we can do our children or grandchildren a big favor by helping them grow comfortable with the idea of relocating when the right time comes.

Give your children a love of travel and some familiarity with other parts of the country early in life. This can help them feel more comfortable later on about moving. Exchange programs, faraway summer camps, family vacations in other states, college in a different region of the country, vacation visits to college friends—these experiences can make it easier for your kids to be at ease with choosing a hometown that has lower costs and risks from warming.

Encouraging your children to pick up portable skills (see Chapter 10 on jobs) can also help them be mobile. Ski instructors, fishermen and dock workers have fewer choices of where they can live than pharmacists, retail store managers, or water engineers.

Where we live is going to matter a lot more tomorrow than it did yesterday. By helping your family to think and feel mobile, you can help them be in the right place at the right time. Remember that mobility doesn't necessarily mean moving your home or your job. It means *being able* to move when it benefits you.

Think simple.

Okay—"think simple" is really a euphemism for "think small."

A shrewd relocation may keep our finances out of real decline, but it isn't likely to fully protect us from rising costs and stagnant incomes. No matter where we live, that squeeze will make many of our lives smaller financially. Americans already sense this. In August 2014, 76 percent of adults lacked confidence that their children's generation would have a better life than they did. That's an all-time high.[4]

If warming is going to bring you higher expenses, flat incomes, and reduced asset values, learning to live more simply—and to enjoy doing so—can make those changes more palatable.

It's hard to downsize.

For most of us, our standard of living defines us—to others and to ourselves. A simpler life will seem like coming down in the world, falling behind the Joneses. The damage to our self-esteem can be very great indeed.

What is downsizing? We're not talking about turning down the thermostat in winter, buying the $18 wine instead of the $30 one, or driving the RV across town to fill up with gas that's 20 cents cheaper. For most of us, there's only so far we can go by pinching pennies. To really protect our family budget, we'll need serious downsizing—a smaller home, simpler pleasures, fewer toys. We'll need reductions in how much energy we use, how often we drive, how often we stay away from home. We'll need to increase how long we keep our clothing and furniture. We may even start making a gradual shift toward new friends whose attitudes reflect ours.

For most of us, to dodge serious cost increases or an income squeeze while building up some savings would mean an uncomfortable decline in lifestyle. If we look at the numbers, then close our eyes and listen carefully, we may hear ourselves saying, "Sorry, Honey, we're going to have to stop doing this," or "How are we going to tell the kids they can't have that?"

Or maybe we hear, "I want a divorce." After all, friction over finances is the second most common reason for couples splitting. So, if outside forces are going to erode our lifestyle, it makes sense to simplify and downsize in advance. On purpose. With a lot of discussion and planning.

There are ways to be happy with less.

So how can we adapt as Darwin suggests? How do we leave behind our level of spending today and create a simpler, more frugal life that protects us against the future costs and risks from warming—but at the same time protects us from disappointed children, gossiping neighbors, and the expectations we've built up for ourselves?[5]

First of all, there's plenty of evidence that less can be more.[6] One school of thought tells us that a society's measures of success bear little relationship to actual wellbeing. Take Gross Domestic Product per capita, for example, and remember that every dollar America spends to clean up oil spills, treat preventable illness, and fight crime improves the nation's GDP. The bigger the spills, the more extensive the epidemic, and the higher the crime rate, the bigger our share of a 'growth economy.'

There are alternative achievement measures. In 2012, the state of Vermont created a Genuine Progress Indicator, based on the Gross Happiness Index conceived by the King of Bhutan. By 2011 the economic elements within Vermont's GPI had risen but the social elements had declined, suggesting that prosperity does not necessarily mean happiness. Vermont's GHI is reduced by the cost of crime, pollution abatement, commuting, and lost leisure time, for instance, while being increased by the value of housework, volunteer work, and higher education.[7]

At the personal level there is the same disconnect between accepted measures of economic success and real personal wellbeing. Above a certain level, more income doesn't necessarily produce more happiness. Memorable happy experiences, which may cost little, provide bigger and longer rewards than nice possessions. Other proven boosters include working less, doing something creative, sleeping more, making and keeping friendships, being grateful, random acts of kindness, smiling at others, reducing TV and the Internet, communicating more without gossip, and connecting strongly with family and community. Exploration, exercise, conscious savoring of current and past activities, supporting a cause, and having more time and freedom of choice are worth any amount of money.

Want a push in that direction? A classic primer on balancing the satisfaction and fulfillment you get from money with that which you get from other sources is *Your Money or your Life*, by Vicki Robin and Joe Dominguez. They stress that "Waste lies not in the number of possessions but in the failure to enjoy them" and go on to provide tips for nurturing attitudes that help with this dilemma.[8]

The earlier your children can learn from your example that happiness need not depend heavily on money, the more likely they will hold that view all their lives. And that lesson can be the biggest legacy you give as they move into the warming world that awaits them.

There are hundreds of books about how to be happy. Virtually all concentrate on changing our values and attitudes, not increasing our spending. So how, in the face of pressures on our personal finances from warming, can we begin to switch our mental standard of living from measures of wealth toward measures of happiness? Here are a few ways to smooth this transition.

Simplify for a cause.

Any serious shift in attitude toward frugality can be easier for us, and feel more credible, if linked to a higher purpose. There are many groups that see simplicity as an important goal in life.

Environmentalists, Minimalists, Homesteaders—there are plenty of movements like these to tag along with or at least take inspiration from. Have a look at the Slow Living, Intentional Living, Downshifting, and Small House movements as well. These can serve two purposes: helping you make ends meet amid rising costs, and supplying different values that you and your family can be proud of. They provide both the rationale and the encouraging friends to help you make the money-saving adjustments you've decided are needed.

Whether or not you link thrift to a specific cause or attitude, there are many other rationales for living more simply. The library is filled with books, and the calendar with workshops, about how simpler living is the key to a higher quality of life, greater self-realization, better health, sexier relationships, reduced clutter, and many other contributors to happiness. These resources can help you make a virtue of necessity and develop pride in a more modest, less financially risky life.

Justify simplicity within your faith.

Your spiritual world may provide inspiration for a simpler life. Scripture would seem to provide strong incentives. The Old Testament says, "How meaningless to think that wealth brings true happiness!" The New Testament tells us, "It is easier for a camel to go through the eye of a needle than for someone who is rich to enter the kingdom of God." And how about "The love of money is the root of all evil?" Finding scripture in all faiths that encourage a change in attitude is easy, but finding a congregation that actually encourages you is probably more effective.

Keep your budget in front of you.

Of course, if you are to benefit from downsizing, you need to actually downsize. Here's where setting and monitoring a budget helps. (Remember? I gave you a budget form back in Chapter 1.) You can track what you are really paying for your chosen way of life, not just some vague gotta-keep-the-expenses-down resolution. Tracking money that flows out of our pockets, checking accounts, and credit cards is time-consuming and boring. It can be a source of conflict with other family members as well. But operating without monitoring a budget is like crossing an ocean without tracking your progress on a chart. You can miss your destination by a lot.

Of course, your goal may not be simply to cut spending. You may want to free up money to drill a new well, build a flood berm, trade to a more economical car, install solar panels, help create a local garden, upgrade your air conditioning, or start a new business that will benefit from the warming trend. All of these are investments that should create future savings and help climate-proof your finances down the road.

Keeping a family budget visible has another purpose. No one wants to be called "cheap," especially by family members, and a good budget helps justify changes in spending. It can show your spouse or children in dollars and cents how cutting back on one family activity is helping to expand others in the future.

Need more tips on tackling the psychological complexities of dowsizing or moving? Read *Rightsizing Your Life: Simplifying Your Surroundings While Keeping What Matters Most* by my friend and college classmate Ciji Ware.[9] It's a cornucopia of practical actions, with an emphasis on ways to reach consensus within the family.

Think provident.

In the face of warming, it will make sense to build a bigger financial cushion than what we're planning today. The joy of a bigger savings account can go a long way to offsetting the pain of a smaller checking balance. Such savings will give us the flexibility to take actions we can't now anticipate, whether it's fixing storm damage, relocating, changing careers, or buying new protective technologies not yet invented.

For most of us, increasing our savings means cutting back on everyday expenses. Not easy. But if you have shifted your attitude toward saving more, there are ways to help you keep that resolution.

Put more money out of temptation.

Automatic payroll transfers to a savings or investment account keep those funds from flowing through your hands in the first place. There are fewer good ways, however, to discourage you from raiding your savings. You could buy bank certificates of deposit (CDs), with up to five-year terms. But the low penalties for early withdrawal provide little discipline, and these days they offer pretty poor interest rates.

Electing to take a 10-year mortgage instead of a 15- or 30-year one forces you to pay down the principal faster, thus building value more quickly in that big piggy bank—your home. As an added benefit, you save tens of thousands of dollars in interest over the life of the loan. Drawbacks include the need to sell or refinance to get at those savings if you really need them, and the risk that putting money into a home may end up having a lower return even than CDs, as we discussed in Chapter 8 on home values.

Tax-deferred savings with an IRA or 401k may not be the way to save for the costs of warming either. They have the advantage of discouraging you from raiding your saving, with a serious penalty if you withdraw money before age 59½. But if your purpose is to save more to help deal with the future costs discussed in this book, those costs may arrive before your retirement.

Another self-enforced savings method, mentioned in Chapter 9 on investments but worth repeating here, is to buy now something you have decided you're going to need anyway in the future—land for a vegetable garden, bicycles, a well, a high-mileage car, prepaid tuition, solar panels or a wind turbine, a pay-down of student debt, or prepaid long-term care insurance. You will be parking your savings in something which, unlike the investment markets, you know will reduce your future costs or have other long-term value to you.

For college expenses, there are 529 Plans that let you invest savings for a child's education at certain colleges, appreciating free of federal taxes. Some states add additional tax benefits. If, however, your child decides to use the money for something other than higher education, the money in a 529 account will be taxed and penalized.

An accountant or financial advisor may be able to steer you to other tax-advantaged means of saving for future needs.

Think multi-generational.

Given the decades over which the effects of warming are predicted to erode Americans' personal finances, some really big costs are slowly building up for coming generations to deal with. As the bumper sticker says, "We don't inherit the earth from our ancestors; we borrow it from our children." While the future will be painful for many young Americans, that need not be completely true for younger generations in *your* family.

Reduce our kids' expenses.

There are two big cost-control gifts we can give our children. The first is being comfortable with frugality. It will be a lot easier for them to live within their income and regularly add to their savings if they grow up conscious that their parents are doing the same thing.

We may think "Okay, I could certainly cut back on my own stuff, but I can't do that to the kids. They have expectations, their peers have expectations, it would be cruel to deprive them." And it's certainly true about young people's recent expectations. A study monitoring materialism in high-school seniors from 1976 to 2007 found that desire for lots of money has increased markedly since the mid-1970s, while willingness to work hard to earn it has decreased. Recent updates confirm this trend.[10]

Yet higher spending is not the expectation of all children, and it needn't be of yours. Beyond teaching them to budget and track expenses, you could be doing them a big favor by helping them learn how to comfortably postpone gratification. You've heard of the Marshmallow Experiment, in which four-year-old children were tested to see if they could resist eating a marshmallow placed in front of them in expectation of soon getting two marshmallows. The researchers tracked the subjects for decades and found that those who were able to postpone gratification at age four did better later in life on measures of money, career and health.[11]

A second way we can help our kids keep their future costs under control is to guide their decisions about where to live and work. As we have seen, location will matter more and more, and they should know how to compare localities with an eye to the future costs of warming.

Improve our kids' instincts.
If we can help the children of our town grow up understanding the cause and effect of warming and its consequences, they will have leverage in creating a safer community. It won't be easy; teaching our children respect for nature and an intuitive belief that a healthy environment is critical to their health and prosperity can be difficult in today's human-dominated world. But you can get help from nature itself.

A study of city kids by Cornell researchers found that children who, before age 11, have opportunities to play in the wild *without adult supervision*—maybe on a camping vacation or in the woods or fields near their house—develop a stronger sense of environmental ethics. Children who encounter nature only in structured settings with adults—in Scouts or on hunting or fishing trips—do not learn the same respect for the environment. These latter children—the majority of us—grow up with an arrogance toward nature and an overconfidence in our ability to control it that has helped cause our current predicament.[12] You might think about organizing regular safe but unsupervised nature experiences for the young children in your life.

Think sharing.

You don't have to see a marina full of unused boats or pass three homeowners riding big mowers in the same street to ask yourself why more people don't share expensive items they use only an hour a week or a few weeks a year. Thanks to the power of the Internet, a revolution in renting, sharing, swapping, and bartering is growing around us. In addition to saving by not needing to own as much stuff, those who use these peer-to-peer services also avoid most of the transaction costs that once made them unattractive. Not only are fees lower today, trustworthiness is seldom an issue.

We covered some of the car- and ride-sharing opportunities in Chapter 5 on transportation. Let's look at a few other ideas. Under the fancy names of 'the sharing economy' or 'collaborative consumption,' these practices are simply reinventions of age-old services, but web technology has greatly reduced the challenge of finding a trustworthy partner.

You can share your everyday stuff.

The University Heights Tool Library in Buffalo, New York holds 9 hedge-trimmers, pruners and loppers; 3 mowers; 10 shovels, spades and a post hole digger; 6 rakes and a wheelbarrow; 30 screwdrivers; 13 paint brushes and rollers; plus dozens of other tools ranging from a spackle trowel to a table saw. The library not only loans these tools to local residents; it organizes youth projects and clean-ups in the neighborhood, saving money and building community.[13]

With almost 800 members and over 35,000 hours exchanged since 2008, the Onion River Exchange in Montpelier serves 28 towns in central Vermont. It's one of the most successful time banks in the U.S. Some services are fairly mundane: a ride to the airport, help cleaning the house, moving a mattress (including truck and driver), or house painting. Some need knowledge, such as baking bread, knitting mittens, computer research, tuning a bike. And some are skilled, like therapeutic massage, herbal medicine, custom art. Members report that, as well as being able to purchase services at a cost of their own time, not their dollars, they value the opportunity to make new friends and enjoy a sense of purpose, belonging and community.[14]

You might even share housing.

We've all heard of Airbnb, which lets people with a space to rent short-term, from a couch to a vacation home, list it on the web for travelers to find. Airbnb handles payments and tries to assure security by vetting both travelers and hosts.

But what about sharing housing on a permanent basis? Cohousing schemes have been around forever. The 20-acre, 77-home village called East Lake Commons, four miles from downtown Atlanta, was designed from the start to help residents keep energy costs down, grow some of their own food, reduce transportation needs, and share costs, skills and time among neighbors. In addition to owned and rental homes, it has a large common house with space for classes, offices, children's play, TV and movies, woodworking, exercise, and overnight guests. A playing field and children's playground surround the common house. Members share values such as simplicity, sustainability, resource sharing, diversity, and community involvement.[15]

Dozens of these cohousing groups—known also as intentional living communities or ecovillages—are scattered across the country. Some are in city centers, others in rural locations. With the right facilities, a low-risk location, and of course like-minded members, cohousing could achieve a high level of cost-sharing and other collaborations that would be a bulwark against the financial costs of warming.[16]

Many other groups do not live together but cooperate to save money, lead simpler lives and cope with the same type of economic and social problems that warming is causing. We have seen how families can share solar panels, backyard gardens, and rainwater storage.

How about shared investments?

Local investment clubs share information and intuition and reduce fees through pooled trades. While stock picking has always been more of a hobby than a proven way to outperform the market, there are some new ways to exchange financial help among individuals.

Microlending, or collecting capital from small donors and lending very small amounts to very small businesses, is best known for its rapid spread in poor countries. The practice has spread, and today there are a dozen or more firms that do the same in the U.S. Anyone needing a few thousand dollars to expand a home, craft, or specialty business, should do a search for *"microlending US"*. You will find Accion, Grameen America, Kiva Zip, and others aimed at small businesses. A company called Prosper offers personal loans, connecting people who want a loan with individual investors who can choose to make a specific loan based on information supplied by the borrower. Prosper sets the rate and manages the transaction and receipt of monthly payments.

National groups promote local sharing.

Becoming a Transition Town is one of the best ways to quickly stimulate ideas and benefit from others' experience when trying to climate-proof your community. The movement started in the U.K. and is based on its founder Rob Hopkins' contention that "life with dramatically lower energy consumption is inevitable, and that it's better to plan for it than to be taken by surprise." Over a thousand Transition Towns operate in 40+ countries, with 150 or so at various stages of maturity in the U.S. Activities vary but often include methods of sharing goods and services.[17]

As Joel Magnuson describes them in his book *The Approaching Great Transformation: Toward a Liveable Post Carbon Economy*, the set of guidelines that Hopkins and other transitioneers have developed are called 'ingredients' because they're "more like a recipe from which each community can choose to use all or part, depending on their circumstances or culture."[18]

Other groups, tracked in LocalCircles.org, perform many of the functions of Transition Towns but are often neighborhood- or church-centered rather than town-wide. Called Resilience Circles, these groups focus more on financial and job security for members, often working closely to help fellow members streamline their spending, borrow small amounts of money, and network for a job. Each circle can have a different emphasis and set of cooperative activities. Like Transition Towns, they provide plenty of help for organizing such a group in your community.[19]

Sharing information and a sense of community can be as important as sharing things. Chuck Collins, founder of the Jamaica Plain New Economy Transition--the 95th Transition Town in the U.S.—also helped create the concept of Resilience Circles. In Jamaica Plain, his groups have gone on to start a community garden, a winter farmer's market, and a local-business incubation project in their bilingual community. They hold an annual State of Our Neighborhood forum, involving hundreds of neighbors, city officials, city councilors and state legislators.[20]

There's an extensive network of similar types of communities in America, but most of us are oblivious to it. Anand Giridharadas, a close observer of financial pressures and the misery they can cause in America, writes, "American poverty is darkened by loneliness; poverty in so many poor countries I've visited is brightened by community. Helping people find other people to lean on—not just government offerings of health care and food stamps, tax cuts and charter schools—seems essential to making this American dream work."[21]

Connecting takes initiative.

Getting started at sharing, renting, swapping and bartering can be uncomfortable for those of us more used to self-reliance, maybe even pride ourselves on it. It will be a whole lot easier to shift our values toward collaborative consumption—and simpler pleasures, frugality and a deliberate lack of ostentation—if we spend time with others who think that way. You might be surprised at the number of people near you who feel as you do and are already involved in various sharing activities.

The best way to identify these people is probably to ask around. If they exist in your town, they won't be hard to find. But certain established groups are easy to connect with. One way is to look on Meetup.com and search for some of these keywords: *simplicity, Transition Towns, collaborative consumption, urban homesteading, cohousing,* and *minimalists.* Of course, not all of these groups will match your needs or temperament, but the search results will give you ideas about where you might start networking. Spending time with these people can help you refine your own thinking and collect referrals to more simpatico groups.

Beyond action organizations, such as Transition Towns and Resilience Circles, there are think tanks such as the Post Carbon Institute, the Center for the New American Dream, and the Institute for Policy Studies that provide ideas and encouragement in coping with many of the risks and costs discussed in this book.

Decentralize, distribute services.
Many neighborhoods and towns are working to share big investments and costs. In previous chapters we've seen groups and towns that are moving away from reliance on existing services and coming together to build and share their own systems for creating, distributing and conserving energy or food. Municipal wind and solar, micro-generators, town farms, community gardens, and farmers' markets can increase reliability and, in some cases, reduce costs.

Many of these cooperative efforts are fostered and monitored by the Institute for Local Self-Reliance, which works to promote innovative local banking, broadband, energy, and waste management programs. They also promote policies to strengthen local independent businesses. Their website is a cornucopia of examples and model systems, with examples of laws and regulations in practice across the country.

You may be thinking this all sounds like a hippie commune, a subculture that kids in their 20s try, then grow out of. The sharing economy may have its roots in those times but, if you look around, you'll notice that those roots are being widely replanted throughout our adult world.

Think self-reliant.

In contrast to sharing risks, resources and costs, there is another approach to the rising problems of food, water, electricity, and other needs. That's a spirit of independence and self-sufficiency.

Training sessions on skills from beekeeping to emergency dentistry, growing healthy vegetables to wood-stove cooking are given at the Sustainable Preparedness Expo, which "attracts attendees from all walks of life, from responsible citizens concerned about disasters to hard-core preppers; from sustainable-living enthusiasts to survivalists."[22] Similar events around the country help families that want to "reclaim noble independence in an unstable world."

In Pasadena, California, the Dervais family were seeking a "home-based, family-centered and self-sufficient way of life" when they started their homestead back in the 1980s. They produce over 6,000 pounds of organic food each year. The surprise is they do it on a tenth of an acre and live on a city street. The Dervais were pioneers in the movement of urban homesteading, growing vegetables and raising chickens, making bread and jam, beer and cheese, using alternative energy sources, and using self-sufficiency skills, all the while remaining close to neighbors and biking to a good job. Today they offer workshops and products for other urban homesteaders.[23]

In my family, one of our sons has for the last five years lived half of each year aboard a small sailboat. His solar panels make him largely self-reliant, with no real need for a marina berth to get electricity. His supply of water can last a fortnight, his diesel fuel and bottled gas a few months. The Internet, via his laptop and cell phone, allows him to make a good living. In ports and anchorages from Marathon Key, Florida to Halifax, Nova Scotia, he has shown up for work in a virtual world at the same national organization nine-to-five every day.

Similar self-sufficient arrangements provide some protections against the threats from warming, but most of us haven't the farm or the boat—let alone the farming or boating skills, the loner temperament, or the thirst for independence— needed to make these lifestyles work long-term.

The concept of self-reliance need not, however, be limited to individual families. As we discussed above, towns, neighborhoods, cohousing units, coops, and other groups can work together to achieve self-sufficiency in various aspects of their lives. Communal agriculture, solar or wind power, shared transportation, and other initiatives can lower the group's dependence on authorities. A fusion of self-reliance with community seems to me to hold more benefits and fewer risks than a one-family or small-group survivalist approach.

Think compassionate.

Compassionate? You may be thinking, "Wait, this book preaches selfishness more than compassion. It talks about self-reliance and argues for a devil-take-the-hindmost approach to choosing a safe place to live."

It's true, the facts about warming do suggest that families who take their own initiatives stand to benefit. But that isn't the whole story. Compassion, charity, and altruism toward those most affected will be among the most important protective steps we can take, for two big reasons.

Do it for their sake.

Tens of millions of people across our country, through no fault of their own, are likely to become miserable, ill, impoverished or worse as the impacts of warming grow. Many of these people are poor already.

There are many reasons why the effects of warming will hurt the poor in America more than others.

1. The poor cannot move as easily as their better-off neighbors and may be caught in less safe, less healthy, poorly-funded hometowns.

2. Getting more skills, finding a climate-proof job, and pushing our communities to take protective steps are not easy for those who do not have a living income, some savings, some higher education, or a history of initiative.

3. Many of the actions called for in this book will be needed in one neighborhood but not in the next. This means it will be natural and proper for planners, decision-makers and bureaucrats to decide which localities should get relief or protections. But this opportunity to discriminate based on need creates an opportunity to discriminate based on other factors, including how influential, affluent, or 'deserving' a community is. This works against the poor, and especially if the wealthy in America increase their resistance to higher taxes, and some continue to insist that "the poor have it easy."[24]

4. If federal, state and local governments are forced to increase their spending on protections against warming, that may further crowd out social service expenditures, many of which go to help the poor.

More than ever, compassion, private charity, and direct assistance from you as a neighbor, your community groups and your church will be needed to help the poor cope with warming.

Do it for your sake.

In helping to protect those potential casualties of warming, you will be protecting your own happiness and wellbeing. Your biggest reasons for helping the most vulnerable are the same as other compassionate acts:

• the satisfactions of having helped the less fortunate and of having taught your children to do the same

• the camaraderie of group projects, and

- not least of all, some relief from guilt.

From a more selfish point of view, by reducing the miseries of those damaged by warming, you will decrease the economic pain, the potential conflict, and the deterioration of your town that becomes inevitable when a portion of the community is in distress, perhaps in revolt.

There's a wide charitable streak in the average American.

A huge number of Americans already think compassionately: sixty percent of us give money to charities, and 34 percent of us volunteer regularly.[25] Existing attitudes of Americans toward the misery of others give us a big head start in making the moral commitments that are needed. Financially, individual donors in America contribute over $200 billion to charity every year, three times as much as all corporations, foundations and bequests together.[26] We perform plenty of quiet acts of kindness for less fortunate people we may not even know; we organize bake sales and car washes; we volunteer at tens of thousands of organizations across the country and around the world— all to alleviate the pain of others. U.S. church attendance is significantly higher than in other industrialized countries and moral issues play a stronger part in our politics.[27] A huge number of Americans vote their moral preferences, even when those clearly contradict their self-interest.[28]

Do it as part of a new, evolving morality.

There is an ethical development likely to have great impact that has yet to surface in America: the acceptance of individual and group responsibility for the effects of warming the atmosphere. In his book *Reason in the Dark*, Dale Jamieson says. "Our everyday morality is flummoxed, silent, or incorrect" regarding the consequences of warming. "Our current rationale tells us it's not our fault; our actions weren't reckless or intentional; we didn't know we were hurting anyone; there were no laws against what we were doing; and anyway, we were thousands of miles away from the scene of the damage."[29]

This is changing. Courts of law, religious thinkers, parents and other arbiters of what is right and wrong seem ready to conclude that warming the earth or failing to protect others from warming-related damage is a crime, a sin, or a moral no-no. In Chapter 10 on jobs, we saw the growth of court cases that are beginning to make this claim. And as the claims grow among those damaged by warming, as well as their sympathizers, it's not hard to imagine one or more accountability movements, with marches on Washington, civil disobedience, even violence.

Established faiths are beginning to see the effects of warming as moral issues. Recent statements from the world's religions affirm "climate change as a moral issue" (Black Church) and call for "new habits as well as new values" (Buddhism) to "safeguard the moral conditions for an authentic human ecology" (Catholicism), and set "a dharmic duty for each of us to do our part in ensuring that we have a functioning, abundant, and bountiful planet" (Hinduism). "An urgent and radical reappraisal is called for" (Islam). "Social justice, sustainable abundance, a healthy Earth, and spiritual fulfillment are inseparable" (Judaism). Finally, "We cannot claim to love God while abusing what belongs to Christ by right of creation, redemption and inheritance" (Evangelicals).[30]

This issue is developing faster internationally than within America. Increasingly urgent and persuasive calls from overseas charities are likely as drought, flooding, famine, and migrations produce misery for millions abroad. One of the main purposes of international climate meetings has been to deal with claims by poor countries for assistance and reparations from America and other rich countries most responsible for warming's causes. Our country may resist moral and legal obligations for damage caused by warming, but the nightly news could sensitize enough Americans to the devastation and pain abroad to the point where the obligation to help becomes an accepted moral attitude among us.

Another moral challenge is growing.

There is an invisible crowd of victims of warming. These are people whose lives and land are being trashed by our activities but whose plight we don't see in the news. We don't set up charities for them or send aid. They aren't close by or influential; and the media never show us their faces. They are America's and the world's grandchildren, the people of the future, the coming generations of humans born decades from now into the hotter and more difficult world we are creating for them.

Our concept of guilt across time is vague at best. It's not surprising we don't concern ourselves much with the safety and happiness of these coming generations. Our technology and political systems were, by and large, improving the world's future, so why change our actions? And it was true: recent generations have had better lives than their forebears.

But that may no longer be true. And if not, it presents an unfamiliar, uncomfortable moral challenge. Today's self-deception about what is needed to dampen future risks, our selfishness in not doing so, and our tiny and reluctant steps to build protections add up to a moral failure—the sort of moral failure worthy of a Save the Grandchildren Foundation.

Think vigilant.

None of us can feel the warming trend on a day-to-day basis. It's obscured by its slowness, disguised among cooler spells, camouflaged within the variability of our weather. Likewise, it will be hard to notice the slow damage from warming to our family finances and lifestyle, hidden as it will be among the income fluctuations, creeping costs, and natural variability of our investments that we consider a normal life. Few of us will be jolted by a sinkhole, a forest fire, or a collapsing bridge. Water shortages may grow to seem normal, and actual food shortages will be few. Our rising medical bills may be attributed to aging; bond issues will postpone tax increases; and an increase in poverty can be ascribed to other causes. No doubt we will hear high-profile news stories about the more dramatic impacts of warming. But they will be in another town. We'll say, "Thank goodness we're not affected!"

But we must be clear-eyed enough to understand that we in fact *are affected*. Over the coming years, the spending of the average American family will be constrained, our incomes more precarious, and our assets eroded. We must learn to notice what's happening to us.

Don't be the frog. Most Americans are going to wait while the water heats up in their particular pot. Blinded by the steam, stoic or angry, they will allow their suffering to grow. Others with different attitudes will see their financial future more clearly and jump to a more climate-proof life.

*Footnotes for this chapter, **Where-To-Live Indicators** for all American towns, and other tools and resources are available at savvyfamilies.org/climateproof, as well as the author's updates, your comments, and other useful information.*

13 GET STARTED NOW!

Most of this book is about what we can do to protect our finances from the effects of warming. But there is also the question of *when*. Let's look first at why we might want to choose "now" or "soon."

Think no-regrets.

If we are to someday look back on today's threats and feel we did all we could to protect our family and community, we need to look ahead now with clear eyes. Warming is unlike most other threats we've faced, and we're likely to find that our everyday instincts and responses cloud or distort our view.

Earlier I suggested you do an assessment of your family's financial strengths and weaknesses in the face of warming. I now suggest you examine your convictions and rationalizations, distractions and extenuations. Here's a checklist of thoughts about the effects of warming that endanger your personal finances most. The more clearly you recognize them, the sooner you'll be able to take ro-regrets actions.

❏ This too will pass.
The past 70 years have provided no painful disruptions like the Great Depression or the World Wars, only little bumps in the road. We've learned to hang in there; progress always got back on track. But warming is different. It won't pass. It's already dialed-in, and it will take decades to stop, centuries to reverse.

❏ It won't happen to me.
After reading this book, you should be able to see which damaging effects of warming are heading your way and which you may be able to dodge. Where you live, what you do for a living, your level of savings, and other factors may protect you. But at least some of the costs and disruptions from warming are definitely going to happen to you.

❏ It doesn't seem that scary.

Because the horrors of a gruesome terrorist attack are easy to imagine, Americans are willing to spend trillions to resist that possible menace. It's much harder to envision slow-developing pain such as tax hikes, asthma, erosion of municipal services, or aborted career paths. Most of us don't apply to warming the same belt-and-suspenders, take-no-risks attitude we apply to terrorism, even though the risks from warming are far greater, closer to home, and more certain.

And many of us, no matter how concerned we may be about the growing costs of warming, are enjoying the warming. A Duke/NYU study finds that 80% of Americans today live in counties that are experiencing more pleasant weather than they did four decades ago—for the moment.[1]

❏ Nobody else is making a move.

If we begin to act differently, we draw attention to ourselves. Taking steps in response to warming isn't a bandwagon, so we can't climb on just yet. But the warming of America, affecting us and our family directly and locally, will give us many opportunities to be individualistic and independent thinkers, to exercise our self-reliance and free choice. We should seize these. We should help to build that bandwagon.

❏ But what can one person do?

"No snowflake in an avalanche ever feels responsible," said Voltaire. It's hard for individuals to see what difference they can make and why they should sacrifice when others won't.

Yes, it will take millions of us acting politically to build some of the defenses we need. But it takes only a few concerned folks to start creating protections for our neighborhood—and only one or two to start taking protective steps within our home and family.

❏ Someone's to blame.

Conspiracy theories can be satisfying and lift responsibility from our shoulders. But even if we choose someone to blame for our costs and pain from warming, that mustn't keep us from doing what we can to protect ourselves against the results of their dastardly actions.

❑ America always finds a way. We will again.

Experience tells us we can cope better than most nations with major threats. We've long relied on our democracy, free market, natural resources, inventiveness, geographic isolation, and common sense to keep us safe from big crises. Think of all the environmental challenges America has tackled. DDT, smog, acid rain, and tobacco smoking lead the list.

But those were threats that, for the most part, we Americans created ourselves. They were local, and a law or two could stop them. Warming is different. The atmosphere, the seas, today's energy and food markets—these are worldwide, largely out of our nation's control.

❑ The free market will protect us.

If you compare the strengths of free-market capitalism with our needs in the face of warming, it's not a good match. To prevent further warming, we'd be asking businesses to replace a profitable energy industry with a new untried one, to trash the value of some big corporate assets such as oil fields, and to cease sales of some popular products.

If we are to adjust to warming, we'll need businesses to do things like forfeit real estate development on big watershed tracts, consider fresh water supplies to be a public good instead of a private asset, artificially boost certain household costs so families are pushed to change generations-old habits, finance major construction projects whose only payback is public cost avoidance, and ease the burdens of warming on the poor.

Where are the incentives? What business leaders wouldn't throw up their hands? There's nothing wrong with the free market. It's just doing its thing.

❑ They'll invent something.

Wouldn't it be wonderful to wake up to a new technology that dramatically slows warming or diverts its effects! Hopeful stuff, but there are many reasons to be skeptical. For one thing, most corporate R&D is not aimed at protecting us from the effects of warming, but at perpetuating the causes of warming. The technological breakthrough of fracking, for example, produces cheap methane, which we can now afford to burn more of, thus actually accelerating warming.

For another, while corporate R&D is focused mostly on near-term profit boosts, federal research programs that focus on long-term improvements have been repeatedly cut and underfunded for years, slowing the advent of both new research and new products.[2]

❑ We can't afford to make changes today. Maybe tomorrow.

It costs money to build defenses, to change careers, to move house, to improve skills. And, as we've seen, the great majority of us don't have the savings needed to make these investments. We need to wait, right?

But wait for what? The last two decades have produced no income growth for most of us. And we're not likely to have more in the bank when the current business cycle begins to head back down again. Even if for good reasons you decide it's the wrong moment for your family to streamline your lifestyle or make other big changes, the sooner you make plans to do so, the easier it will be when you feel the time has arrived.

❑ Democracy will protect us.

How likely are our elected officials to protect Americans' family finances from the costs of warming? So far Congress and the State Houses show little signs of creating public works programs to safeguard communities, regulations to stop dangerous behavior, or funds for protective measures, disaster planning, mass education campaigns, or government research that can help us deal with the consequences of warming.[3] Those signs that say *Emergency Evacuation Route - for information tune to 870 am* are okay, but voters and taxpayers are entitled to programs that help prevent the emergency in the first place.

Shouldn't we be writing our Senator, getting out the vote, and supporting mass movements for the policies we want? If recent research is correct, that won't work. A big study found that the wishes of economic elites and organized groups representing businesses correlate pretty well with whether or not a piece of U.S. legislation is passed. But the wishes of individual Americans, even when we are almost unanimous, show no correlation at all![4]

We're lucky that many effective steps to dodge the threats of warming can be taken within the family and the local community without relying on American democracy.

❑ We can adapt.

We may be tempted to take reassurance from the popular words 'adaptation' and 'sustainability.' We mustn't. They imply that we'll be able to 'sustain' our current lifestyle at its current level if only we make a few 'adaptations.' That's unlikely. The word 'resilience' is even more misleading if it says to us that we can absorb blows from warming and bounce back fully.

❑ There's always hope.

Yes, but hope can freeze us. If we're in danger of heart disease, the hope that genetic therapy will someday cure us may tempt us to continue avoiding exercise and healthy food. And our hopes that technology will someday save us from the impacts of warming are encouraged by those who have a big stake in the status quo, such as energy companies. After all, the longer consumers wait in hope, the longer we use their products. One example: "clean coal" is publicized heavily by those who benefit from our continued use of coal. To most independent engineers that technology seems a near impossibility.

Rescue by the cavalry is a persistent American image, but so is self-reliance. It makes no sense to wait for inventors, lawmakers, and corporate decision-makers across the country to shield our families from the consequences of warming when we can already take dozens of personal and local steps ourselves.

Did you put a check mark against any of the thoughts you recognized as yours? If you can resist these and other excuses for procrastinating or rationalizing inaction, you are more likely to strengthen your personal finances and start building the flexibility and resilience that will maintain wellbeing and happiness. Best of all, you may someday hear a child of yours say, "You know, I was thinking about all those irritating family decisions you made when I was growing up. Thanks for making them. I'm much better off today than a lot of my friends from back then."

If, like most of us, you need an encouraging vision of the future to help with morale while you take painful decisions and difficult actions, I suggest reading Jonathon Porritt's *The World We Made*. This fictional work looks back from 2050 at both the disastrous effects of warming—

economic, social and physical—over the 35 years, and the difficult steps the world took to adapt and in many ways improve.[5]

Getting ahead of the crowd

Our everyday clichés reinforce the importance of good timing. We get in on the ground floor or we miss the bus. An idea takes off or the bubble bursts. Fisheries collapse, markets crash, videos go viral, dominoes fall, and situations spiral out of control.

If you're thinking about taking a no-regrets approach to climate-proofing your family budget, assets and happiness, getting the timing right can be key. What you do is important; *when* you do it can be even more so.

Maybe we have plenty of time. But relatively small, often unpredictable, causes can trigger big irreversible effects. The moment when change becomes inevitable and starts to accelerate is called a "tipping point.[6]" It can signal a big opportunity, or it can slam a door in our face. Taking advantage of tipping points means you are not just ahead of the curve— you're ahead of the crowd.

Nature has tipping points.

Most climate scientists believe the planet has already passed one major tipping point. The concentration of atmospheric CO_2, they tell us, has increased to a level that guarantees warming of at least 2°C, probably 4°C, even if CO_2 emissions stopped today.

The best-known cause of sea-level rise is the melting of polar snowpack and glaciers. And ice melt may have passed the tipping point and is now unstoppable. The ice stored on top of Greenland alone, if it all melted, could raise the world's oceans 24 feet. Water from the West Antarctic ice sheet could eventually add another 14 feet.

The melting is accelerating. As more of the Arctic Ocean becomes ice-free in the summer, the water absorbs more heat from sunlight than the ice did. In Greenland, melting exposes darker snow that now absorbs more heat than the lighter snow did.[7]

A big potential driver of warming is the Arctic's permafrost, frozen soil that covers almost a quarter of the Northern Hemisphere across Canada, Alaska, Greenland and Siberia. Permafrost contains large amounts of methane only a few degrees below its freezing point. As permafrost reaches the thawing point, the methane, a powerful cause of atmospheric warming, is released—another big tipping point.

In addition, billions of tons of methane hydrates, a crystal similar to ice, lie just below the surface on the East Siberian Arctic shelf. As the Arctic Ocean warms, this huge store of methane could start to seep steadily, maybe even belch, into the atmosphere.[8]

Public consciousness has tipping points.
Another humongous storm like Katrina or Sandy could tip coastal residents' awareness of the costs of warming over the edge. This could be true too for those far from the actual storm.

When it comes to our jobs and investments, the legal world could suddenly change the impacts of warming on private and corporate assets. How would America change if the courts start deciding . . .

- . . . that companies, national or local, can be sued for their impact on warming?

- . . . that local governments can greatly expand eminent domain and property rights of owners can be forcefully purchased to benefit the neighborhood?

- . . . that governments actually own and regulate all water sources (including groundwater and rainwater)?

- . . . that towns can hold back free-market initiatives to protect their residents?

- . . . or that stricter fiduciary responsibilities apply to your investment managers in the face of climate risks?

These far-reaching decisions would likely change public sentiment about a lot of things, not least the value of homes and corporate securities.

Still another arena in which a sea change in thought is possible is organized religion. Many American churches believe that God promised "that the earth and those living on it will never again be destroyed by a flood." There are 52 million American Baptists, and in 2007 their leaders urged them to reject government-mandated reductions in greenhouse gas emissions.[9] Yet polls show that many Baptists are increasingly worried about the effects of warming, and that sections of the church are doing something about it.[10] A shift in the pronouncements from leaders of the Baptists and other large religious groups could suddenly create millions of American families suddenly determined to protect themselves.

Government policy-making has tipping points.

As this book goes to press, Senator Sheldon Whitehouse (D. RI) has given his 143rd weekly "Time To Wake Up" speech on the floor of the U.S. Senate, elucidating the reasons why Congress needs to take action to protect the nation against warming. Despite his fact-filled exhortations, which began in 2012, Congress has done virtually nothing about warming. But that will change—and when it does, it could happen suddenly.

At the state and municipal level, similar actions may be quickly recognized as necessary. Corroding gas pipes under city streets are a source of atmospheric methane. You can look at a map of Boston dotted with hundreds of symbols indicating the locations of gas leaks. Not all U.S. cities have dilapidated gas pipes, but most have not been mapped and measured.[11] Boston's aging gas lines could trigger a financial tipping point when the city's gas utility is forced, with or without a court order, to ask residents for the billions it will cost to fix the problem.

It will pay to be on the lookout for policy turning points—from the federal level down to our counties and towns. On the positive side, newly supported government-sponsored infrastructure projects could create local jobs for those in the right location and vocation. New co-op laws could brighten the prospect for investing or working locally. On the negative, sudden shifts in government policy are likely to create new taxes and land-use restrictions which, while beneficial, could slow economic expansion locally and exacerbate political conflict.

Markets have tipping points.

It takes decades for nature and years for public opinion and government policies to change. But prices, especially asset prices, can change overnight.

Home prices in particular can boom or bust quickly. As John Englander puts it in his eye-opening book about sea-level rise, *High Tide on Main Street: Rising Sea Level and the Coming Coastal Crisis*, property values will likely go underwater long before the property does.[12] The opposite can happen in safer towns.

This is not the first time a more appealing climate has sparked a real estate boom. In the winter of 1922, the developers of Miami Beach placed a sign in New York's Times Square and other northern locations that said: "It's June in Miami." The resulting rush saw six million people arrive in Florida over the next three years, bidding up property prices.[13]

Around 1974, a residential real estate boom began in California. One-story bungalows in Santa Monica rose ten times in price between 1974 and 1980.[14]

Magazine articles that could influence home values have already begun appearing in consumer media titled:

- "Spared by Climate Change: The 10 best cities to ride out hot times"
- "Screwed by Climate Change: 10 cities that will be hardest hit"
- "14 U.S. Cities that Could Disappear over The Next Century, Thanks to Global Warming"

Many areas are cruising for a fall and may wake up to these threats suddenly. An expanding drought, another big hurricane somewhere, lots of municipal bankruptcies, or a craze among talking heads in the media could fill certain lawns with "Price Reduced" signs. Locally, new municipal leadership, a tax referendum, a prolonged water cut, publication of a pessimistic city plan and, of course, a damaging storm can turn a spotlight on the town, spooking homeowners and investors into a stampede to sell.

These changes in value could apply not just to a home's location, but also to its size or type. If family budgets shrink while heating, cooling, property taxes and other costs rise, 1,800-square-foot houses may be in great demand while 4,000-square-footers languish. South-facing or well-insulated homes could command a premium. Small yards may become more in demand than beautiful lawns.

If we're thinking of moving but miss the tipping point in a quickly changing market, we can lose two ways: first, we get less if we sell, and second, the homes that would suit us in a safer city may jump in price. As we saw in Chapter 8 on our housing costs, it could pay to sell early in an endangered town, even if you choose to stay on in a rental.

Stock market values are harder to perceive. There will be tipping points in investment values, but the average investor is unlikely to see them coming, even if the media is beginning to focus on the effects of warming on stock prices. Recent articles include:

- "Investing in Climate Change: A 25-stock index"
- "Global Warming—What's the Long-Term Investment Strategy?"
- "7 Industries at Greatest Risk from Climate Change"
- "Hot Planet, Hot Stocks"
- "Meet the companies that are Going to Get Rich from Global Warming"

Again, unlike property and job markets, your chances to get the timing right on buying and selling securities, no matter how much research you do, are low. There's plenty of evidence that investors, whether amateur or professional, who try to time the market systematically miss the up elevator. As John Bogle, founder of the Vanguard Group of mutual funds, tells us, "After nearly 50 years in this business, I do not know of anybody who has done it successfully and consistently."[15]

Your own tipping points

It would be ideal to take actions to dodge the various costs of warming, each at the optimal moment just before it arrives or begins to accelerate. You'd avoid bad stuff, make your move just as good stuff is happening, and not waste time or money by being early or late.

But even if you could see those ideal moments coming, your timing will be driven mostly by your own circumstances and needs. This means there's another set of tipping points you need to anticipate: the ones within your family. Here are some ideas for using those tipping points to make better decisions now, ahead of the crowd.

Do the no-brainers now.

We've looked at many steps you can take right away to start climate-proofing your finances: reducing food waste, changing the family's diet, doing more trips on foot or bike, trading in an expensive-to-run car, fixing the bad drainage around your house, volunteering or getting involved with a social enterprise.

When it comes to taking steps to dodge the effects of climate change, most of America is following Mark Twain's tongue-in-cheek policy, "Never put off 'til tomorrow what you can do the day after tomorrow." But you can use the easy actions as a chance to break a procrastination habit, and also as a chance to demonstrate to your family, friends and neighbors—and yourself—that you really intend to climate-proof your life. It alerts everyone and gives them time to prepare for more and bigger changes ahead.

Move ahead with research and planning.

Many actions can be taken soon, without much effort or money, but which will need a little advance research. Even if you don't actually move for years, or ever, you can start learning about whether your hometown is where you and, more importantly, your children will want to be long-term. If what you find worries you, you can start looking at alternative places to live. With that research behind you, you're in a position to make quicker decisions if the time comes.

Whether or not you are considering a move, before you start a backyard vegetable garden, you may need to test the soil, then enrich it with compost or install pipes and barrels to collect rainwater. If you have decided to steer your career toward a climate-proof industry, you may need to start enhancing your skills at night classes.

There can be value in getting to know people with whom you might someday share rides, a neighborhood garden, flood protections, a bank of solar panels. Cultivating neighborhood friendships and finding mentors can take time. If you find or start a chapter of Transition Towns or Resilience Circles, you'll have a proven way to start building these community connections.

And if you are thinking that your town, not just your home, will need some climate-proofing—protecting the watershed, adjusting land-use policies, armoring historic sites, or reclaiming wastewater—then start pushing local government now. It's never too early to start recruiting and electing leaders who will be attuned to safeguarding your town from the physical and financial threats of warming.

Start now on actions with long lead times.
You may be considering climate-proofing actions that take a long time to bear fruit, such as building up your savings, or gradually interesting your kids in skills and careers likely to have strong future demand.

If so, you will want to recall President Kennedy's story about "the great French Marshal Lyautey, who once asked his gardener to plant a tree. The gardener objected that the tree was slow-growing and would not reach maturity for a hundred years. The Marshal replied, "In that case, there is no time to lose; plant it this afternoon."[16]

Start working on emotional barriers.
Stresses from dealing with the effects of warming won't be up there with the death of a spouse, divorce, or time in jail. But a serious effort to redesign your family's life in the face of warming could involve other items high on the list of Life's Most Stressful Events. These include changes to your financial state and living conditions, plus your personal habits, place of residence, social activities, and school.[17]

Not every family can make the adjustments without pain, conflict and resentment. Keeping up with the Joneses is an American right on a par with the pursuit of happiness. Taking pleasure in a higher savings rate, less expensive vacations and pastimes, and more community service will seem perverse to many. The emotional steps needed to help other family members free themselves from 20th-century spending and lifestyle habits, and create a new self-image and renewed morale can take months, maybe years.

But if you begin now imagining, exploring, and discussing your options, that moment when your family is ready to change location or lifestyle or attitude will come sooner—and less painfully. You'll be psychologically ready to shift your lives away from danger.

Some big decisions are best made in stages.
Moving can be done in stages—for instance, by selling your home first, renting in the old or new town for a while, and then buying in a new

location. The same may be true for a career change if, on a consulting or part-time basis, you can stay in your old field or start in a new one. This approach may reduce not only the logistical complexities and the emotional impact of abrupt change, but also the risk of making hard-to-reverse decisions.

Sometimes, not often, it's best to wait.

Installing solar may have a big payback for you—eventually—but a better payback could be in holding off until photovoltaic efficiency goes higher and prices lower, or until your area reaches grid-parity. That doesn't mean, however, that it's too early to find or create a south-facing location for your eventual solar panels, start saving the money to buy them, and lobby the utility commission to improve net-metering policies.

Likewise, starting a backyard or neighborhood garden can wait if supermarket prices are still far below our costs for seed, tools and labor. But getting started with soil-testing and rainwater catchment planning need not wait.

Beyond simply finding specific parts of a project that can benefit from an early start, there are advantages to starting the decision-making process now, even if we know we won't act on some of those decisions until later. Most of us need time to simply get used to a new idea. Emotionally, a big decision can get easier the longer we, and our family, live with the idea, imagining the consequences and dealing with our second thoughts before we finally make the call.

Look ahead for natural family decision points.

It's impossible to identify many external turning points, such as the top or bottom of the stock market or the next big flood. But you can more easily predict the moments in your family's life when it will be easier to make big changes. You may regret missing such moments.

Take relocating, for instance. You can examine your multi-year calendar for moving dates. Many of these will be milestones: kids changing schools, the arrival of a child, an expected promotion or inheritance, the empty nest, retirement, the need for a bigger or smaller home, etc. At those moments you have more elbow room to take new and important decisions about your hometown, your career, your level of savings.

Think competitively.

There is a devil-take-the-hindmost aspect to relocating, shifting careers, and making some of the other changes discussed in this book. Today most of the country is in ignorance of what's ahead. A few years from now, the light bulb may have gone on and the rush to safety started in earnest.

Even without a nudge from warming, eleven thousand Americans will be turning 65 every day for the next 15 years. They will be elbowing each other in the race to downsize and make other lifestyle changes.[18] In particular, their need for smaller homes, low-cost hometowns, and greater savings may compete with yours as you take steps to climate-proof your life.

Is this your family?

Close your eyes and see your life a decade from now. Your family is not hostage to energy costs because you live where your cooling bills are low and you can walk or bike to most daily destinations. Your town and state finances are in good shape, your leaders clued-in and proactive. The water supply is plentiful, and the air is healthy. Flooding is unlikely. Your local farmers, plus a neighbor's vegetable garden in which you share the work on weekends, provide a measure of security to your food supply.

Your lifestyle is fun, but more modest than before. Sure, photos of your former big house and lawn, the faraway vacations, and the toys in the old garage make you nostalgic. It took some painful attitude adjustments, but downsizing freed up money to deal comfortably with the higher costs of daily life plus some increasingly needed charity. You have a high savings rate, and your nest egg is now much bigger than you planned ten years ago. You sleep well, knowing your no-regrets decisions have created a buffer against further pressures and a cushion to pass on to the next generation in your family, which will face even stronger pressures.

You and your children have made heads-up decisions to acquire skills and choose careers in resilient sectors of the economy. Your savings are invested in relatively climate-proof securities, including some local enterprises. Your home has increased in price, thanks to the press of newcomers from other parts of the country who belatedly saw what you saw earlier and have been arriving steadily. Your highly saleable home gives you the mobility to make further moves if circumstances change. To a large extent, your family has managed to dodge the financial penalties from warming, while other families have paid heavily for their lack of initiative.

If this is, in fact, your family ten years from now, it's likely that today you're seeing America's future more clearly than others and are contemplating some important, perhaps painful, decisions: where to live, what to study, and how to be happy with a simpler life and more frugal pleasures. You have to a large measure climate-proofed your personal finances, your lifestyle and your family's future. Congratulations!

ACKNOWLEDGMENTS

Writing a book about warming and personal finances has turned out to be just one more step in my extended education on both subjects. My teachers have included Beth Milham, Tina Dolan, Chris Wilhite, and Fred Unger, who were among those who originally helped me tune in to the effects of warming.

It was John Deputy who woke me to the idea that most of us are, by nature, far less interested in saving the planet than in saving our wallets, and thus more likely to take steps against the effects of warming than against its causes.

As I began to promote this notion, Tony Cook helped persuade me that a book might reach more people than my blog or the energy-related educational events I was organizing.

I thank these thoughtful friends for teaching me some of the fundamentals that underpin *Climate-Proof*.

Of course, my ideas, attitudes and choice of examples have been heavily influenced by the many original thinkers whom I quote throughout the book, as well as by friends including Earl Leiken, Gael and Bill Crimmins, and Tom Gallagher.

I am particularly grateful to my editor, Chris Murray, for helping turn my blog-style screed into a more structured and balanced book. Other readers whose editorial suggestions I have valued include Samantha Briggs, Greg Gunther, Ben Stookey, Diane Young and Crane Stookey.

My many-talented friend Joanna Detz designed the book's interior and cover. Todd Larson did the proofreading.

The information sources I have used are *Climate-Proof*'s foundations. The book's footnotes, along with the *Where-to-Live Indicators* and other materials, are available online at SavvyFamilies.org/climateproof. I'm grateful for the work done by database manager Leigh Ann Smith, site designer Joanna Detz, and web developers Brad Mering and Katie Lovelace to create the Savvy Families site.

If you find yourself smelling hot muffins as you read, it's because I wrote the book in the Empire Tea & Coffee Shop, sitting near the ovens. I was often reminded as I wrote that the young people who took such good care of me there—including Chelsea, Bridget, Kat, Josh, Jen, Bianca, Sarah, Jade and others—are the generation whose lives will be most strongly shaped by the effects of warming and by the tactics they choose in protecting themselves.

Finally, I want to give a special thank-you hug to my strongest supporter and most thorough and sensitive editor, my wife Hilary.

THE AUTHOR

Like many Americans, David Stookey has become concerned by the dangers from global warming. Unlike most, however, David has been looking beyond cracking soil and higher tides to the everyday impacts of warming on the average American's wallet and way of life. Which expenses in the family budget are likely to balloon? Where should we live to enjoy better economic protection from climate change? What are the right skills for a changing workplace?

Stookey's appreciation of the natural world has been molded by climbing expeditions in the Sierra Nevada, a solo transatlantic sailing race, a year living off the grid, and other experiences he treasures.

His interest in financial issues comes from a career as vice-president at an economic forecasting firm, CEO of high-tech venture-backed companies, business consultant in Tehran, debt collector in Hong Kong, and a Harvard MBA.

The urge to find and spread useful how-to's led him to become a business-literacy trainer to Fortune 500 firms, an editor and publisher of a magazine on a little-known sport, and a compiler of an online directory serving another sport.

In his community, his efforts to help neighbors protect themselves from the effects of warming include an annual Energy Independence Day Expo and a year-long Neighborhood Energy Challenge in partnership with his state electric/gas utility. He serves on the board of ecoRI News, a regional environmental news service.

Stookey is president of the Savvy Families Institute, helping to educate Americans about the personal financial threats that lie ahead thanks to warming, and the many steps they can take to dodge them.

Stookey's primary qualifications for writing this book, however, are a big-hearted wife, three optimistic children, a modest income, and a concern to protect them all. He believes such credentials should entitle any of us to look ahead at the effects of warming and share what we see with others.

INDEX

4

4H Club, 28

5

51st state, 182
529 Plans, 199

A

Accion microlending, 203
Agriculture. See Food & Agriculture
Ahead of the crowd. See Timing
Airbnb, 202
Airports, 64, 67, 135
Albedo effect, 14
Albuquerque, NM, 72
Algae as fuel, 35
Allentown, PA, 97
Allergies, 58, 143
    where to live, 60
Allstate, 120
Amarillo, TX, 176
American Psychological
    Association, 57
American Red Cross, 58
American Society of Civil
    Engineers, 56, 75, 81, 82
Anaerobic digestion, 35
Annapolis, MD, 81
Antarctic, 216
Anti-American sentiment, 109
Aqua America, 139

Aquifers, 14, 83, 90, 119, 164,
    183
    saltwater intrusion, 121
Arab Spring, 108
Arctic, 65, 69, 216
Armoring shoreline, 123
Asset Owners Disclosure Project,
    152
Assets
    corporate, 147, 217
    stranded, 149, 213
    threats to our, 5
Asthma, 54, 58, 60, 143
    where to live, 60
Asthma & Allergy Foundation of
    America, 60
Atlanta, GA, 59, 202
Attitudes
    ahead of the crowd, 216
    compassion, 206–10
    mobility, 190–94
    multi-generational, 199–201
    provident, 198–99
    self-reliant, 205–6
    sharing, 201–5
    simple (small), 194
    vigilance, 210
Austin, TX, 70, 183
Avocado production, 16

B

B Corporation, 148
Baca County, CO, 175

Balanced budget requirement, 85

Bangladesh, 107, 108

Bankruptcies

from healthcare costs, 53

municipal, 165, 175

Baptists, 217

Barnhart, TX, 38

Bartering skills, 170

Best Development Practices, 90

Bethlehem, PA, 97

Biking, 73–74

sharing a bike, 74

Biotechnology, 144

Black Church, 209

Blanco River, 123

Boating industry, 84

Bogle, John, 220

Boise City, OK, 15

Boston, MA, 58, 218

Boulder, CO, 95

Brand, Stewart, *Whole Earth Discipline, An Ecopragmatist Manifesto*, 33, 111

Bridgeport, CA, 134

Bridges, 64

Brookings Institution, 2, 72, 172

Brookline, MA, 176

Bucks County, PA, 28

Buddhism, 209

Budgetting, 7–10, 197

bookmark, 8

budget sheet, v

calculators, 10

online services, 10

spreadsheet, 10

Buffalo, NY, 201

Buffet, Warren, 88

Building

restrictions, 92

Bureau of Labor Statistics (BLS)

Consumer Expenditure Survey, 10

Occupational Employment Projections, 171

C

Calculators, budget, 10

CalPERS, 153

Cambridge, MA, 86

Cape May, NJ, 121

Cape Vincent, NY, 130

Carbon tax, 67–68, 112, 114

how it works, 40–42

reimbursement, 41

Careers. See Jobs

Carlsbad, CA, 140

Cars

high-mileage, 43, 70

second, 70

sharing, 70

Catholicism, 209

Cedar City, UT, 50

Center for the New American Dream, 204

Charity, 18, 208

Charles City, IA, 91

Charleston, SC, 80

Charleston, WV, 89

Chicago, IL, 59

heat wave, 54

Chickens, 27, 206

Children and grandchildren. See Future generations

China's water shortage, 14

Chipotle, 16

Civil rights, 164

Clean Edge Index, 141

Climate bonds, 149

Climate change. *See* Warming

Club of Rome, 146

CO_2, 19, 96, 216

   capture & sequestration, 145

Coastal Property Guide, Rhode Island, 124

Coastkeeper, 92

Coffee rust plague, 17

Cohousing, 202

Collins, Chuck, Jamaica Plain, New Economy Enterprise Hub, 203

Colorado River, 13

Columbus, OH, 134

Community and Regional Resilience Institute, 179

community gardens, 25, 26, 28, 29, 205

Community supported agriculture (CSA), 32

Compassion, 206–10

Conflict, 89, 181–87

   costs, 6

   international. *See* U.S. military

   migration, 183

   resolution taught in school, 186

   the poor, 184

Congress, U.S., 104, 106, 214

Congressional Budget Office, 41, 67

Conspiracy theories, 212

Construction

   finance, 143

   investments, 142–43

   jobs, 160

   relocating power utilities, 143

Cooking, 30

Cooling needs, 49–50

Cooperation, 184–87

Cooperatives

   employee, 170

   laws, 218

Copenhagen Climate Summit, 109

Coralville, IA, 126

Corn Belt, 16

Corn yields, 16

Cost of living, 115, 173

Cravens, Gwyneth, *Power to Save the World, The Truth About Nuclear Energy*, 33

Credit risk, municipal and state, 101

Cuba's Special Period, 26

Cyclone Marian, 110

D

Dairy farming, 15

Dallas, TX, 29

Danville, VA, 173

DAXglobal Nuclear Energy Index, 142

Debt

   average American family, 3

   home foreclosure, 3

   student loans, 3

Decentralized services, 205

Degree days, 49–50

Delcourt, Paul & Hazel, *Living Well in the Age of Global Warming*, 179

Democracy, 184, 214

Denver, CO, 59, 90

Dervais family, 205

Detroit, MI, 121

Diego Garcia, 105

Distributed services, 205

Doiron, Roger, 26–27

Downshifting, 196
Downsizing, 194
Drainage, 123
Drought, 13
   local risk of, iii
   Santa Cruz, iii, 57
Dunedin, FL, 118
Dust Bowl of the 1930s, 15

E

Earnings, 4, 132
   and skills, 168, 172
   stagnation, 4, 138
   where to live, 171
East Lake Commons, 202
East Siberian Arctic shelf, 217
Eating less, 30
Economic activity, 4, 84, 128, 172
El Paso, TX, 50
Electric power, 36
   and heat, 36
   and sea-level rise, 36
   biomass, 44
   cooperatives, 44
   cost, 39
   declining use, 34
   future needs, 33
   hydro, 35, 44
   solar. See Solar power
   wind. See Wind power
Electric utilities
   and solar, 37, 44
Emotional barriers, 192, 222
Employment. See Jobs
Energy
   heating and cooling needs, 49–
      50

   where to live, 48–52
Energy audit, 42
Englander, John, *High Tide on Main Street*, 218
Enterprise Car Share, 70
Environmental ethics learned early, 200
Environmental Protection Agency (EPA), 55, 61, 80, 185
Erie County Water Authority, 82
Erosion, 123
Evangelicals, 209
Evergreen Cooperatives, 170
Excuses, 211–15
Exxon Mobil, 151

F

Fair Oaks, CA, 28
Fallow fields, 16–17
Famine, 106, 111
Farmers' markets, 22–23, 32, 205
Federal Bureau of Investigation (FBI), 21
Federal Climate Disruption Costs, 106
Federal Crop Insurance, 18
Federal Emergency Management Agency (FEMA), 63, 93, 105
Federal government
   insurance programs, 105
   lower your taxes, 114
   resistance to climate-proofing, 104, 113
Federal Highway Trust Fund, 66
Financial advisers, iv
Fiscalini Farms, 35
Fishing industry, 18–19, 84
Fitch Ratings, 101
Floating buildings, 125

Floating homes, 206

Flood Control America, 126, 158

Flood insurance, 123

   for renters, 123

   out of the flood zone, 123

Flood zone

   expanding, 118, 135

   maps, 136

Flooding

   floating buildings, 125

   flood-proofing buildings, 125

   moving a house, 126

   population affected, 79

   raising buildings, 125

   waterproof fence, 126

Food & Agriculture

   commodity investing, 146

   food security, 21

   international problems, 107

   limits to local, 25

   local, 21–25

   meat prices, 17

   plant hardiness zones, 31

   price speculation, 19

   processing, 17

   rising prices, 12, 16

   soil quality, 31

   undernourished Americans, 12

   waste, 30

   where to live, 30–32

Food banks, 18

Food for Women, Infants, and Children (WIC), 18, 28

Food hubs, 24

Food miles, 19

Food pyramid, 21

Foodshed Alliance, 28

Foreign aid. *See* Non-military aid

Forest fires. *See* Wildfires

Fracking, 34, 38, 39, 163

Free market, 213, 217

Freon prices, 55

Fuel taxes, 66

Full Circle, 23

Future generations, i, 6, 87, 199–201, 209, 215

   and moving, 193

   learning enironmental ethics, 200

   learning simplicity, 196

G

Gainesville, FL, 37, 51

Garden clubs, 29

Gary, IN, 98

Generations X and Y. *See* Future generations

Genetically-engineered food, 111, 144

George's Bank, 18

Getaround, 71

Giles Slade, *American Exodus*, 180

Giridharadas, Anand, 204

Global warming. *See* Warming

Globe, AZ, 134

Gloucester, MA, 84

GMO Commodity Index, 146

Golf courses, 84

Goodell, Jeff, *Rolling Stone*, 84

Gore, Al, *An Inconvenient Truth*, ii

Grameen America microlending, 203

Grand Rapids, 80

Grange, 28

Great Lakes, 69, 121

Great Recession, 146, 172, 191

Green bonds, 149

Green City Market, 23

Green Climate Fund, 109

Greenland, 216

Greenville, SC, 72

Greenwashing, 152

Grid parity, 45, 163

Gross Domestic Product, false indicator, 195

Gross Happiness Index, 195

Groundwater. See Aquifers

Growing your own food, 25–29

Guam, 105

H

Hancock County, ME, 22

Hansen, Jim, 109

Happiness, 195–96

Hartford, CT, 176

Hawaiian Electric Industries, 37

Health and healthcare, 84

costs, 62

investments, 143

quality, 62

where to live, 60–62

Heat island effect, 59

Heat waves, 54–55, 58

effect on crops, 15

Heating needs, 49–50

Hertz On Demand, 70

Highways & roads

abandonment, 87–88

conditions by state, 75–76

cost of bad roads, 67

engineering standards, 64

erosion, 64

heat damage, 64

privatizing, 76–77

sea-level rise, 65

trucking, 69

Hinduism, 209

Hine, Dougald, 3

Historic sites, 81

Hoboken, NJ, 79, 176

Home value, 6, 218

as investment, 131

drought risk, 128

flood risk, 129

insurance rates, 120

mortgage term, 130

storm and flood risk, 119

town reassessment, 129

Home vegetable garden, 26–29

Homeless, 3

Homeowners insurance, 120

Homeowners' Guide to Retrofitting, Six Ways to Protect Your House from Flooding, 125

Homesteaders, 196

Honesdale, PA, 28

Honeybees, 16

Hopkins, Rob, Transition Towns, 203

Housing, shared, 202

Hudson River Valley, 179

Humanitarian assistance, U.S., 109–11

Hurricane Isabel, 81

Hurricane Katrina, 160

Hurricane Sandy, 36, 55, 63, 119, 143, 151, 160

Hybrid cars, 43

Hydroelectric power, 39

Hydroponics, 27

Hypocrisy Index, 152

I

Ikea, 141

Illinois Farmers Insurance
lawsuits, 120

Illinois underfunded pensions, 89

Income. *See* Earnings

Income taxes, 114–15

Indianapolis, IN, 98

Indus River, 108

Infrastructure
airports, 64
bridges, 64
ports and waterways, 65
rail, 63
roads, 64, 65, 67, 69
waterways, 65, 68

Insolation, 50

Institute for Local Self-Reliance,
205
John Farrell, 45
Stacy Mitchell, 169

Institute for Policy Studies, 204

Insulation, weatherization, 42

Intentional Living, 196

International climate finance, 110

International Living magazine, 180

International Monetary Fund, 19

Investing, 220
agricultural, other commodities,
146–47
clean energy, 141
climate or green bonds, 149
construction, 142–43
defensive, 154
education, 155

genetically-engineered food,
144
healthcare, 143
home solar, 155
information, 152
insurance, 147
locally, 155
minerals, 146
municipal bonds, 151
necessities, 154–55
nuclear energy, 142
overvalued real estate, 151
rental property, 132
risks disclosed in offerings, 149
social enterprises, 148
solar energy, 141
stranded assets, 149
technolgy, 145
water desalinization,
purification, 140
water rights, 139–40

Investor Network on Climate Risk,
153

Irrigation, iii, 160, 161, 166

Islam, 209

Ivanpah Solar Electric, 142

J

Jackson, MS, 176

Jamaica Plain, MA, 178
JP Resiliency Measures Project,
178
New Economy Enterprise Hub,
26, 170, 203

Jamieson, Dale, *Reason in the
Dark*, 208

Jefferson County, AL, 175

Jobs
building construction, 161

consulting, advice, 163–64

heavy consruction, 160

law, mediation, 164–65

list of promising, 165

local, 94, 169

moving buildings, 162

real estate, moving families, 161

skills, automatable, 167

skills, old-fashioned, 168–69

skills, portable, 167–69

start-ups, 172

titles -v- descriptions, 157

where-to-live, 171

with local companies, 169

Judaism, 209

Just-in-time delivery, 20

K

Kennedy International Airport, 65

Kingsnorth, Paul, 3

Kitchen Gardeners International, 27

Kiva microlending, 203

Knoxville, TN, 60

Kunstler, James Howard, *The Long Emergency*, 179, 184

L

La Guardia airport, 65

Lake Huron, 68

Lake Mead, 13, 14, 91

Lake Michigan, 68

Land trusts, 92

to protect local agriculture, 21

Las Vegas, NV, 91

League of American Bicyclists, 74

Lewisburg, WV, 50

Liability claims, 165

Libby's, 16

Liberty Mountain Resort, 148

Life's Most Stressful Events, 222

Little Compton, RI, 124

Livestock, 15, 17

Livingston, MT, 51

Lloyd's of London, 165

Local

businesses, 94

Institute for Local Self-Reliance, 45

Institute for Local Self-Reliance, 169, 205

investing, 155

jobs, 169

limits to food, 25

reasons to shop, 169

Location. See Where to live

Long Beach Island, NJ, 185

Los Angeles, CA, 59

Lovins, Amory, *Reinventing Fire*, 35

Lyautey, Marshall, 222

Lyft, 70

Lynn, MA, 86

M

Magnuson, Joel, *The Approaching Great Transformation*, 203

Mairs & Powers Midwest investment funds, 156

Malthus, Thomas Robert, 146

Maple sugar, 15

Marijuana growers as mentors, 29

Marshall, MI, 64

Materialism, among high school seniors, 200

McKibben, Bill, *Eaarth*, 48

Meetup.com, 204

Mental health, 57

Mentors

  finding, 204, 221

  marijuana growers, 29

  recent immigrants, 29

Methane, 35, 38, 217

Miami, FL, 84, 219

Microlending, 28, 202

Migration

  of agriculture infrastructure, 15

  source of conflict, 183

Minerals uncovered by warming,
  146

Minimalists, 196

Mint online service, 10

Mississippi River, 68

Missouri River, 68

Mobility, 172, 190–94

  advance visits, 192

  reasons for decline, 191

  renting, 132, 193, 223

  tackling emotional barriers, 192

Monmouth County, NJ, 175

Montpelier, VT, 201

Moody's Investors Service, 98, 101

Morality, new elements, 208–10

Municipal finances

  borrowing, 86–87

  credit risk, 101

  fees and fines, 85–86

  influencing officials, 99

  new ideas, 97

  non-politicized, 185

  quality of officials, 94

  quality of planning, 95

  revenues, 86

  service cuts, 66, 87–88

  sin taxes, 85

  split-rate property taxation, 97

  town-owned solar, 205

  underfunded pensions, 88–89

  where-to-live, 99–103

Muslim world, 109

N

Nags Head, NC, 99

Napa-Sonoma Valley, 121

NASDAQ OMX Global Water Index,
  141

National Aeronautics and Space
  Administration (NASA), 14, 48,
  109

National Aeronautics and Space
  Administration (NASA), 16

National Association of Clean
  Water Agencies, 56

National Bureau of Economic
  Research, 2

National Climatic Data Center, 49

National Flood Insurance Program
  (NFIP), 93, 105

National Geographic, 15

National Renewable Energy
  Laboratory, 50

National Resources Defense
  Council, 106

*National Security and the
  Accelerating Risks of Climate
  Change*, 106

National Water and Climate
  Center, 51

Natural Resources Conservation
  Service, 51

Natural Resources Defense
  Council, iii, 100, 133

Neglect, cost of, 5

New Bedford, MA, 18

New Economy Enterprise Hub, 170

New Haven, CT, 118

New Jersey plans, 96

New Orleans, LA, 125

New York City, 59, 63, 80, 81, 86, 97, 143, 160

   sea-level rise, 36

Newman's Own, 148

Newport, RI, 81

NOAA, 135

Non-military aid, 109–11

No-regrets actions, iv, 42, 114, 155, 158, 169, 190, 211, 216

Norfolk, VA, 130

North Carolina, Local Government Commission, 96

Northeast Ohio Regional Sewer District, 182

Nuclear power, 33, 47–48

   investments, 142

O

Ogallala Aquifer, 14, 21, See Aquifers

Oil & natural gas

   demand, 34–35

   prices, 34–35

Oklahoma Food Cooperative, 24

Onion River Exchange, 201

Orman, Suze, The 9 Steps to Financial Freedom, 10

Osceola, AR, 134

Owen, David, Conundrum, 20

Oyster Creek Generating Station, 36

P

Pendleton, OR, 46

Permafrost, 216

Petroleum refineries, and water, 38

Philadelphia, PA, 59

Photovoltaic. See Solar

Plant Hardiness Zones, 15, 31

Platt River, 19

Politics

   local government, 185

   red and blue counties, 186

Pollen, 53

Pollination, 16

Poor communities, 184, 204, 207–9

Porritt, Jonathon, The World We Made, 215

Port Angeles, WA, 176

Port Fourchon, LA, 65

Portland, ME, 56, 92

Post Carbon Institute, 204

Powerton, IL electric plant, 36

Precipitation increasing, 13, 55, 56, 80, 91

Preparedness planning quality, 100

Privatizing

   roads, 76–77

   water, 98

Procrastination, 214

Property Assessed Clean Energy (PACE), 46

Property rights, 92, 217

Property taxes, 129

   limits, 85

Prosper microlending, 203

Public transit, 72

Pumpkin yields, 16

Q

Quadrennial Defense Review, 105

R

Rail system, Vermont, 63

Raleigh, NC, 92

Ramsey, Dave, *Total Money Makeover*, 7

Rationalizations, 211–15

Real estate

agents, iv, 130, 161

development, 21, 84, 90, 92, 164, 185

jobs, 161

overvalued, 129, 151

Rebound effect, 71–74

Recession, 7

Regional Access, 24

Regulations and ordinances, ii, 92, 161, 205

to encourage local food, 21, 22

Rehoboth, MA, 43

Religious attitudes, 209, 217

Relocating public structures, 81

Relocation Accounts, tax free, 165

Renting, 132

when moving, 193, 223

Research & Development, 214

Resilience Circles, 203, 221

Resilience, Americans' family finances, 2

Riverkeeper, 92

Robin, Vicki and Joe Dominguez, *Your Money or Your Life*, 196

Rochester, NY, 85

Rocky Mountains, 13, 14, 21, 90

Roofs, green, 59, 161

Roofs, white, 59

Rubin, Robert, 104

Russia, crop destruction, 107

S

S&P Dow Jones Global Water Index, 141

S&P Goldman Sachs Commodity Index, 146

Sacramento, CA, 176

Salisbury, MA, 183

San Antonio, TX, 51, 83

San Francisco, 22, 119

Santa Barbara, CA, 122

Santa Cruz, CA, ii–iv, 57

Santa Monica, CA, 219

Satellite Beach, FL, 130

Sausalito, CA, 126

Saving, 198–99

retirement, 2

savings rate in America, 2

Savvy Families Where-To-Live Indicators, 134, 177, 181

School Lunch Program, 18

School of Government, University of NC, 96

Seafood. See Fishing indusry

Sea-level rise, iv, 99, 164

armoring shoreline, 123–25

Seaport City, 143

Seaports, 65

Seattle, WA, 50, 59

Securities and Exchange Commission (SEC), 153

Seffner, FL, 118

Self-reliance, 205–6

Sewage systems

combined sewer overflows (CSO), 61, 80–81

raw sewage releases, 55

Shaker Heights, OH, 176

Sharing

bicycles, 74
cars and rides, 70
housing, 202
investments, 202–3
time banks, 201
tools, 201
Shiller, Robert, 131
Shuman, Michael, *Local Dollars, Local Sense*, 24, 156
Sierra Nevada Mountains, 14
Simplifying, 194–98
    for a cause, 196–97
    within your faith, 197
Sinkhole. See Subsidence
Skiing industry, 84
Skills. See Jobs
    self-sufficiency, 206
Slow Living, 196
Small House movement, 196
Smith, Paul, 109
Snowmelt, 21
Snowpack and snowmelt, 13–14
Social enterprises, 148
Social justice, 184
Social Vulnerability Index, 175
Soil quality, 31
Solar City, 43, 46
Solar power, 33, 35, 52
    costs, 43
    financing, 46
    group purchases, 44
    insolation, 50
    investments, 141
    jobs, 162
    passive solar buildings, 161
    sharing, 43
    timing, 45–46

Soup kitchens, 18
Sperling's Cities Ranked and Rated, 178
Split-rate property taxation, 97
Stamford, CT, 46, 173
Standard & Poor's, 101
Stanford University, 35
Start-ups, job creation, 172
State of Our Neighborhood forum, 204
States' rights, 94
Stern, Nicholas, *The Economics of Climate Change*, 149
Storm surge. See Flooding
Stranded Assets, 147, 149, 213
Subsidence, 118, 119
Sullivan County, PA, 175
Summit County, CO, 29
Supplemental Nutrition Assistance Program (SNAP or Food Stamps), 18, 28
Sustainable Preparedness Expo, 205
Syria, 107

T

Tax burden by state, 100
Taxes, income, 114–15
Taxes, municipal. See Municipal finances
Terrorism, 21, 108–9
The Federal Crop Insurance Program (FCIP), 105
Timing, 216–24
    delay, v
    gradual, insidious decline, 7
Tipping points
    government policies, 218
    markets, 218–20

nature, 216–17
personal, 220–24
public consciousness, 217–18
Titley, Rear Admiral David, 104
Toledo, OH, 56
Tools
Where-To-Live Indicators, 180
Topsoil, 14
Tourism, 85, 162
Town farms, 205
Trade-offs, location, 181
Transit Score, 72
Transition Towns, 203, 221
Transportation costs
of food, 20
where to live, 74–76
Trees for cooling, 59
Tropical Storm Irene, 63
Twain, Mark, 221

U

U.S. Department of Agriculture, 21
U.S. economy, slowdown, 7
Uber, 70
Union of Concerned Scientists, 55
University Heights Tool Library, 201
University of California, Cooperative Extension Service, 28
Urban farms, 22
Urban homesteading, 206
US Agency for International Development, 110
US Conference of Mayors, 96
US Department of Agriculture, 19
US Government Accountability Office (GAO), 104

US government property, 105
US Military
bases, 105
conflict, 107–9
humanitarian missions, 106, 110
mission change, 106
stabilization, peacekeeping, 106
User fees, tolls, 66

V

Vail, CO, 13
Vermont's Genuine Progress Indicator, 195
Victory gardens, 25
Vigilance, 210
Violence and crime, 57
Voltaire, 212

W

Waldrum, Josh, 70
Walk Score, 72
Walkable neighborhoods, 73
Ware, Ciji, *Rightsizing Your Life*, 198
Warming
probability of, ii
terminology, ii
Warming penalty, 225
earnings, 173
transportation, 77
Warren County, NJ, 97
Warwick, RI, 90
Washington DC, 59
Wastewater. *See* Sewage systems
Water
auctions, 17
desalinization, purification, 140

dry landscaping, 128
free-market price, 122
municipal, 82–83, 134
private ownership, 139–40
privatizing utility, 98
reducing use, 127
restrictions, iii, 31
reuse, 91, 128, 140
rising costs, 121
transport, 140
watershed protection, 90
well-water costs, 122
where-to-live, 133
xeriscaping, 127
Water Supply Sustainability Index, iii, 133
Waterkeeper, 92
Westerly, RI, 79
Westminster, MA, 90
Where to live, 11
    children, 200
    comparative data, 177–79
    conflict, 181–87
    cooperation, 184–87
    effect on earnings, 4
    energy, 48–52
    food, 30–32
    heatlh, 60–62
    jobs, 171–73
    municipal finances, 99

overseas, 180
Social Vulnerability Index, 175
solar or wind, 50–52
transportation, 74–76
water, 133
Where-To-Live Indicators, v–vii, 8, 11
    forecasting value, 180
    not the whole story, 180
    trade-offs, 181
Whitehouse, Hon. Senator Sheldon, 218
Wichita Falls, TX, 91
Wildfires, 83, 119
Wimberley, TX, 183
Wind power, 33, 35, 43, 44, 52
    jobs, 162
World Food Programme, 111
World Health Organization, 143

X

Xeriscaping, 127

Y

Yodlee online service, 10

Z

Zip microlending, 203
ZipCar, 70
Zoning, 21, 22, 43, 90, 165, 183

	Latest	%Change	
Earned income before taxes			
Other income before taxes			
Federal income taxes			
State/local income/sales taxes, fees			
Social Security, pensions withheld			
Income after taxes			
Expenditures			
Food, at home and out, incl. alcohol			
Housing (owned)			
Mortgage interest and charges			
Property taxes			
Insurance, maintenance, repairs			
Rent			
Utilities, fuels, and public services			
Natural gas			
Electricity			
Heating, cooling, cooking fuels			
Telephone			
Water and other public services			
Transportation			
Vehicle purchase incl. interest			
Gasoline and motor oil			
Maintenance and repairs			
Vehicle insurance			
Public and other transportation			
Health care, including insurance			
Charity			
Education & reading			
Other			
Other			
Total Expenditures			
Saving, incl life insurance			
Market value of owned home			